"In this highly readable volume, Darrell Whiteman at last shares with us the fruit of decades of reflection and practical experience. Peppered with provocative concepts and illustrated with numerous stories, this text is sure to launch lively discussions. Readers will be stimulated to become better students of culture and more effective cultural bridge-builders for the gospel."

—**Craig Ott**, Trinity Evangelical Divinity School

"Every Christian who responds to God's invitation to proclaim the gospel—with one's words and one's life—within an unfamiliar culture will benefit greatly from the practical wisdom distilled in this book. A seasoned teacher and one of America's leading missiological anthropologists, Whiteman proposes an incarnational model of ministry that will challenge and inspire teachers, students, and practitioners of mission to be more attentive to their own cultures and the cultures of their hosts."

—**Thomas John Hastings**, editor, *International Bulletin of Mission Research*; retired executive director, OMSC@PTS

"Drawing from decades spent coaching and mentoring missionaries and from deep knowledge of cultural anthropology, Whiteman has written a helpful and easy-to-read book for everyone involved in day-to-day cross-cultural ministry. It is filled with vivid illustrations and practical suggestions for learning about culture, coping with culture shock, developing close trust relationships with local people, and communicating the gospel wisely and well."

—**Robert J. Priest**, Taylor University (emeritus)

"This is the book I have been waiting for. As a student in Darrell's seminary class on anthropology for Christian witness, I was both inspired and challenged by his insights from anthropology for missions today. He captivated the class with a unique combination of humor, wisdom, and probing questions. It was truly a life-transforming experience. I have often wondered what was Darrell's 'secret sauce.' That secret sauce is now captured in this book. It is an invaluable resource for professors and trainers of intercultural workers. Based on his decades-long experience training others in a wide array of contexts, he provides a teaching approach that is tried and true ⸺ ⸺ in my own teaching."

—W. Ja   ·y

"I was mesmerized the first time I attende   ⸺y
he made Jesus come alive, unpacked the c   ⸺ıy
interacted with the class left a significant impression on me. After hearing him speak many times since, I was thrilled to learn that Darrell has recorded his thoughts and experiences in a book. It's about time! I am especially excited to share this tool with the burgeoning missions movement spreading from Ethiopia to the ends of the earth."

—**Richard Coleman**, cross cultural witness, TMS Global & EvaSUE

"Whiteman, globally renowned missiological anthropologist, has expertly woven together various strands of his life and ministry—academic scholarship as an anthropologist, missionary service in Papua New Guinea, professor at Asbury Theological Seminary, and master trainer of thousands of cross-cultural witnesses around the world—to produce this magnificent tapestry, *Crossing Cultures with the Gospel*. As his student and colleague, with immense joy I recommend this magnum opus, written with profound wisdom and great lucidity for 'such a time as this.'"

—**PrabhuSingh Vedhamanickam**, South Asia Institute of Advanced Christian Studies, Bangalore, India

"Whiteman's gift to us in this book is a magnificent tour de force, an eloquent summary of a life lived helping people imitate God's self-emptying, incarnational love as they participate in God's mission. It is warm, wise, inspiring, beautifully written, passionate, eminently practical, and deeply challenging. It should be read by every missionary but also by any disciple who yearns to minister faithfully, creatively, and effectively in today's multicultural church and world."

—**Stephen Bevans, SVD**, Catholic Theological Union, Chicago (emeritus)

"It is not every day that you come across a missiological text that should be required reading for every current and future cross-cultural worker. *Crossing Cultures with the Gospel*, however, is such a text. With over forty-five years of cross-cultural experience, Whiteman's engaging approach to missiological anthropology invites both the novice and veteran missionary to explore anew the centrality of culture in cross-cultural ministry. Filled with scholarly insight, hard-earned wisdom, and personal reflection, Whiteman provides practical anthropological tools and perspectives that are essential for effective cross-cultural witness. *Crossing Cultures with the Gospel* is an invaluable missiological resource that scholars, mission practitioners, and mission educators will return to again and again."

—**Sarita Gallagher Edwards**, author of *Christ among the Nations: Narratives of Transformation in Global Mission*

"When I first met Darrell on a mission trip to a remote area in northern Kenya, I was struck by his genuine interest in and deep insights into the local cultures and the gospel. Since then I have had the distinct privilege of being trained and mentored by him. In this book he deftly explores key topics of culture, incarnational ministry, worldview, culture shock, and effective communication. He has had the privilege of not only training on these topics but also living out the truths as he serves across the globe. I wholeheartedly endorse this significant book for all of us who are spiritual pilgrims—crossing cultures with the gospel in an ever-changing world."

—**Duncan Olumbe**, regional director, Interserve

CROSSING CULTURES WITH THE GOSPEL

CROSSING CULTURES
WITH THE
GOSPEL

Anthropological Wisdom
for Effective Christian Witness

Darrell Whiteman

Foreword by Miriam Adeney

Baker Academic
a division of Baker Publishing Group
Grand Rapids, Michigan

Published by Baker Academic
a division of Baker Publishing Group
Grand Rapids, Michigan
www.bakeracademic.com

Printed in the United States of America

Library of Congress Cataloging-in-Publication Data
Names: Whiteman, Darrell L., author.
Title: Crossing cultures with the gospel : anthropological wisdom for effective Christian witness / Darrell Whiteman.
Description: Grand Rapids, Michigan : Baker Academic, a division of Baker Publishing Group, [2024] | Includes bibliographical references and index.
Identifiers: LCCN 2023026223 | ISBN 9781540960467 (paperback) | ISBN 9781540967374 (casebound) | ISBN 9781493429547 (ebook) | ISBN 9781493429554 (pdf)
Subjects: LCSH: Missions—Anthropological aspects. | Christianity and culture. | Intercultural communication—Religious aspects—Christianity. | Interpersonal relations—Religious aspects—Christianity. | Cultural relations. | Globalization—Religious aspects—Christianity.
Classification: LCC BV2063 .W455 2024 | DDC 266—dc23/eng/20230823
LC record available at https://lccn.loc.gov/2023026223

The table in chapter 3 is from Charles Kraft's *Christianity in Culture: A Study in Biblical Theologizing in Cross-Cultural Perspective*, revised 25th anniversary edition (Maryknoll, NY: Orbis Books, 2005), p. 49. Used with permission.

The Holmes-Rahe Stress Inventory table in chapter 10 is from Thomas H. Holmes and Minoru Masuda, "Life Change and Illness Susceptibility," in *Stressful Life Events: Their Nature and Effects*, edited by Barbara Dohrenwend and Bruce Dohrenwend (Hoboken: John Wiley & Sons, 1974), p. 52. Copyright © 1974, by John Wiley and Sons, Inc. Used by permission.

Unless otherwise indicated, Scripture quotations are from the Good News Translation in Today's English Version-Second Edition. Copyright © 1992 by American Bible Society. Used by permission.

Scripture quotations labeled CEV are from the Contemporary English Version © 1991, 1992, 1995 by American Bible Society. Used by permission.

Scripture quotations labeled KJV are from the King James Version of the Bible.

Scripture quotations labeled NIV are from THE HOLY BIBLE, NEW INTERNATIONAL VERSION®, NIV® Copyright © 1973, 1978, 1984, 2011 by Biblica, Inc.® Used by permission. All rights reserved worldwide.

Unless otherwise indicated, figures are created by Darrell Whiteman and designed by Baker Publishing Group.

Baker Publishing Group publications use paper produced from sustainable forestry practices and post-consumer waste whenever possible.

24   25   26   27   28   29   30   7   6   5   4   3   2   1

To the memory of my father, G. Edgar Whiteman,
who was truly a man of God in his short-lived life,
and to my lifelong companion, Laurie,
who has accompanied me on this journey
with patience and encouragement along the way

Contents

PART 5 Growing into Effective Communicators

Foreword

The Disposition to Become a Friend

MIRIAM ADENEY

Every steamy June we used to descend on Techny Towers, we members of the American Society of Missiology, pushing through O'Hare Airport from all parts of the continent. Headquarters of the Society of the Divine Word, a Catholic missionary movement, Techny Towers was a few acres with its own postal code. It sheltered a parish church with soaring arches, painted murals, and marble floors; a seminary whose Vietnamese and Latino students swished past in long robes; a garden; a duck pond where frogs croaked; a missionary retirement home; and a cemetery. Parish to mission, cradle to grave, garden to table: Christian community lived whole.

"I'm off to the cemetery," Darrell would say, as he headed to Louis Luzbetak's grave. Luzbetak was a Society of the Divine Word missionary who authored *The Church and Cultures* in 1963. He and Eugene Nida had tethered post-war American missiology for their successors: William Smalley, Charles Kraft, Paul Hiebert, and others. Through the decades, as Darrell worked tirelessly to keep missiology flourishing, he never forgot that we stand on the shoulders of others, our ancestors. So, he walked out to spend a moment with Luzbetak.

Today, in spite of education and technology, we live in dystopian times. There is so much wrong with the world and the church, so many flash points that could catch fire and erupt. Human beings are still as self-centered as ever. Thoughtful people wonder, *Is there hope?*

There is. Our hope bursts out of the resurrection. There are crucifixions, yes. But beyond Jesus's cross explodes the resurrection. There is evil, yes, but when evil has done its worst, here comes restoration. A way appears. Dreams are restored. Hope is reborn. What profoundly good news, and how amazing that it is available to every people.

This is what motivates Darrell's life work: good news for all. Yet he is motivated by more than just beliefs. Darrell has always insisted that the gospel is lived through bodies, through sweat and weariness and achievements and celebratory pizzas—or fried crickets—not just through abstract ideas and doctrines. The gospel is expressed in particulars honed by the ways of life of people with distinct heritages in diverse parts of the world—islands and snowy alpine mountains, jungles and urban high-rises.

How can we shape our Christian communication so that it makes sense to such people in their own terms? That is the focus of this book. Drawing on forty-five years of teaching and training, Darrell explains how to cope with culture shock. How to "bond." How to build a bicultural identity. How to "exegete the context." He illustrates how language shapes our mental categories. How worldviews condition behavioral changes. How our American values affect the way we see others. Charts and checklists, strategies and steps, dangers and disciplines all enliven the text.

"Just take a stab at it!" is not the way we train surgeons. Nor should we train missionaries that way. Well-meaning but ignorant witnesses can cause harm, dishonor God's name, and burn over the ground for future witnesses.

So how do we learn about a culture? What questions do we ask? How do we record the data? Or interpret it? Darrell teaches us how to practice participant observation, the fundamental research technique for anthropologists. Extended immersion, analytical skills, curiosity, and the ability to listen are illustrated.

This book goes beyond asking "How?" to also ask "Why?" Jesus's incarnation is the most profound reason for taking local cultures seriously. Jesus never ate cheeseburgers, just fish and hummus. Jesus never spoke English or French, just Aramaic, Greek, and Hebrew. He limited himself by becoming human, but beyond that he limited himself even more by living as a Palestinian Jew, as a relatively poor carpenter in a society oppressed by a colonial power. In this concentration, Jesus affirmed and honored a specific local context.

Is this not a model for us? Each cultural heritage is precious. Yes, cultural sins must be judged, but cultures themselves are gifts of God. Endowed with creativity, peoples have imagined diverse architectures and cuisines and music and economic exchanges and family patterns. The resulting global mosaic is a glory to God. It enriches God's world.

Or does it? Cultural distinctives seem to be flattening out. Wherever we look, people drink Coke, watch blockbuster movies, and order over the internet. Pilots follow the same rules globally. So do doctors. Students take similar exams. Languages can be translated with apps. Citizens migrate. Young people have new ideas. Everybody everywhere may experience the same epidemic. Do cultural differences really matter that much anymore?

Yes, cultures still matter. Every one of us comes from a community with a story, however garbled it may be. We are not cogs in a machine. We are not just robots or animals or producers or consumers or statistics. We are not interchangeable with everyone else. In spite of change, particular precious heritages—core continuities—flow on. We deserve the respect of having our stories taken seriously.

Pig feasts in the South Pacific flavored Darrell's original missiology, which he expressed in his keystone work *Melanesians and Missionaries*. Today Darrell's students celebrate with dim sum and egg flower soup and roast duck, or with chai and samosas and the elusive tastes of masalas. In both China and India Darrell is at work mentoring learners, as both of these great nations shape missionaries to serve inside and outside their borders.

Darrell is also at home behind a banquet podium with a microphone in hand, decked out in a suit and tie (always partnered by sandals and socks and his trademark bushy beard). Or he may be hunkered down on muddy knees, troweling the tulips in his yard. Everywhere, his joy in people in their cultural contexts, in learning, in the global church, and in the community of missiologists animates him. Everywhere his dancing eyebrows, big smile, and irrepressible aliveness vibrate. Everywhere he demonstrates what he recommends as an essential quality for a successful missionary: the disposition to become a friend. This book distills that vitality into wisdom.

Preface

For forty-five years I have been training students, pastors, and cross-cultural witnesses with an understanding of some basic anthropological tools and perspectives that will enable them to cross cultural barriers with the gospel. The number of people who have participated in this training is upwards of five thousand, and they are scattered around the globe in India, China, Kenya, Philippines, Brazil, Cuba, and elsewhere.

A common response to my teaching has frequently been, "If I had known this before I ventured out into cross-cultural ministry, I would have been far more effective and lasted a lot longer. Why haven't I heard this before? Is there more where this came from?" In response, I could only point to a few scattered articles I had written and tell them about books that had helped shape my understanding of crossing cultures with the gospel, such as Charles Kraft's *Christianity in Culture* (1979) and Paul Hiebert's *Anthropological Insights for Missionaries* (1985), but that's about all I could say. I slowly came to realize that this teaching and training is a gift that God has given to me and through me, and therefore I am responsible to pass it on to others.

And now the time has come for me to pass this on to you. My prayer is that the insights and perspective, and perhaps even some wisdom, in the pages that follow will encourage and also challenge you. As a follower of Jesus, I've come to believe that the gospel is for everyone, without exception. But it must be understood and lived out in a wide variety of different cultures in the present and throughout different eras of history in the past. In other words, the universal gospel takes on particular forms as it encounters people in different cultures across space and engages people in different eras through time. The eternal gospel must connect with the changing world if it's going to have any relevance and transforming power in their personal lives and in their community life.

Why is a book like this needed today? Seventy years ago, the great Bible translator and anthropological linguist, Eugene Nida, wrote *Customs and Cultures: Anthropology for Christian Missions* (1954). You may wonder, *Hasn't the mission world already learned all of these anthropological principles and intercultural lessons?* I wish I could say an unqualified yes, but I can't. As we move into the postcolonial era, and as the former mission *fields* are increasingly becoming a global mission *force*, I often see the same lack of cross-cultural understanding and awareness as was too often characteristic of previous generations of missionaries. Confusing the gospel with their own culture or their denomination's interpretation of the gospel is a rampant problem everywhere I've observed cross-cultural ministry.

I have written this book to challenge you, the reader, to confront your ethnocentrism, to discover how much of your understanding of biblical truth has been shaped by your culture, and to adjust your lifestyle to one that is more appropriate for cross-cultural ministry where you live. I've also written to encourage you, to remind you that God has not left God's self without a witness in every culture, among every people group, at every era of human history. It is God's mission in the world that we join, not our mission. We can also be encouraged by the fact that Jesus promised to be with us throughout the process of crossing cultures with the gospel.

Another way I hope to encourage the reader is through my in-depth discussion of the problem of culture shock. I've given a fair amount of space to discussing it because every cross-cultural witness goes through it in one form or another. I identify what it is and what causes it, and I've suggested ways we can overcome it and have a long-lasting, effective ministry instead of leaving the host society prematurely because we could never adapt to the local culture.

Many people, places, and events have shaped my understanding of cross-cultural ministry, and I acknowledge some of those "giants in the field" in the pages that follow. I struggled to complete this book, and there were times of discouragement and periods of lack of confidence that what I was writing would make a difference in the kingdom of God. I wondered at times if I would ever finish the book, and so finally I went to one of my former graduate students, Jay Moon, and suggested that we reverse roles. I asked him to become my mentor and I would gladly be his student in order to push this project across the finish line. It worked and I am eternally grateful for his important role in helping me complete this writing. To God be the glory.

1

Conversion of the Missionary

A new broom sweeps well, but the old broom knows all the corners. (New experience is good, but wisdom is better.)

Builsa proverb, Ghana

W hat do you mean that missionaries need to be converted. I thought missionaries simply converted others?" asked a bewildered student of missiology. I had just finished the keynote address at the 2022 American Society of Missiology annual meeting at Notre Dame. I chuckled to myself because I have answered this same question over a thousand times. I realized that my experiences as a missiological anthropologist over the past forty-five years are still valid for those practicing mission today. The hard (and at times painful) lessons I have learned are still as relevant as they were when I first started my own missionary journey. Many times I have said to myself, "I wish someone had taught me this when I first started. I could have avoided a lot of headaches!"

The theme of the conference in 2022 was "The Ongoing Conversion of a Missionary," and the title of my address was "The Conversion of a Missionary: A Missiological Study of Acts 10."[1] I argued that every effective missionary must undergo two conversions. The first conversion is our conversion to Christ as Lord of all our life. Then I noted how the apostle Peter had to undergo a second conversion to cleanse him of his ethnocentrism before he could lead the gentile

---

1. That keynote address was published in the January 2023 issue of *Missiology*. See D. Whiteman 2023b, 19–30.

Roman centurion Cornelius and his household to faith in Christ. My talk lasted only thirty-three minutes, but the Q&A afterward went on for nearly an hour. What happened to "electrify the audience," as one participant described it? Another said, "As you responded to difficult questions and often told a story from somewhere in the world to illustrate your point, you were drawing on a long life of experience and wisdom."

As I thought about the response to my keynote address, I realized that over a lifetime of living in many parts of the world, I have studied what it means to become a follower of Jesus and remain within one's own culture. The insights from missiological anthropology are as valuable today as they have ever been in our increasingly globalized and urbanized world. So I invite you to journey with me through this fascinating field and apply the ideas, concepts, and examples to your own life and ministry.

My goal is to share with you the wisdom I have learned over the past four decades as a missiological anthropologist. My hope is to bring you along on the journey God has invited me into. In the process, you will both laugh at my mistakes and marvel at God's interventions. I didn't start off with the wisdom I have now. Actually, I started off quite naive.

My Story

I grew up in Michigan in a conservative Wesleyan tradition in which missionaries were given the highest place of spiritual honor. It was as if we had an unspoken spiritual pyramid with missionaries at the top, pastors in the middle, and ordinary laypeople at the bottom. So of course I wanted to become a missionary when I grew up. "Why not aim for the top of the spiritual hierarchy?" I mused. But even though missionaries occupied the upper echelons of the spiritual pyramid, some kinds of missionaries were perceived to have more spiritual value than others. For example, Bible translators were near the top of my spiritual pyramid because they had to be really intelligent, jungle savvy, and extremely dedicated to spend twenty years translating the New Testament. But at the apex of the pyramid resided medical missionaries. Why medical missionaries? Perhaps because they were perceived to sacrifice even more than regular missionaries. I read everything I could about medical missionaries, and I knew I wanted to become like them, minus martyrdom, of course.

I enrolled in college as a premed student, taking classes in chemistry, biology, anatomy and physiology, microbiology, and other physical sciences. In my third year of college, I transferred to Seattle Pacific College and acquired a new academic adviser. When he asked me what I wanted to become when I grew up, I told him I wanted to be a medical missionary. "Then you better take a course in anthropology," he recommended. I had never even heard of the discipline, but I trusted his counsel and so enrolled in my first anthropology class.[2] It was love at first sight, for I discovered an academic discipline that fit me as a person. I proceeded to take as many anthropology and other social science courses as I could in my final two years, and I graduated in 1969 in the middle of the Vietnam War. What was I to do with my life now?

Starting My Cross-Cultural Journey

My church invited me to go to the Democratic Republic of Congo and help restart the mission that had been "blown out of the water" by rebel uprising. They were looking for two young men who were expendable, and so I volunteered. Two years in the Congo would postpone having to go to Vietnam and would give me an opportunity to seek God's guidance about what to do with my life. Should I continue pursuing a vocation as a medical missionary or do further study in anthropology? I asked God to show me a clear path for my life and vocation. The first six months I felt I should continue along the medical missionary path because I witnessed so much human suffering, and this was before HIV/AIDS invaded the continent.

This was the beginning of the postcolonial era and the waning days of missionary compounds. We were kept busy running here and there, completing one task after another. There wasn't much time left to develop deep personal relationships with local people. I remember once making a trip to buy supplies, bouncing along rough dirt roads in our Land Rover to the Rwandan capital city of Kigali. My conversation with my missionary colleague that day was about all the things we needed to do to keep the mission running smoothly. We were focused on completing tasks around Bibles, books, and Band-Aids—the three traditional avenues of cross-cultural ministry. It seemed like we didn't have much interest in understanding the African people at the deeper level of their worldview. And besides, it would take too much time to dig into their culture like that.

I also noticed that the missionaries didn't seem very interested in exploring whether Christianity was connecting to the deepest levels of the Africans' worldview. This was the same place where twenty-four years later the Rwandan genocide would occur. The missionaries seemed content for Christianity to reside on the surface level of behavioral and religious change. Slowly I came to the conclusion that I could make a more significant contribution to the missionary enterprise as an anthropologist than as a medical missionary. I remember

2. I tell the story of my life as a missiological anthropologist in Whiteman 2023c.

as though it were yesterday the day I told my missionary colleagues that at the end of my term of service, I was going to return to the United States and pursue graduate studies in anthropology rather than go to medical school.

"Throwing My Life Away"

They did not greet my announcement with enthusiasm. To the contrary, they were very upset with me and told me I would end up throwing my life away. "We've never met a Christian anthropologist," they said. "Why do you think you can become the first one? Even if your Christian faith does survive and you are able to remain a Christian, there's nothing of value in the field of anthropology for missionary work. It is just about human evolution and digging up old bones." So, with that kind of "encouragement," off I went to graduate school in anthropology.

As I studied anthropology, my passion for Christian mission only increased, and now I had some tools to contribute to it. Following fieldwork in the Solomon Islands and the successful defense of my dissertation, my wife, Laurie, and I were invited to serve in Melanesia, where I was able to use my training in anthropology to help train missionaries in understanding the Melanesian context of their ministry. From that day to this, for the past forty-five years, I have been passionate about helping missionaries connect the gospel to the deepest part of people's worldview and culture. In the process, I have trained several thousand missionaries from many denominations and ecclesial traditions, mentored scores of doctoral students in the field of missiological anthropology, and contributed to the field through writing and editing.[3] My research has focused on the cross-cultural adjustment of missionaries and the planting and fostering of indigenous expressions of Christianity that missiological anthropologists would come to call the contextualization of the gospel.

Helpful Friends

In my missionary and missiological pilgrimage of discovering the ways in which the gospel connects to people's cultures, I have been greatly helped, encouraged, and inspired by several missiological anthropologists who went before me.

The first of these giants was the brilliant linguist and Bible translator Eugene Nida (1914–2011), who in 1954 published *Customs and Cultures: Anthropology for*

---

3. From 1989 to 2002, I was the editor for the American Society of Missiology's academic journal *Missiology: An International Review*. This journal continued a previous publication called *Practical Anthropology* (1953–72), which had grown to nearly five thousand subscriptions.

Christian Missions, which was one of the earliest and arguably most significant books connecting anthropology to mission.[4]

Another friend in the journey was Charles Kraft (1932–). His book *Christianity in Culture* (1979) helped me see how so much of our cross-cultural ministry has missed the mark because it wasn't "receptor oriented" and didn't engage people at their worldview level. Later, his *Anthropology for Christian Witness* (1996) would provide a textbook in cultural anthropology for cross-cultural ministry.

Alan Tippett (1911–88) was an Australian Methodist missionary in Fiji for twenty years and then earned a PhD in anthropology, studying under the famous Homer Barnett at the University of Oregon. Tippett adopted me as a missiological son and introduced me to his research in his groundbreaking book, *Solomon Islands Christianity* (1967), which spurred my own doctoral research among Anglicans in the Solomon Islands.[5]

The person I consider the "dean" of missiological anthropology is Paul G. Hiebert (1932–2007), who wrote *Anthropological Insights for Missionaries* (1985). Hiebert's engaging and creative models of culture convincingly show how our own culture shapes our understanding of the gospel. In this well-written and engaging book, Hiebert discusses cultural differences and the message we communicate, the cultural differences we encounter as missionaries, and how to create a bicultural community in cross-cultural ministry. We are all indebted to Paul Hiebert.

The most important missiological anthropology book from a Catholic perspective is Louis Luzbetak's *The Church and Cultures: An Applied Anthropology for the Religious Worker* (1970), which was completely revised and published as *The Church and Cultures: New Perspectives in Missiological Anthropology* in 1988. This remains the premier missiological anthropology text from a Catholic perspective.[6]

Additional books written by anthropologists with a focus on applied anthropology for missions include Marvin K. Mayers's *Christianity Confronts Culture: A Strategy for Cross-Cultural Evangelism* (1974, 1987) and Michael Rynkiewich's *Soul, Self, and Society: A Postmodern Anthropology for Mission in a Postcolonial World* (2011).[7]

---

4. For a fascinating biography of Eugene Nida and especially discussion of his impact on Bible translation, see Stine 2004.

5. Tippett wrote the foreword to my book *Melanesians and Missionaries* (1983). For more on Tippett and his contributions to missiology, see Whiteman 1992, 1994; and Hovey 2019.

6. Taber wrote a glowing review of this book, calling it "one of the most significant missiological books of the last quarter of this century" (1990, 104).

7. For a brief history of the development of missiological anthropology, see Whiteman 2003.

Following in the tradition of Nida, Kraft, Tippett, Hiebert, Luzbetak, and Mayers, the present book is *not* an introduction to cultural anthropology from a Christian perspective, such as *Introducing Cultural Anthropology: A Christian Perspective* by Brian Howell and Jenell Paris (2011, 2019) or *Cultural Anthropology: A Christian Perspective* by Stephen Grunlan and Marvin Mayers (1979, 1988). Rather, the purpose of this book is to share the anthropological wisdom I have gained to assist cross-cultural ministry. This is the field of missiological anthropology.[8]

The goal of this book is to encourage and empower missionaries, who I will frequently refer to as cross-cultural witnesses, from every region of the globe and from every theological perspective to become more effective, to serve longer, and to thrive, not just survive, in their cross-cultural ministry (see Alma 2011). Several themes in this book will resonate with this goal:

1. Uncovering and understanding some of the challenges and problems encountered in cross-cultural communication of the gospel.
2. Recognizing and embracing the theological concept of the incarnation as a biblical model for cross-cultural ministry.
3. Encouraging contextualization of the gospel by understanding the dynamic relationship between Christianity and culture, between God's eternal Word and a changing world (cf. Conn 1984).

Training Others

As an anthropologist serving the church and mission for the past forty-five years, I have traveled to many parts of the world—China, India, Kenya, Cuba, Brazil, Philippines, and Papua New Guinea, to name a few—to train people for cross-cultural ministry. I confess that my teaching and training haven't always been met with a warm initial reception.

The answer I often give to "Why haven't we heard this before?" is that there are so few Christian anthropologists in the world, and even fewer have used their

---

8. The application of anthropology to mission was earlier called missionary anthropology. See especially Smalley 1963, 1967, and 1978, which contain reprinted articles published in the journal *Practical Anthropology*. These are very practical applications of anthropological knowledge, perspectives, and theories to various challenges and opportunities in mission. *Practical Anthropology* was published six times a year and ran from 1953 to 1972. In 1973, the newly established American Society of Missiology began publishing the journal *Missiology*, which took over from *Practical Anthropology*. The masthead of *Missiology* carries the phrase "continuing *Practical Anthropology*." The first editor of the newly inaugurated journal was missiological anthropologist Alan Tippett. The American Society of Missiology and its journal *Missiology* continue to explore the field of missiological anthropology. I served as the fourth editor of *Missiology* (1989–2002) and always remembered that our journal began in the field of missiological anthropology.

training as professional anthropologists to serve God's mission in the world. My motivation for publishing this book, in the sunsetting of my professional vocation, is to help fill the void and to respond to the lack of understanding of and appreciation for the value and importance of an anthropological perspective in cross-cultural ministry.

The Structure of This Book

We will begin this journey of crossing cultures with the gospel by first examining the concept of culture. We start here because unless the gospel connects deeply with the culture of a people, there will be very little transformation. New Zealand missiological anthropologist Gerald A. Arbuckle, in his book *Earthing the Gospel: An Inculturation Handbook for Pastoral Workers*, says that evangelization "demands the *insertion* of the Gospel within the very heart of a culture" (1990, 18). It is imperative as cross-cultural witnesses that we understand the concept of culture, for it is within a culture that people come to find meaning in their existence, understand the gospel as it relates to their personal and corporate life, and become followers of Jesus and join in fellowship with others. There are of course legitimate critiques of the concept of culture when we overextend its usefulness and make generalizations about people and essentialize and stereotype them. Part 1 will therefore build a foundation of understanding culture so we'll better understand what we are crossing when we talk about crossing cultures with the gospel.

Part 2 will focus on the biblical basis for how we cross cultures with the gospel. I will argue that the incarnation—God entering human history through the person of Jesus the Jew—is more than a theological doctrine, as important as that is to Christian faith. The incarnation is also a model of how we are to enter another culture and identify with people. I call it incarnational identification, and it is the basic approach I take throughout the book.

Equipped with an understanding of culture and with Jesus as our model for developing cross-cultural relationships, we sally forth, only to quickly bump up against significant problems. We soon discover that enthusiasm for and knowledge of the Bible are not enough to cross cultures with the gospel. So in part 3 we will address some common issues that can cause communication problems. As we begin to identify with people, it doesn't take us long to discover significant worldview differences. Another cross-cultural communication challenge doesn't involve words at all. It comes from the many messages we send that are nonverbal, which are called paramessages. We frequently send unintended messages that sometimes contradict the verbal message we want to proclaim. The next problem we will address involves cultural forms. If we don't use cultural forms that make sense in a particular culture, then we may not convey the meaning we wish to communicate, which can lead to significant miscommunication, misunderstanding, and even mistrust. We'll conclude this section on communication problems by addressing the use of space in communicating with others.

Part 4 will take on the subject of culture shock, which is often an unwelcome, but unavoidable, side effect of crossing cultures with the gospel. The problem with culture shock is that it often goes undiagnosed, so people don't understand what is happening to them, why they are so depressed, and why they feel discouraged and wonder if they are good enough to participate in God's mission in the world. We will address the problem of culture shock as an occupational disease of people who are suddenly transplanted from one culture to another.

How can we become more effective communicators? This will be the focus of part 5. In chapter 12, I will demonstrate how we can discover cultural differences through some time-tested anthropological methods of conducting fieldwork, such as participant observation and learning how to be a good ethnographer in the midst of our cross-cultural ministry. One of the biggest challenges of crossing cultures with the gospel is that we are unaware of our own worldview assumptions. Naively, we think the way we see the world is the way the world really is for everyone. We therefore spend too much of our energy trying to convince others to see the world the way we do. So in chapter 13, we will explore some of the dominant values and worldview themes that impact our cross-cultural ministry. We will examine how sometimes our faith can be shaped by our culture as much as it is by biblical values.[9] Finally, in chapter 14, we will look at two strategies for overcoming many of the problems outlined in this book. The first strategy is a short-term one called bonding, which occurs in the early days and weeks in another culture. The long-term strategy, following the biblical model of incarnational identification, is to become a bicultural person who can freely move in and out of different cultures, feel at home in both, and make contributions to the community, society, and culture.

While I encourage my students to learn from all of the literature they can, nothing beats listening to wisdom gained from actual cross-cultural experiences. After all, the new broom can sweep nicely, *but* the old broom knows the corners of the room! Research (e.g., Taylor 1997; Hay et al. 2007) documents a fairly high attrition rate across all cultures of cross-cultural witnesses. We simply need the wisdom and insight of others in order to navigate the complexities of cross-cultural life and ministry. My great desire is to see the attrition rate

9. For example, Richards and O'Brien 2012 illustrates this principle very convincingly.

decrease and the rate of satisfaction and fulfillment increase for the sake of the kingdom of God and God's mission in the world, which we are invited to join.

Missionary Conversion

Let's get back to that student asking the question about missionary conversion. I had just given the keynote address "The Conversion of a Missionary: A Missiological Study of Acts 10," in which I argued that every missionary is in need of two conversions. If you are reading this book, then you have probably experienced the first spiritual conversion to Christ as Lord and Savior. Many cross-cultural witnesses have, but not many have experienced the second conversion of becoming aware of the impact their culture has on them, gaining a deep understanding of others, and discovering where the Holy Spirit has already been at work before they arrived on the scene. So, I invite you to journey with me through the fascinating field of missiological anthropology and to apply the ideas, concepts, and examples to your own life and ministry. In the process, I hope you experience your own second conversion!

PART 1

The Concept of Culture

2

Understanding Culture in Mission

He who does not travel thinks his mother is the world's best cook. (If we don't experience other cultures, we'll think our own is the best.)

Kikuyu proverb, Kenya

W e're no longer headhunters; we're Christians," they insisted. "What do these Campus Crusade people mean when they say we should compare our life before and after we became Christians? We don't have a *before* and *after* time. Does this mean we aren't Christians?" Questions like these arose one day when my wife, Laurie, and I were living in a small village on the island of Santa Isabel in the Solomon Islands in 1977–78. A number of villagers came to talk to me about what it meant to share their faith as Christians in the Anglican tradition. They had encountered a new teaching from Campus Crusade for Christ (now CRU) that was instructing them on how to prepare their personal testimony. They were told to talk about their life *before* they became a Christian and compare it to *after* they had become a Christian. The villagers were utterly confused. "We have always been Anglican Christians, for several generations now," they said. "Are we not Christians simply because we cannot explain our faith in their terms?"

This encounter was a clash of two very different cultures—an individualistic culture versus a collectivist and community-oriented culture.[1] It represented

1. For further discussion on the significance of these two very different cultures as they relate to evangelism and mission, see Moon and Simon 2021, 49–52; and Richards and James 2020.

two different theologies shaped by contrasting cultures. It was fueled by contrasting understandings of what a Christian is. If the goal of Campus Crusade was to get these Solomon Islanders to understand the "Four Spiritual Laws" and invite Jesus into their hearts, then it is unlikely they were successful. The Campus Crusaders and the Solomon Islanders did not understand each other because they did not know and appreciate the culture from which the other came.

This is a simple example of why culture matters and why we must understand the culture of the other in cross-cultural ministry. We will explore in this chapter the concept of culture, which is foundational for effective ministry within and between cultures.

Effective cross-cultural ministry and discipleship require one to be able to form, develop, and maintain personal relationships. If we try to do evangelism and discipleship without establishing a relationship with the potential follower of Jesus, then we will likely fail. Our effort to evangelize will not be perceived as good news; it will be confusing news, irrelevant news, or, even worse, bad news. To develop meaningful relationships with others, we must understand their culture, which shapes their ideas, influences their attitudes, and affects how they live, think, and behave. Before we can understand the specific culture of a people, however, we need to understand the concept of culture, and that is our task in part 1. Not everyone in mission will agree with this.

I have encountered opposition to my teaching from some theologians. For example, a systematic theologian sent two of his students into my Anthropology for Christian Mission class essentially as spies to report back to him what I was teaching. Imagine my surprise one day when they confessed that they had been sent to my course to spy on me but in the process had been converted. They were now thoroughly convinced of the importance of understanding culture for mission and discipleship and that biblical knowledge and systematic theology were necessary but not sufficient for effectively serving in cross-cultural ministry. The pushback I occasionally hear goes something like this: "There are thousands of missionaries all over the world with only biblical and theological training, if that much. They certainly aren't anthropologists, and yet they appear to have an effective ministry." Yes, that is true, but unless we understand the culture of the people among whom we live and serve, we will likely miscommunicate, despite our depth of biblical and theological knowledge.

So how important is the concept of culture for effective cross-cultural ministry? Missionary anthropologist Louis Luzbetak, in his book *The Church and Cultures*, says, "The concept of culture is . . . the anthropologist's most significant contribution to the missionary endeavor. Nothing could be more fundamental than a proper understanding of the term. A failure to grasp the nature of culture would be a failure to grasp much of the nature of missionary work itself" (1970, 59). Luzbetak is saying that if we don't understand what culture is, then we don't really understand what missionary work is all about. How many missionaries have been properly trained and have learned some ethnographic skills that enable them to understand the concept of culture? Unfortunately, very few. This is because cross-cultural and anthropological training has historically had a low priority in preparing people for cross-cultural ministry. We're going to try to rectify some of that deficiency in this chapter. Let's begin with a definition of culture.

Definitions of Culture

We need to begin by noting what I do *not* mean by the word *culture*. A popular use of the term, borrowed from the French, is related to a person who enjoys fine arts and follows careful etiquette as a *cultured* person, in contrast to those who supposedly aren't cultured. For example, when we see travel brochures for Paris, London, Hong Kong, Tokyo, or New York advertising "cultural events," they are frequently referring to museums, ballets, orchestras, musical productions, plays, and other aspects of "high culture."

In contrast to this popular understanding of the term, *culture* in the anthropological sense refers to the entire human-made environment in which people live (Herskovits 1955), not just fine arts and "proper" manners. The concept of culture includes the music of Brahms, Beethoven, and Bach but also the Beach Boys, the Beatles, and Beyoncé. The anthropological use of the term is a broad concept that encompasses the norms, values, customs, traditions, habits, skills, knowledge, beliefs, and whole way of life of a group of people. As we'll discover throughout this book, understanding the concept of culture is crucial for effective ministry, whether within your own culture or in another.[2]

Anthropologists have offered hundreds of definitions of this important term (cf. Kroeber and Kluckhohn 1952; and Weiss 1973). Occasionally the usefulness of the term has been debated among academic anthropologists. The definitions have changed over time from a more static, bounded set to understanding culture as dynamic, changing, complex, and porous. Howell and Paris view culture as "internally diverse, always changing, and affected by power" (2019, 44).

The concept of culture from a social science perspective is relatively recent. Edward Burnett Tylor gave us the first scientific definition of culture in English.[3]

2. Luzbetak has a very thorough discussion on the nature of culture that covers the historical development of the term in anthropology and applies it to missiological anthropology today (1988, 133–222).

3. An earlier definition in German appeared about thirty years prior to Tylor's definition.

In 1871, Tylor wrote, "Culture is that complex whole which includes knowledge, belief, art, morals, law, custom, and any other capabilities and habits acquired by [human beings] as [members] of a society" (1871, 1). One hundred years later, Clifford Geertz, often a favorite of missiological anthropologists, defined culture as "a system of inherited conceptions expressed in symbolic forms by means of which [people] communicate, perpetuate, and develop their knowledge about and attitudes toward life" (1973, 89). Geertz would say that the purpose of culture is to impose meaning on the world and make it understandable.

Sometimes when we are new to a place, we don't understand what is happening or how to behave appropriately, and this may leave us confused. James Spradley and David McCurdy explain why this happens: "Culture is the acquired knowledge people use to interpret experience and generate social behavior" (1975, 5). Michael Rynkiewich, in a comprehensive and more postmodern definition, argues that "culture is a more or less integrated system of knowledge, values and feelings that people use to define reality (worldview), interpret their experiences, and generate appropriate strategies for living; a system that people learn from other people around them and share with people in a social setting; a system that people use to adapt to their spiritual, social, and physical environment; and a system that people use to innovate in order to change themselves as their environment changes" (2011, 19). Finally, Howell and Paris offer a contemporary definition of culture: "Culture is the total way of life of a group of people that is learned, dynamic, shared, power laden, and integrated" (2019, 40).

When we understand a culture different from our own, we can interpret people's experiences in that culture and make sense of what they're doing and thinking. We can also learn to behave in ways that are appropriate for that context. It is so important in ministry to take the time and to expend the energy to learn about another culture so that we can understand what's going on and act in a manner that's culturally appropriate.

Speaking as an anthropologist and not as a theologian, I believe culture is what separates human beings from all other animals that are a part of God's creation. We are animals in the sense of our biological creation—that is, we are Homo sapiens—but we are fundamentally different from all other animals that God created in that we are the only ones with culture, which influences who we become. Moreover, we are the only animals created in God's image. Therefore, culture must be a very important part of our God-given being and identity. I like to think of culture as a gift of God's grace. M. A. C. Warren, in his introduction to John V. Taylor's The Primal Vision, says, "Our first task in approaching another culture, another religion, is to take off our shoes, for the place we are approaching is holy. Else we may find ourselves treading on men's dreams. More serious still, we may forget that God was here before our arrival" (Taylor 1963, 10).

Culture is what enables us to distinguish between cultural and noncultural—natural, organic, chemical, or geological—things. For example, if you are walking through a forest and come across a table and chairs, your first thought would not be, *What a strange-looking tree without any leaves.* No, you would immediately know that human beings had been there before you, because that table and chairs are a cultural by-product of some person's ideas and creative skill. Culture transforms natural, geological, or organic things into cultural things, like a table and chairs. Culture, then, is primarily a mental phenomenon consisting of ideas, values, and feelings that lead to behaviors and the creation of material and nonmaterial products. Figure 2.1 shows this relationship.

Figure 2.1
Sequential Elements in the Creation of Culture

The Danger of Reifying, Essentializing, and Totalizing Culture

Because it is such a powerful influence in shaping our ideas, values, and feelings, I sometimes refer to culture as a straitjacket that fits comfortably. But we must raise two cautions here. We must be aware of the tendency to reify culture—that is, to assume culture has a life of its own, irrespective of the human beings who create and change it. When we reify culture, we can easily assume that it controls us. But culture does nothing. People make decisions, react to events, behave in certain ways, and create products. Culture does not do those things. So when thinking about or learning about the culture of a particular group of people who appear resistant to the gospel, we must be careful not to assume that their culture *causes* them to reject the gospel. For example, when Protestant missionaries arrived in Korea and Japan in 1884, they believed that Korean culture was open to the gospel and that Japanese culture made people resistant to accepting the gospel.

Misunderstanding what culture is can also lead to another problem: we essentialize or totalize culture, thereby removing agency from the people who participate and live in a particular society. Among postmodern anthropologists today, this is the number one "sin" that must be avoided (cf. Rynkiewich 2011, 38–39). If we essentialize culture, we unconsciously assume that everyone in that culture acts or thinks in similar ways. Essentializing culture causes us to ignore the tremendous diversity within any given culture and to create stereotypes of people, such as, "Mexicans are . . . ," "Americans always . . . ," "Those people . . . " We do this all the time, often unconsciously. Miriam Adeney warns against this, noting that "God doesn't stereotype us, but meets us each as the exceptions we are, with our multiple and overlapping identities, our unique pilgrimages, and our individual quirks. God doesn't slot us into pigeonholes" (2015, 96).

Craig Ott, in a creative and brilliant article, suggests a solution to two extremes in our understanding of the concept of culture. He writes, "The concept of culture has long been central to mission theory and practice. However, current understandings of culture can easily fall into one of two extremes: on the one hand, essentialist views of culture can easily lead to stereotyping, and on the other hand, extreme postcolonial cultural hybridization theories reject typologies of cultural differences altogether and tend to disregard empirical research on cultural differences" (2022, 63).

In some recent missiological discussions, there has been a trend of lumping people into generalized categories of guilt, shame, and fear cultures.[4] These categories can be helpful in evangelism and mission, but we need to be careful not to overgeneralize—that is, essentialize. I have argued elsewhere that we shouldn't jump on the latest missiological bandwagon in hopes of achieving quick results with a minimum of life investment (Whiteman 2018). This can easily happen if we essentialize and assume that all people within a given culture are the same. We must avoid essentializing and totalizing culture because sometimes there is as much variation within a culture as there is between cultures.

Avoiding essentializing and reifying culture means we take it seriously but don't idealize it or, worse, idolize it. To underscore the dynamic nature of culture with the present global flows of ideas, people, and products, we can say that culture is changing, constructed, contested, contingent, contextual, complex, and creative. Some postmodern anthropologists today believe the concept of culture is no longer valid or useful in explaining human societies because it doesn't make sufficient room for personal agency in the way we create and innovate or that it doesn't adequately account for the role of power and inequality

4. For recent discussions on this topic of guilt, shame, and fear cultures in mission, see Beech 2018; Cozens 2018; deNeui 2017; Flanders and Mischke 2020; Georges 2017, 2019; Georges and Baker 2016; Mischke 2015; Moon and Simon 2021; Muller 2000; Richards and James 2020; and Wu 2019.

in societies (e.g., Brightman 1995; and Fischer 2007).[5] These critiques of the concept of culture are good because they remind us to avoid the reification of culture, to make room for agency, and to understand culture as dynamic and changing, not static and fixed. If we keep these precautions in mind, then the concept of culture can be relevant and helpful, especially as it informs how we understand and practice cross-cultural ministry.

Attributes of Culture

Let's build on the foundation of what culture is and discuss some attributes that are important for cross-cultural ministry: culture is learned, culture is shared, and culture is acquired as a member of society.

Culture Is Learned

When we say that culture is learned, we mean it is not biologically inherited; it is not an instinct. In other words, there is not a gene on our chromosomes for culture. In some ways, it would be nice if there were, because then as part of our preparation for cross-cultural ministry, we could splice in a gene for learning another language or understanding another culture. When we're struggling to comprehend another language or make sense of cultural differences, it is tempting to wish that God had created us so that we could simply do genetic programming and take all the hard work out of the process. But God did not create us that way. Instead, we have to learn everything. And unfortunately, it is true, the older we become, the more difficult it is to learn another language or make sense of a different culture. I frequently tell parents engaged in cross-cultural ministry that they are giving their children a great gift of learning more than one language and understanding more than one culture. The earlier the better when it comes to learning a second language and culture.

Let's consider a hypothetical experiment. What if we took a baby born in Beijing, China, before June 4, 1989, and brought that baby to Atlanta, Georgia? After twenty years, will she have a natural proclivity for using chopsticks? No. Will she speak Chinese? No, she will speak English with a Southern accent. What is the likelihood she'll be a communist? It is unlikely. Depending on the family in which she was raised, she is more likely to be a Southern Baptist Christian. There will be nothing Chinese about her, other than her physical appearance, which may lead people to initially conclude that she is "Chinese." But to be Chinese, she would have had to learn all the Chinese aspects of culture.

5. For an excellent review of the concept of culture and its strengths and weaknesses in and beyond anthropology, see Fox and King 2020; and Silverman 2020.

She would not have inherited them biologically. And so, because she was raised in the United States, she will not be culturally Chinese.

You may be protesting, "But aren't there some instincts? What about sin? Everyone sins, so this must certainly be instinctive." It is true that sin is universal, but what is defined as sin varies from one culture to another, as T. Wayne Dye (1976) and Robert J. Priest (1994) have persuasively argued. We have a propensity to sin, a bent toward sinning, and of course without the help of the Holy Spirit within us, we would not be able to overcome this tendency to sin. If we had an instinct for sin, then everyone would sin the same way, but that does not happen. Perhaps figure 2.2 will help explain this concept.

Figure 2.2
The Continuum of Behavior

Instinctual Behavior   Learned Behavior

If we were to line up all the animals in the animal kingdom, they would fall somewhere along this continuum between instinctual and learned behavior. Insects would be to the far left because their behavior is more instinctual. Human beings would be to the extreme right because our behavior is learned. Other primates, such as chimpanzees and gorillas, would be near the learned behavior end of the continuum, but they wouldn't occupy the same space on the continuum as human beings.

Alfred Kroeber explains the difference between instinct and learned behavior. He wrote in 1917, which accounts for his choice of words and ethnocentric perspective, but his insights are as important today as they were over one hundred years ago. Kroeber writes, "Take a couple of ant eggs, of the right sex, unhatched eggs, freshly laid. Blot out every individual and every other egg of the species. Give the pair a little attention as regards warmth, moisture, protection, and food. The whole of ant 'society,' every one of the abilities, powers, accomplishments, and activities of the species . . . will be reproduced, and reproduced without diminution, in one generation" (1917, 177). In this example, the whole of ant society is reproduced from just two ants because their behavior is genetically programmed.

"But," says Kroeber,

> place on a desert island or in a circumvallation two or three hundred human infants of the best stock from the highest class of the most civilized nation; furnish them the necessary incubation and nourishment; leave them in total isolation

from their kind; and what shall we have? The civilization from which they were torn? One tenth of it? No, not any fraction; nor a fraction of the civilizational attainments of the rudest savage tribe. Only a pair or a troop of mutes, without arts, knowledge, fire, order, or religion. Civilization would be blotted out within these confines—not disintegrated, not cut to the quick, but obliterated in one sweep. (1917, 177)

In other words, Kroeber is suggesting that if human beings were somehow raised without human contact, they would not turn out to be human, with all the normal human characteristics that we associate with them, such as fire, order, art, music, religion, language, and so on. Ants don't need the presence of other ants to know how to function in ant "society" because their behavior is genetically programmed, but human beings must be in the company of others if they are to become fully functioning human beings.

Is Kroeber's argument only a theoretical possibility, or is there some basis for it in fact? Unfortunately, his hypothetical example of children being raised without human contact is all too real. We know them as feral children—human beings who have somehow been able to survive without human contact but who, when they are discovered, have very few if any human characteristics.

The first scientifically documented case is known as the Wild Boy of Aveyron. He was discovered in the mountainous forest in the Aveyron district of southern France in January 1800. In a carefully researched and well-documented book by Harlan Lane (1979), we learn that a farmer found this boy, estimated to be around twelve or thirteen years old, digging in his garden looking for something to eat. Although he had human characteristics, he walked on all fours and acted more like a dog than a human being. The farmer sold him to a traveling circus, who put him on display as a bizarre phenomenon. Eventually, the remarkable French psychologist Jean-Marc-Gaspard Itard (1774–1838) learned about this boy, bought him from the circus, and brought him to Paris, where he tried to work with him. He gave him the name Victor, but Victor never really developed as a fully functioning human being and died around age twenty-eight. The Wild Boy of Aveyron created quite a stir in the European scientific community because the nurture versus nature debate was raging at this time.

This story illustrates what can happen when a human being is not raised in the company of other humans and does not learn a language and culture. When I first learned about these feral children, they were disturbing to me on a number of levels. For one thing, where was the image of God in them? Where did original sin reside? This is not the place to probe such theological questions, but they do make us vividly aware of the importance of culture in our development as human beings created in the image of God.

The example of feral children also underscores the importance of the kind of culture we create in our homes that our children are exposed to in the early months and years of their lives. When our son was born, I was writing my doctoral dissertation in anthropology on the impact of Anglican Christianity in the Solomon Islands. Arguably, I knew more about that topic than any other living person at the time, but I felt as if I knew nothing about how to introduce my son to a culture in our home that would reflect biblical values and pour out generous portions of love and ample discipline. It was a sobering thought to realize how significant would be the culture of our family that my son was exposed to in the early months and years of his life and the responsibility and privilege my wife and I had to create it.

Learning through our culture is critical to our formation and growth as human beings, but strangely, I have encountered many Christians who find this revelation that culture is learned and not biologically inherited to be rather disturbing. But what this knowledge reveals to me is that God uses culture, not genes and chromosomes, to shape us into what God wants us to become. The more we reflect the values of the kingdom of God, and the more we take on the mind of Christ (1 Cor. 2:16), the more we can influence our culture with values that are consistent with God's character. Figure 2.3 illustrates the relationship between a biological *Homo sapiens* and a cultural human being.

Figure 2.3
The Role of Culture in the Creation of Human Beings

Most animals eat and drink whenever the urge arises, but human beings eat and drink at certain prescribed times and feel hungry when those times arrive. The number of meals per day ranges from one meal a day in some parts of Africa up to six small meals in some areas of Scandinavia. Culture is also powerful in the sense that it tells us what foods are appropriate and which ones are not. Some foods we can eat without any difficulty, other kinds of food we cannot eat. They are culturally inappropriate.

I remember one of my students from Japan who dropped by my office one day to bring me a gift from home. He had just received a care package and was anxious to share it with his professor, so I invited him into my office. Then he peeled off the top of his Tupperware container, and there floating in soy sauce were grasshoppers. "Would you like to taste a grasshopper?" he asked me with excitement. I knew that all of my teaching on incarnational identification was on the line at that very moment (more on this in chap. 4). I had no choice. I had to accept his gracious gift. So I gingerly pulled out a grasshopper from the container, shook off the excess soy sauce, and popped it into my mouth. To my surprise, it was delicious. The texture was a little off, but the flavor was wonderful. And then I surprised him when I asked for a second helping! He later confided in me about some personal concerns. He knew he could share them only with someone he knew he could trust and who would listen. So swallowing a grasshopper did more than satiate my appetite—it built a bridge of trust.

Several years later after he graduated, I met him again at Yale Divinity School, and he asked me if I remembered the time he dropped by my office with some marinated grasshoppers. "Oh yes," I said, "I've never forgotten that." He then went on to say how he had offered those grasshoppers to all of his professors, but only six of them had been willing to try them. And then he said, "And you were the only one who asked for a second helping." Culture was at play in influencing his American professors about whether they could eat marinated grasshoppers, a delicacy in Japan.

There are human needs that we all share with the whole of humanity. These are given, biological needs. But the way these needs are met is through cultural means, and these are in no way universal but vary from society to society. The well-known British anthropologist Bronislaw Malinowski (1884–1942), born in Cracow, Poland, developed what he called a Permanent Vital Sequence that is incorporated into all cultures to explain the relationship between biological and psychological needs and the cultural ways in which those needs are met in order to bring satisfaction (1944, 77). His scheme is depicted in figure 2.4.

Malinowski's Permanent Vital Sequence is a useful conceptual tool for understanding the concept of culture, and for the non-anthropologist who wants to begin to understand another culture, Malinowski's scheme is a good starting point. Because all persons have the same needs (impulses in Malinowski's terms), we often erroneously assume that all persons meet those needs in the same way. Malinowski's approach helps us to be aware that *various cultures meet the same needs in different ways.* This opens the door for us to begin

Figure 2.4
Malinowski's Permanent Vital Sequence

Impulse	Act	Satisfaction
Biological and Psychological	*Cultural*	*Biological and Psychological*

understanding people in another culture, which is an important step toward effective cross-cultural evangelism.

Malinowski goes on to describe what he calls the basic human needs:

1. Metabolism—the need for oxygen, liquid, and food
2. Reproduction—the sex drive
3. Bodily comforts—maintaining a tolerable level of temperature, humidity, and so on
4. Safety—the prevention of bodily injuries by mechanical accident, attack from animals, and from other human beings
5. Movement—activity, exercise, sports, and so on
6. Growth—maturation, enculturation, and love
7. Health—the maintenance and repair of the biological organism (1944, 91)[6]

I would argue that we are on solid, empirical ground in suggesting an eighth universal or basic need in all human beings. I call this a religious need, a psychological impulse that is met culturally in very different ways. This is a contributing factor to why there are so many religions in the world. I believe, however, that this need is fully met only as human beings come into a relationship with Jesus Christ and grow toward spiritual maturity and into the full stature of Christ (Eph. 4:13).

Culture Is Shared

The second attribute of culture is as important as the first. Culture is not only learned but also shared. It is not enough to learn a culture; it has to be shared with others for it to become part of the society. This, of course, is the social basis of evangelism. It is not enough for me to know Christ personally. I have to share that understanding, share that experience with others so that it can become a part of their lives and the gospel can transform their culture. And, of course, when Christians from other cultures share their experience of following Jesus, it helps us gain a broader and deeper understanding of God. We learn from each other. Anthropologically, this is the reason for sharing our faith with others.

Let's be anthropologists for a moment and transport ourselves to a village in the Highlands of Papua New Guinea. We are amazed at the beauty of the mountainous landscape, and because of the mile-high altitude, we'll enjoy the springlike weather year-round. We see people inhabiting a common territory,

---

6. Malinowski also discusses the various cultural responses people have to needs (1994, 91).

and we call it a village. They are interacting to achieve common goals, and we call that a society. But where is their culture?

We see a man thatching the roof on his house, and we notice the kind of sago palm leaves and bamboo poles he is using. What really captures our attention, however, is that many men in his kinship group are helping with the repair. They are singing and having a grand time, and it looks more like a party or celebration than work, but they are getting the work done.

We see a woman disciplining her child, and if we are Americans (shorthand for those who live in the United States; I recognize that people north and south of the border also consider themselves North Americans), we'll probably ask ourselves, "Why did she take so long to discipline the child? If I were his parent, I would have done it a long time ago, because the child seems to be very disrespectful to his mother from my perspective." We note what the child did to incur his mother's wrath, and eventually she does discipline the child. We note, however, that she uses the opportunity as a teaching moment instead of violently spanking the child.

We also see women working in their gardens, often with a baby strapped to their backs. They are working their sweet potato mounds, and it turns out that they are rather good horticulturalists.

Six months pass, and we start to see a pattern emerge. People exhibit these behaviors in a similar fashion for similar reasons. In fact, the uniformities of behavior are the outward, observable expressions of their culture, which they carry in their minds. In other words, they share these ideas on how to thatch a roof, to discipline a child, and grow a garden. As they share these ideas, the ideas become part of their culture. In the spirit of cognitive anthropologist Ward Goodenough (1971, 1981), we can say that culture consists of the shared models people carry in their minds for perceiving, relating to, and interpreting the world around them. In this sense, culture is an abstraction from reality similar to a map, which is also an abstraction from reality. A map mirrors reality by showing us the most important geographical features, such as roads, rivers, towns, and so on. If you are living in Shanghai, a map of China will not show the location of your house. It is too abstract. To find your house on a map, we'll need a neighborhood map. Then to find your bedroom, we'll need a map of your house.

Culture is shared, so as we share our mental maps of reality, it enables us to create appropriate behavior and interpret our experience in a society. But culture as a mental or cognitive map shows only the most significant aspects of people's behavior, not the details. Culture gives us themes that we must follow as human beings in a society, but we all have our individual interpretations and variations on those themes. For example, a North American cultural theme is that one wears clothes in public, even if it is an unbearably hot day. So, when we get up in the morning and hear that the temperature will be 95 degrees Fahrenheit or 35 degrees Celsius, we don't debate within ourselves whether to wear clothes. That decision has been made for us by our culture. What we may debate is what to wear, and if we are typical North Americans, we will be certain to wear something different today from what we wore yesterday.

Just as a map is a guide to direct people through geographical space, so culture is a mental map that makes it possible to find one's way in a society. Culture provides answers to life's questions from the cradle to the grave, and this provides security and to some degree predictability. Ironically, culture not only gives answers to life's questions but tells us what questions to ask.

Now, if we have the wrong road map and we follow it and get lost, how do we feel? We are likely to feel insecure, maybe even frightened. We'll be frustrated, maybe even angry. Perhaps we feel stupid and incompetent. This is what happens when we go to Singapore for cross-cultural ministry with a mental map that we learned growing up in Perry County, Mississippi. We naturally expect our Mississippi mental map to work in Singapore, but it doesn't. If we try to use our Mississippi map, then we are going to feel lost. We're going to get frustrated and angry. We're likely to become depressed and wonder if we are even good enough for God's service. When we operate in our host society using only the mental map of our home culture, it will lead to misunderstanding, which contributes to our experience of culture shock. We'll address this later in this book (see under "Psychological and Spiritual Depression" in chap. 10). Culture shock occurs when we are in a new situation but are relying on an old mental map from back home, which will lead us astray every time.

I'll never forget my first day in the village of Gnulahage on Santa Isabel in the Solomon Islands. It was May 19, 1977, and we had spent six years preparing for this day. We landed on the shore with all our earthly belongings in a few suitcases and some string bags. After we got out of the canoe and came ashore, we walked through a coconut plantation and then a mile inland through the jungle. Suddenly, we came upon a clearing with about twenty houses made out of palm leaves and bamboo poles. With pride, the group who met us pointed to a newer-looking house built on stilts and said, "That's your house we built for you."

We climbed up the steps to enter the house and put all our stuff on the floor. I noticed a fifteen-foot-long log along one side of the room. I wondered to myself what it was for, but within a few minutes, I discovered its use. It seemed as if every child in the village was sitting on the log watching every move we made. For many of those children, we were the first white people they had ever seen.

I remember kneeling on the floor to go through our belongings and getting overwhelmed, on the verge of panic, wondering, *What have I gotten us into?* I turned to my wife and said, "I think I've made the biggest mistake of my life. I don't know what we're doing here." Of course, I knew in my head why we were there, but emotionally and psychologically I wasn't so sure, and I certainly was not confident.

The only solution to my plight was to get out of that grass hut and into the village, talking with people, building relationships, and finding my way around. Unless I did that, I would never learn their mental maps, those aspects of their culture that they share with others in their society. A year later, we left the village of Gnulahage for the first time. What had happened in that intervening year? I had been able to learn part of the culture, to move and navigate in that society without getting permanently lost. I had learned some aspects of their culture. Now, finally, I was a Solomon Islander! Right? No, not at all, not even close! But I had learned a great deal of their mental map. I had learned to operate in ways that were appropriate in their culture. To paraphrase Spradley and McCurdy's definition given earlier, I had learned enough of the culture of that village to be able to understand what was happening and to behave in ways that were acceptable to the people in that village.

This is one way of describing and understanding culture. It is a mental map, and our task as cross-cultural witnesses is to learn the mental map of local people among whom we are living and serving. Once, after talking to a group of missionaries about the importance of learning the mental map of the people, a missionary told me, "I have been working and living in Macau for fifteen years, and I have to confess. I don't want to tell anybody else this, but I'm going to tell you. I don't know Chinese people. I really don't. I have been so busy doing everything else, but I really do not know why Chinese people are the way they are. Your talk has really been convicting to me."

Christian and Missionary Alliance missionary H. Myron Bromley (1925–2016) served among the Dani in the Baliem Valley of Irian Jaya on the island of New Guinea in Indonesia for nearly forty years. He graduated with a PhD from Yale in 1972 in anthropological linguistics and became a brilliant linguist. He came to know the Dani language and culture at the deepest level. When I visited the Baliem Valley in 1981 and met Bromley, the Dani told me, "Dr. Bromley knows our language and culture better than we do." How was that possible? It was possible because Bromley was able to create a mental map of the Dani language and culture that was a composite of many aspects of their culture.

As cross-cultural witnesses of the gospel, we must learn the mental map of those among whom we have come to live and serve. However, we must always remember that this mental map is never static, like a geographical map printed on paper. It is dynamic, with flows of ideas coming from many parts of the world. Missiological anthropologist Kenneth Nehrbass reminds us that globalization has made us even more aware of the diversity of cultures. The complexity of mental maps has underscored the importance of acquiring cultural competence[7] in relating to others and understanding that culture is shared, from one person to another, from one society to another (Nehrbass 2016). We've said that culture is learned, not biologically inherited, and it is something that is shared from one person to another, not just an idiosyncratic idea that a person dreams up. We turn next to discuss the context in which we learn and share culture.

Culture Is Acquired as a Member of Society

The third and final attribute of culture we will consider is that we acquire culture as members of a society. If "culture" ultimately refers to ideas in people's minds, then "society" refers to the people themselves. Society is an enduring aggregate of people that continues through time despite the death or birth of individual persons.

We learn and share our culture in the context of a specific society. Culture as a design for living tells us how a society will cooperate in securing food, in keeping warm, and in producing offspring. Culture is the mental map that tells a society how to function effectively. However, what happens when the mental map of how to navigate in a society no longer works as effectively as it once did? When cultures change quickly due to a variety of causes, such as environmental catastrophes, colonial invasion, warfare, or forced migration, anomie and cultural dysfunction can result.

Culture is a gift of God's grace and can be used for positive ends, but it is also capable of being pressed into horrible, evil purposes, reflecting the sinfulness of human beings. This is why the kingdom of God is a beautiful blueprint of how to live together in harmony in every society.[8]

In 1789, a man by the name of George Washington put his hand on a Bible and was sworn in as the first president of the United States. Two hundred years later in 1989, another man by the name of George put his hand on the same Bible and was sworn in as the forty-first president of the United States, George Herbert Walker Bush. In this two-hundred-year period, a few people had lived

---

7. David Livermore (2009, 2015, 2022) is one of the leading experts in the area of understanding and acquiring cultural intelligence, which is an indispensable skill for cross-cultural witnesses.

8. See Miriam Adeney's *Kingdom without Borders* (2009) for a fascinating story of the diversity of cultural expression that make up Christianity around the globe.

over half the time, but most had lived considerably less than that, and no one alive in 1789 was still alive in 1989. The culture had changed radically, but the society still existed. However, societies don't last forever. If a culture becomes dysfunctional and brings death and despair instead of hope and survival, and if the culture can't cope with environmental and human threats from outside, then the society will disintegrate over time.

We learn our culture mostly unconsciously from our society, and because societies are not isolated in this present age of globalization and urbanization, this means that the culture is changing more rapidly and more extensively than during any previous period of human history.

In every society, there are social roles waiting to be occupied and played by someone. When we enter a society from outside, it is important that we understand what role we are playing, what social position we are occupying in that society. We must be aware of not only what role we think we are occupying but, more importantly, what role our host society has assigned to us. We will be perceived as credible if we play well the role that a society assigns to us.

The role we call "missionary" may not even exist in a society or may not be the most effective role for us to play. A popular mission role today, flying under the banner of "business as mission" (BAM), is the role of a businessperson.[9] Since it is often easier to get a visa as a businessperson than it is to acquire a religious visa in many countries, many missionaries go as businesspeople. Their "platform" is a business enterprise, which presumably gives them some protective cover enabling them to legally reside in the country of their ministry. Unfortunately, however, many business-as-mission people are poor businesspeople, their businesses make little to no profit, and they contribute nothing to the local economy. But because they are supposed to be playing the role of a businessperson in that society, they can come across as duplicitous at best and dishonest at worst. An important question to ask ourselves is, What role in the host society can I occupy, and do competently, that will give me legitimate access to local people and enable me to live out the gospel authentically and with integrity in their context?

I remember an occasion when I spoke to a group of missionaries to share the results of my sabbatical research. For eight months, I had studied their cross-cultural adjustment and the degree to which they were developing close personal relationships with Hong Kong Chinese. I began my report by thanking them for welcoming my family and me into their mission and telling them

---

9. The following books related to business as mission give an overview of the field, showing strengths and weaknesses: Johnson 2009; Lai 2015; Russell 2010; Steffen and Barnett 2006; and Yamamori and Eldred 2003.

how much we had enjoyed our time in Hong Kong. Then I said that, based on my research, my first recommendation was that they all resign and go home. Imagine the kick in their teeth they must have felt and the look on their faces. They were understandably shocked and upset with the findings from my research and my subsequent recommendation. After a pregnant pause in my oral report, I went on to suggest that after resigning their present positions, they ought to come back to Hong Kong and occupy normal roles in Hong Kong Chinese society. I suggested that some of them should become taxicab drivers, others teachers, and still others businesspeople, roles that would be normally found in Hong Kong society. The problem was that the role of missionary was almost nonexistent among the Hong Kong Chinese, and it wasn't a role they were attracted to, understood, or trusted. Consequently, it was difficult for missionaries to relate in normal, everyday ways to Chinese people. One of the missionaries in the group was a medical doctor and worked in a clinic. His role was easily understood by the Hong Kong Chinese, and he was able to develop meaningful, trusting relationships with them.

Church planters in Japan and Taiwan similarly have a difficult time relating to the very people among whom they want to plant a church. This is because the role of church planter does not naturally exist in these societies. Some missionaries who have discovered that their role does not exist in the society have joined sports clubs or other groups to help them relate to other human beings in natural ways. One missionary family in Japan discovered that one of the unexpected bonuses of putting their children in Japanese schools was that they were able to connect with and relate naturally to the Japanese parents of the other students.

Because the role of missionary either does not make sense to people or does not exist in many places in the world today, it is important that we occupy a social position and play a role that will enable us to develop normal relationships with people.

There are strengths and weaknesses of going into other societies as a crosscultural witness under the umbrella of a tentmaker. Tentmakers are those who find employment in the country that allows them to make a living there, but they are also committed to finding ways of communicating the gospel across cultural boundaries in the context of their business (Acts 18:1–4). The main strength of a tentmaker is that you have a legitimate role in the society, and you are able to occupy a natural role that makes it easier for local people to relate to you, and you to them. The major weakness of the role of tentmaker is that, if you don't have a strong missional base of support, it is easy to become overwhelmed with the business end of your role. This may mean you have little time or energy left to do the evangelism and ministry part of tentmaking.

CHAPTER SUMMARY

In this chapter, we defined the concept of culture, explaining how the anthropological use of the term is very different from the colloquial "arts and culture" understanding that one may read in the Sunday edition of the *New York Times*. I primarily take a mentalistic approach to the concept of culture, seeing it as ideas in a person's mind, and something that, along with values and feelings, is expressed in people's behavior. Thus part of our task as cross-cultural witnesses is to understand the mental maps of the people among whom we serve. We have also noted three attributes of culture: it is learned, not biologically inherited; it is shared with others in the society, which is the anthropological basis for why we share our faith; and it is acquired as a member of society.

3

The Functions of Culture

It is no longer possible to be a Christian shut up in the narrow confines of one's own community, or country. . . . The cosmos is our home. The world is our family. The peoples are our neighbor. . . . Collective history is our task.

Kairos Central America (1988)

he Tzeltal of southern Mexico, descendants of the ancient Maya, were a despised group, isolated, abused, oppressed, exploited, and understandably hostile toward the outside world. They were riddled with disease from inadequate hygiene and nutrition and were suffering from the scourge of rampant alcoholism. They were a textbook example of how a society can fall apart and become dysfunctional. According to Marianna Slocum, a Bible translator who lived among the Tzeltal from 1941 to 1964, one seldom heard music in the Tzeltal villages, and there was a noticeable absence of joy and laughter. Into this dismal cultural context came cross-cultural communicators of the gospel. The New Testament was translated into the highland Oxchuc dialect and the lowland Bachajon dialect, and the Tzeltal began responding to the Word of God in their own language, which they called "The Good Seed." Conversion to Christ first followed family groups along already existing kinship structures, then communities, and then dialect areas, with subsequent change in every aspect of their lives. Slocum says that before the Tzeltal had vernacular Scripture, the factors that prohibited their development were geographical isolation, monolingualism, and illiteracy, but the dominant factor was the all-pervasive fear of witchcraft, a spiritual barrier that could be overcome only by spiritual means. However, those spiritual means were available in the translated Scriptures. As the Tzeltal responded to the Bible, individuals and communities were transformed, for the truth of Scripture did clearly set them free, and the culture experienced positive change in educational, economic, medical, social, and spiritual domains.[1]

This story illustrates how culture functions as a system and how a change in one area, whether negative or positive, can bring changes to other areas of the system.

Culture as a System

When we describe culture as a system, we mean that the different parts of a culture are integrated and related to each other. Consequently, a change in one aspect of a culture will cause changes in other parts. I call this functional integration. The human body is a good example of how a system functions. When there is illness or injury in one part of the body, it doesn't stay isolated there but spreads to other parts and can eventually affect the whole body. Culture is similar, and it can help us to think of culture as a system.

We can conceptually divide culture into three large areas, as illustrated in figure 3.1: ideology, economy and technology, and social relations. The lines between the areas are dotted to indicate that these are not impermeable borders but rather porous lines of demarcation that allow aspects of each of the areas to flow easily into the others.

Figure 3.1
The Functional Integration of Culture

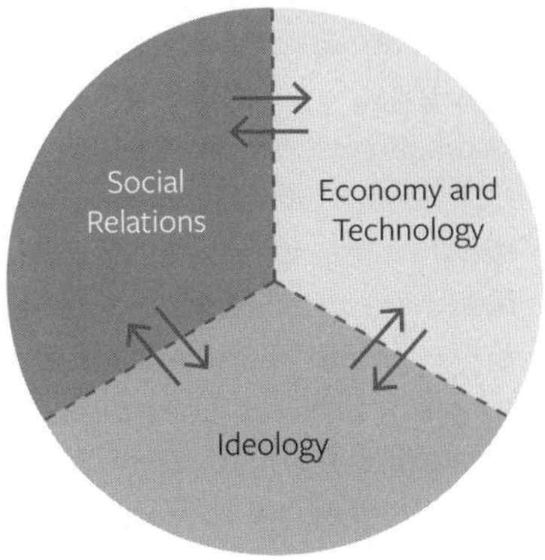

1. This story is in Slocum 1988. My discussion of this case study is in Whiteman 1990, 120–41.

Let me briefly describe each of these:

Ideology includes values, beliefs, worldview, religion, and so on.
Economy and technology include all the areas by which people make a living and the things they make.
Social relations include all aspects of how people relate to each other in a culture.

An example of functional integration in US society is the automobile. The automobile is primarily a piece of technology, and at one time it was one of the most significant indicators of and contributors to the economy in the United States. In fact, in previous generations, it was common to hear the phrase "As General Motors goes, so goes the country." But the importance of the automobile has reached far beyond being just a piece of technology or a contributor to the economy in our society. Now we've come to acknowledge that automobiles are a major producer of greenhouse gases, which contribute to climate change. Henry Ford in 1906 would never have imagined that driving a gas-guzzling automobile would become a moral issue for environmentalists. The automobile is also used as a status symbol in an attempt to communicate one's relative importance in the culture. It has been used for years as a haven of privacy for teenagers and many others. It has altered our neighborhoods and the way we relate to or ignore our neighbors. It has also come to dominate church life so that congregations are no longer made up primarily of people who live and work together and walk to church in what we used to call a parish. Rather, congregations consist of people who drive to church and may never see each other except for an hour on Sunday morning, and the size of the parking lot has now become a litmus test for the spiritual vitality of a church. The automobile has affected our social relationships, our ideology, and our economy. It is integrated into nearly every aspect of our culture.

When teaching people in cross-cultural ministry, I ask them to identify which part of the cultural system (ideology, economy and technology, or social relations) they see as their primary area of ministry. Most people indicate social relations, and usually the fewest people identify with economy and technology. Then I ask them to go through the four Gospels and note where Jesus put most of his emphasis. Most participants in my seminars indicate ideology as the primary focus of Jesus's ministry, followed by social relations and last but not least by economy and technology. However, Jesus said far more about money, the poor, earning a living, and other economic aspects of life than about anything else. His parables are full of economic issues. Jesus's emphasis on the economic dimensions of society is not just a substantial difference of focus in his ministry but an overwhelming difference. Of course, you could argue that when he talked about money, he was also concerned about people's values and beliefs. That is exactly the point! Jesus understood the integrated nature of culture and that our attitude toward money and material things affects every other aspect of our culture. Financial adviser Ron Blue notes, "16 out of 38 of Christ's parables deal with money; more is said in the New Testament about money than heaven and hell combined; five times more is said about money than about prayer; and while there are more than 500 verses on both prayer and faith, there are over 2000 verses dealing with money and possessions" (2016, 22). According to the *Crown Biblical Financial Study*, there are 2,350 verses on how to handle money and possessions in the Bible (Crown Financial Ministries 2007).

If you are engaged in cross-cultural ministry, where is your mission organization paying you to work? Many of us are engaged in some form of evangelism and church planting, which we would see as fitting into the ideological sector of the cultural system. Many young people in mission today feel more comfortable working in the social-relations sector with young women caught in sex trafficking, children living on the streets, refugee and migrant resettlement, and many other social-relations areas. I want to encourage followers of Jesus to make certain their ministry touches people in all three areas. It is not so important where we start our ministry—in the ideology, economy and technology, or social relations part of the cultural system—as long as we don't stop there. In other words, our cross-cultural ministry should connect with all aspects of the culture.

Unfortunately, many of us in the evangelical tradition have taken the gospel and split it apart. As a result, we talk about evangelism as separate from social responsibility. We tend to stereotype "liberals" as those concerned with issues of social justice, while "conservatives" are concerned with evangelism and church planting. Jesus never did that kind of bifurcation of the gospel, and we shouldn't either. We have been given a whole gospel that is redeeming and transforming all aspects of people's lives. If we are not making an impact on the economy and technology in the society through our faith, then something is wrong. If we're not seeing social relationships transformed by the power of the gospel, then something's gone wrong with the harvest. I submit that we cannot do the "spiritual" side of cross-cultural ministry unless we are aware of these other dimensions of culture. The kingdom of God is about far more than getting a ticket to heaven.

If one's job description is church planter, that's fine, but planting a church in another culture involves economic issues, it involves technology, and it certainly involves social relationships and social justice. Sure, it is fueled and informed by an ideology, by values and beliefs, but it is about so much more.

Cultural Ideals versus Actual Behavior

A cultural system becomes a guide for living in a society, and what is taught to each generation is the ideal pattern for living. These ideals include the many ways we are expected to behave as well as values and beliefs we are expected to hold. Often, we are not consciously aware of the values and beliefs because they seem so natural to us. Each individual in the society then determines their actual behavior. We are taught the ideal, but we don't always practice it. This is why culture is open, flexible, and changing, not closed, bounded, or static.

So we have the ideal configuration that is taught in contrast to the actual behavior that is followed. For example, in American culture, we say, "Little boys don't hit little girls." Nevertheless, one day our young son is playing with the little girl next door. They get into a dispute, and our little boy hauls off and hits the girl next door. How do we respond? We don't change our ideal that "little boys don't hit little girls," but we may change the boundaries of what we will tolerate. We may end up saying, "Boys will be boys." Now, if our son grows up and marries the girl next door, but he still has a propensity for slapping her around, we no longer say, "Boys will be boys." Instead, he is removed from society because of his domestic violence, for he has become an unstable threat to his wife and family.

So what is the relationship between the ideal that is taught and the actual behavior that is followed? Figure 3.2 illustrates this.

A general rule of culture is that the closer the actual behavior is to the ideal, the more stable the society becomes. And the reverse is true as well. The further the actual behavior is from the ideal that is taught, the more unstable the society becomes. When the ideal and the actual are similar, we can anticipate one another's behavior. This predictability brings stability to a society.

Generally, the ideal configuration in a culture is the most stable part and changes slowly, whereas the actual behavior can change quickly from one decade or generation to another. In many societies today, cultural and social change,

Figure 3.2
Ideal Culture vs. Actual Culture

Ideals

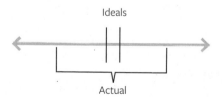

Actual

fueled by globalization and urbanization, are happening so rapidly that the actual behavior of people is getting further and further from the ideal of their society, and so chaos is happening on many levels. If we were to apply this model to Edward Gibbons's six-volume study *The History of the Decline and Fall of the Roman Empire* (1776–89), we would see the same phenomenon occurring. With each generation, the actual behavior moved further from the cultural ideal, until eventually there was a total collapse of the society. There was no longer enough moral and social glue to hold the society together.

We can apply this model of cultural ideals versus actual behavior to our traffic laws and speed limits. If the speed limit on a US highway is 65 mph, that is the ideal, but we can probably drive 70 mph and get away with it. I was once driving 76 mph, which was 11 mph over the speed limit, and got stopped by the police. I naively asked the policeman if he could give me a stiff warning instead of a ticket, and I promised to be more careful about my driving in the future. He smiled and said, "If you had been going 10 mph or less over the speed limit, then I could have given you a stiff warning, but because you were going 11 mph over, the law requires that I give you a ticket."

In this model, anthropologists have discovered an interesting phenomenon related to theological truth. There is no known society in which people are able to live up to their cultural ideals. Every society falls short. This sounds very similar to the idea of sin. As Romans 3:23 tells us, "For all have sinned, and come short of the glory of God" (KJV). When we examine the cultural ideals of societies around the world, we make another interesting discovery. These cultural ideals are similar from one society to another, and they are all similar to the Ten Commandments. For example, in nearly every human society, there are prohibitions against adultery, murder, and stealing as well as the positive value of honoring and respecting parents. Anthropologist Robert Edgerton wrote a controversial and politically incorrect book called *Sick Societies: Challenging the Myth of Primitive Harmony* (1992), in which he argues that all societies are sick, but some are sicker than others. I would submit that this sickness comes primarily from sin and that it is expressed in people's inability to live up to their own cultural ideals, many of which are similar to values communicated in the Ten Commandments.

Perhaps a good starting point in cross-cultural ministry is to empower people, guided by Scripture and through the power of the Holy Spirit, to live up to their cultural ideals, helping them to close the gap between their actual behavior and what their society says their ideal behavior should be. This can be a first step on the pilgrimage of following Jesus. Moreover, in the cultural ideals of many societies, we see evidence of God's prevenient grace at work. We know from the promises of Scripture that God has not left God's self without a witness in every culture at every period of human history (Acts 17:22–28; Rom. 1:20).

Am I suggesting that living up to the standards of one's cultural ideals is the same thing as following Jesus, as spelled out in the Gospels? No, they are not the same, but they are often not far apart, because despite the culture from which we come, we are all human beings created in God's image. So an effective starting point for any kind of evangelism is helping people live up to their own cultural ideals and from there encouraging the critique of those ideals using the values of the kingdom of God.

Analysis of Culture

A culture can be analyzed in a number of ways. One older but nevertheless very helpful approach is suggested by anthropologist Ralph Linton in his book *The Study of Man* (1936, 272–75). He developed a way to analyze a culture based on how individuals participate in the culture. Linton notes that the content of every culture can be divided into four categories: universals, specialties, alternatives, and individual peculiarities. We will briefly discuss each of these areas.

Universals

Universals are "those ideas, habits, and conditioned emotional responses which are common to all sane adult members of the society" (Linton 1936, 272). In this category, we find a society's values, beliefs, worldview, and unconscious assumptions. Universals in a culture are what members of a society have in common. It is those aspects of culture that are so deeply assumed that they can say, "It goes without saying . . ." Examples of universals within a culture (not to be confused with universals that all cultures have in common) are the use of a particular language, patterns of dress, housing styles, and ideal patterns for social relationships.

Specialties

Specialties are "those elements of culture which are shared by the members of certain socially recognized categories of individuals, but not shared by the total population" (Linton 1936, 272). Examples of specialties include cultural and social differences between men and women, and between adults and children. Different professions, such as teachers, preachers, doctors, farmers, factory workers, and stockbrokers, have certain cultural elements that members share in common with each other but not with the total society. For example, if an American male college professor shows up to teach a class cradling a doll in his arms, he is going to raise some concerns about his mental health among his students. His behavior may be appropriate for a female child but not for an adult male. The category of specialties is where we also find the characteristics of a social class, and that is why there are such large cultural differences between the wealthy and the poor that cover much more than just a difference in annual income. The gap between the wealthy and the poor in every society is as much a cultural gap as an economic one.

Alternatives

Alternatives are "cultural traits shared by certain individuals, but not all members of society, or even all members of a socially recognized group" (Linton 1936, 273). In this category, we find a wide range of cultural elements, everything from the atypical ideas and habits of a particular family to different schools of painting and architecture. Alternatives represent different reactions to the same situations or different techniques for achieving the same end. Examples of alternatives include styles of clothing, hairstyles, and various forms of transportation. Different denominations within the Christian church are a good example of alternatives.

Individual Peculiarities

Individual peculiarities are the "results of childhood experience" (Linton 1936, 274). Examples of this include a person with an abnormal fear of fire, a craftsman's individual technique, a professor's style of lecturing, and an individual's expression of religious faith.

Core Culture and Fluid Zones

The four categories discussed above represent an individual's participation in a culture. It is important in analyzing a culture that we are careful not to generalize from one category to another. For example, assuming that alternatives are universals, or assuming that they should be, will lead to stereotyping and robbing people of their agency.

We can build on this model of analyzing culture and note that every culture can be divided into a core culture and a fluid zone (see fig. 3.3).

In the core culture, we find a society's cultural universals and specialties. The core culture is very resistant to change, and if it does change, it often takes a long time. The fluid zone contains alternatives and individual peculiarities. Change in this part of a culture happens more quickly and easily. Societies that are technologically simple, such as Papua New Guinea, tend to have a

Figure 3.3
Culture as Core Culture and Fluid Zone

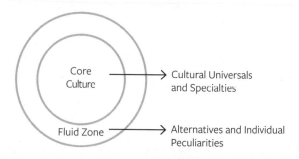

large core culture and a small fluid zone. Technologically highly developed societies, such as Germany, have a larger fluid zone and a smaller core culture (see fig. 3.4).

This theory of culture has important implications for church workers and cross-cultural witnesses whose primary goal is to advocate for change in the core culture more than in the fluid zone. The very part of the culture that we want to influence with gospel values turns out to be the most resistant to change. We therefore can tend to focus on change in the fluid zone, since people are more responsive there. However, changes in the fluid zone will not necessarily mean that changes in the core culture will follow.

This model of culture helps explain why there can seemingly be a change in individuals' behavior so that the society looks like it has been "Christianized," but at the deeper level of values and worldview, there has been very little change at all. During times of crisis, people readily revert back to traditional

Figure 3.4
Papua New Guinea Society and German Society

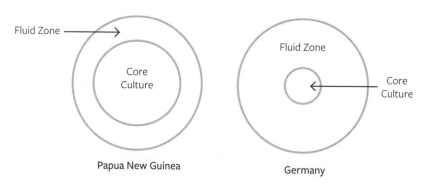

practices and explanations, because this is where they find more security and predictability in their society.

Perhaps a word of caution is necessary, or at least a nuanced interpretation of this model will be helpful. Due to globalization and urbanization, the core culture is being subjected to more change today than in previous generations. Bryant Myers, in his award-winning book *Engaging Globalization: The Poor, Christian Mission, and Our Hyperconnected World* (2017), documents the impact of globalization on cultures around the world and the church's often inadequate response to it. Similarly, Kenneth Nehrbass, in *God's Image and Global Cultures: Integrating Faith and Culture in the Twenty-First Century*, notes that

> in the twentieth century Christians recognized the value of studying culture—
> and *cultures*—so that they could go "out there" and be effective witnesses over-
> seas. Increasingly, though, we are recognizing that a good grasp of how culture
> influences our thoughts, behavior, and faith is essential for understanding our-
> selves and others, and for developing effective practices in business, education,
> and just about every other social endeavor. In the past few decades, the phe-
> nomenon of globalization—rapidly increasing cultural diversity—has moved the
> study of culture from an exotic subject to a core competency in any discipline.
> (2016, xv)

The Impact of Culture on the Individual

Here we move from discussing culture as a system to focusing on the im-
pact of culture on the individual. In doing so, we have to keep in balance the powerful influence of culture on people and the importance of personal agency in decision-making and lifestyle choices.

Learning one's culture is a kind of indoctrination, insofar as it makes one blind to other possible ways of behaving. In fact, the individual learns his or her lessons so well that (in spite of their intellect and free will) their actions, assumptions, motivations, and values, the things they make and do, the speech they use, and the very thoughts they think seldom conflict in any major way with those of their group. In other words, through the process of enculturation, individuals learn the standard behavior that is expected of them in the society. Mechanisms of social control, such as formal laws and informal gossip, pressure individuals to abide by the expected behavioral norms, thus keeping their actual behavior fairly close to the cultural ideals that are taught in their society, which in turn brings them security and predictability. An individual's behaviors, ideas, values, and feelings become so automatic and natural that they take their culture for granted and assume that this is perfectly normal, never

realizing there may be other ways of speaking, thinking, and acting that are just as proper, just as human, as their own.

Another way of conceptualizing the impact of culture on the individual is to say that we are thoroughly immersed in and totally influenced by our culture. Not only is our behavior governed by our culture, but our thinking process is also pervasively influenced by it. This kind of talk feels too deterministic, especially to Americans, but there is much truth in it.

For example, how many colors are in the rainbow? When I ask a North American audience, they frequently respond with the number seven and then say, "Red, orange, yellow, green, blue, indigo, and violet." But much to our surprise, if we ask people in other cultures, we'll get a different number, usually fewer than seven, and some of the obvious colors are "missing" from their list. For example, Japanese traditionally make no distinction between blue and green. They use the term *aiyoi* for the color of green grass and for the color of the blue sky. In the Telegu language of South India, there is no word for orange. But one of the simplest conceptions of color terms is found among the Hanunóo, who live on the island of Mindoro in the Philippines, in an environment that is partly tropical forest and partly grassland. Anthropologist Harold Conklin found that the complex Hanunóo system of color classification could be reduced to just four terms associated with lightness and darkness, wetness and dryness (1955). So, for the Hanunóo in the Philippines, all the colors in the rainbow are reduced to only four terms.

The "correct" answer to the question "How many colors are in the rainbow?" is that there are thousands, if not millions. Colors have different wavelengths of light, but different cultures select certain wavelengths and lump them together and refer to them as a certain color. The English language enables us to distinguish red from orange and orange from yellow. In other words, our perception of reality (in this case color) is significantly determined by our culture. The Thomas theorem, developed by sociologist William I. Thomas, reminds us that whether something is real or imagined, it is real in its consequences (Thomas and Thomas 1928).

Let's look at another example. In many Asian cultures, such as Chinese, people tend to think in a continuum of possibilities, and so their language makes distinctions of degree more than distinctions of kind. For example, we say something is clean or unclean. Chinese language is more adept at speaking of degrees of cleanliness. In contrast to Chinese speakers, North American English speakers who have been influenced by Greek thought since the Enlightenment tend to think in either/or categories rather than in a continuum of possibilities. This either/or thinking plays out in our political system. If you are caught up in a denominational tug-of-war for power, you are either with the fundamentalists or on the side of the liberals. It seems like we are forced into one position to the exclusion of the other. We think in terms of either/or instead of both/and, and this is one of the reasons Americans have become so polarized.

Now, how do we interact with people who think more in continuums than in either/or categories? How do we introduce them to the gospel and to Christ? Do we have to encourage them to first change their worldview before they can follow Christ? Do they have to learn English before they can adequately understand what it means to be a Christian? You may smile and say, "How absurd," but in fact we often act as if they do. We find it very difficult to talk and witness to people who think in continuums when we think in either/or, black-and-white categories.

The late well-known Japanese theologian Kosuke Koyama (1929–2009) and I were speaking once at a conference on Bible translation at Princeton Seminary. He was speaking from an Asian perspective on the role of Bible translation in developing indigenous theologies. After we had both addressed the audience, I asked him how he dealt with the tension of being a Japanese and a Christian at the same time. He responded, "How did you know that that is an ongoing tension in my life?" He went on to say, "I love the Buddha. Buddhism has taught me so much about harmony with nature, about how to relate with other human beings so that we have harmony and smoothness in our relationships. There's no question, Buddhism has had a profound influence on my life. But I love Jesus so much more."

His response blew me away. I wasn't prepared for it. Was he a closet universalist? Was he advocating a sloppy syncretism in which we have a little bit of Buddha and a little bit of Jesus all mixed together? No, he gave a very Japanese Christian response. But many American evangelicals would have been more comfortable with an answer that went like this: "I love Jesus, and therefore I have turned my back on the Buddha. Because I am a follower of Jesus now, I have denounced my Buddhist background and now see it as demonic." But Koyama was a Japanese Christian, not an American Christian, and so he said, "I love the Buddha, but I love Jesus so much more."

I confess that this provocative illustration of the impact of culture on the individual pushes the limits of my theological categories. If the gospel is true, as I believe it is, then that means it can become incarnate in every culture around the world and down through time, including among people who think in continuums instead of either/or categories. This need not be a cause for concern, because this is the way God has designed God's mission in the world. As Lamin Sanneh says, Christianity, unlike Islam, demands to be translated into every language, culture, and society (2009, 1).

So, where lies the burden of proof of whether people can become followers of Jesus and think in continuums rather than either/or categories? The burden of proof is for me to enter into the world of linguistic continuums and learn how to communicate Jesus as Lord over all of it. So when I hear an Asian Christian say, "I love the Buddha, but I love Jesus more," I have to recognize that this person's worldview is very different from mine, but we are both children of God and followers of Jesus. If Christianity is true, then people can become followers of Jesus in every language and every culture. There are no exceptions. So, imagine how disturbed I was when Japanese students would tell me they couldn't be Japanese and Christian at the same time.

E. Randolph Richards and Brandon O'Brien underscore how our culture shapes the way we read, understand, and interpret the Bible. In their breakthrough book, *Misreading Scripture with Western Eyes: Removing Cultural Blinders to Better Understand the Bible*, they argue that "the majority of our worldview, like the majority of an iceberg, is unconscious, below the water line. The part we notice—what we wear, eat, say, and consciously believe—is really only the visible tip. The majority of these powerful, shaping influences lurks below the surface, out of plain sight. More significantly, the massive underwater section is the part that sinks ships. Another way to say this is that *the most powerful cultural values are those that go without being said*" (2012, 12).

I remember an incident in a class I was teaching on the power of culture to shape our values and perception of reality. One young man couldn't take it any longer and raised his hand. I called on him, and his anger and frustration just erupted. "Mr. Whiteman, maybe everyone else is influenced by their culture, but I'm not. I'm my own man, my own person. I do my own thing. I think my own thoughts. I go my own way." He continued for several minutes, and then when he calmed down, I said to him, "Thank you for giving us the perfect definition of what a young American male should be. That's precisely what your culture says you should be. Your response right now was thoroughly American. It wasn't a Chinese, or a Melanesian, or an African response. It was an American one." His mouth dropped open with surprise, and he said, "Is that what you have been trying to teach us about the power of culture?" I responded, "Yes, and you have demonstrated before this whole class in just a few minutes what I have been trying to teach the last two hours."

When we don't recognize how culture impacts who we are, we frequently assume that human nature—which we all have—is the same thing as our cultural nature. We confuse the two. We certainly do have a human nature that is both sinful and created in the image of God. We have a biological temperament and a certain personality. But culture takes our *human* nature and shapes and molds it into a *cultural* nature. This is why the radical statement "We are totally immersed in and influenced by our culture," as frightening as it may seem to Americans, is in fact true. When we confuse cultural conditioning with human nature, it can cause real conflict in cross-cultural situations and is certainly a contributing factor in culture shock, which we will discuss in depth in part 4.

We now turn to one of those perceptions shaped by our culture that influences how we relate to those we see as undeveloped, backward, Third World, or even primitive.

What Is a "Primitive" Culture?

At first glance, this topic seems to be inappropriate, and certainly a politically incorrect topic to discuss, but I believe it is important to do so. The concept of "primitive people" has affected us greatly in the West, and although today one seldom hears people referring to others as "primitive," the idea has nevertheless pervaded much of our mission thinking[2] and shapes our attitudes toward immigrants. The notion of "primitive people" lurks in our subconscious and influences our perceptions and interactions with "the Other." Tite Tiénou reflects on a sermon titled "The Plan That Will Not Fail" preached by missiologist David Hesselgrave in May 2008. Tiénou writes, "Hesselgrave's introductory remarks included the following statements, 'Romans chapter 1 refers to primitive, tribal peoples' and 'Romans chapter 2 refers to Greeks, Romans, civilized peoples, and Jews.' I could not believe what I was hearing from the lips of this senior evangelical missiologist. I wondered to myself, 'What in the text suggests these categories to him?'" (2016, 322–23). We have been strongly influenced by nineteenth-century evolutionary thought known as social evolution, which rates all cultures in comparison to our own. While many conservative Christians are concerned about the threat biological evolution poses to their faith, they have often agreed with the theory of social evolution without realizing it, which could be a far greater threat to Christianity than biological evolution ever could be.

Nineteenth-century cultural evolutionists, such as Lewis Henry Morgan, Edward B. Tylor, Herbert Spencer, James G. Frazer, and a host of others, saw all social and cultural life as evolving from simple to complex, from homogeneous to heterogeneous, and they applied their evolutionary scheme to whole societies as well as to institutions within those societies. So, for example, they divided the whole of humanity into three levels: savages, barbarians, and civilized (see

2. See Tiénou 1991, which discusses how anthropologists invented the concept of the primitive to explain cultural differences in the nineteenth century but have now completely discredited it. Nevertheless, the idea of the primitive is still influencing some mission thinking, although normally with less offensive language.

Figure 3.5
Social Evolutionary Pyramid

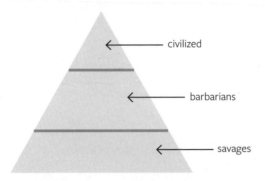

fig. 3.5). Institutions were also perceived to evolve, such as magic evolving into religion and religion evolving into science.

We in the West have strengths in technological development and hence military power. Technology, of course, is only one aspect of a culture, as we learned in the section "Culture as a System." However, because we assume our technological superiority, we also assume that all other aspects of our culture are superior as well—our system of democratic government, our capitalistic economic system, our values of independence and self-reliance, and our formal education. We have poured so much of our energy into technological developments that we have created social disorientation and disruption at nearly every level of our society. Our marriages are often unstable, whether we're Christians or not. Our quest for freedom and individualism destroys close friendships and neighborliness. Our extreme competitiveness is ripping our society apart, and yet we continue to judge it as superior to all others and insist that we are the superpower of the world.

When I conduct cross-cultural training for cross-cultural witnesses, I often ask if anyone has seen in the news lately that the Solomon Islands in the South Pacific is planning to develop a space program and hopes to land a person on the moon in twenty-five years. No one ever admits to seeing that news story, and then I confess I haven't either, and I won't. Most of these Melanesian people have a simple technology of farming, still living in grass huts and bathing in the river, so there is no way that in twenty-five years they will have the technology to enter the space age.

Now, let's go back to the social evolutionary pyramid, which divides cultures into three levels (see fig. 3.5). Is there some truth in that pyramid, that not all cultures are the same, that some are more "civilized" than others? Yes, there is, but the criteria used to distinguish the three levels of human society is technology. It's true. Some societies are technologically more sophisticated and developed than others. What would happen to the pyramid, however, if we chose different criteria by which to judge and rate different cultures? What if we chose social relations instead of technology? Who would end up on the bottom as "savages"? It wouldn't be our Melanesian friends, for they would be at the top as the most "civilized." If we have to rate other cultures in relation to our own, let's at least be more honest and open in naming the criteria we are using to draw our pyramid (see fig. 3.6).

Figure 3.6
Inverted Pyramid of Social Evolution

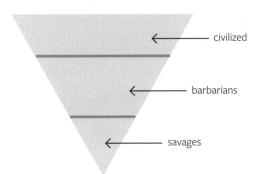

In the early decades of the twentieth century, a French philosopher, sociologist, and anthropologist by the name of Lucien Lévy-Bruhl (1857–1939) wrote about people at the bottom of the social evolutionary ladder as having a primitive mentality (1910, 1923), and he spoke of people like my Solomon Islander friends as being "pre-logical." His writing spurred a great deal of anthropological research, and his ideas were soundly refuted, which he admitted before he died in 1939. What we now know, thanks to this abundance of anthropological research, is that human beings everywhere think in approximately the same manner. In other words, there are no cultures where people are "pre-logical" in their thinking, nor do people in some cultures think concretely while people in others are able to think abstractly.

If this is true, then why do we come to such different conclusions about all kinds of things in life? The reason we don't reach the same conclusions from one culture to another is not because we think differently but because different cultures have a different set of premises and assumptions. The following chart, based on Charles Kraft's *Christianity in Culture*, illustrates beautifully how different assumptions give rise to different conclusions.

Cultural Feature	Assumption	Conclusion
Clothing	1. Immodest to go naked (US)	1. Must wear clothes, even to bed
	2. One covers one's body only if hiding something (Gava people, Nigeria)	2. Go naked to prove oneself
	3. For ornamentation only (Higi people, Nigeria)	3. Wear on "occasion"; rearrange or change in public
Buying	1. Impersonal, economic transaction (US)	1. Fixed prices; no interest in seller as a person; get it over quickly
	2. Social, person-to-person transaction (Africa, Asia, Latin America)	2. Dicker over price; establish personal relationship; take time
Youthfulness	1. Desirable (US)	1. Look young; act young; wear cosmetics
	2. Tolerated; to be overcome (Africa)	2. Prove yourself mature; don't act young
Age	1. Undesirable (US)	1. Dreaded; old people unwanted
	2. Desirable (Africa)	2. Old people revered
Education	1. Primarily formal; outside home; teacher-centered (US)	1. Formal schools; hired specialists
	2. Primarily informal; in the home; learner-centered; traditional (Africa)	2. Learn by doing, discipleship, proverbs, and folktales
Family	1. Centered around spouses (US)	1. Compatibility of spouses all-important
	2. For the children (Africa)	2. Mother-child relationship paramount
Rapid Change	1. Good; change = "progress" (US)	1. Encourages rapid change and innovation
	2. Threat to security (Africa)	2. Conservatism valued; aim at stability

Source: Kraft 2005, 49.

This table reminds us that the reason people in different cultures come to such different conclusions about various aspects of their culture is not because they are "primitive" and less developed. It is because their starting assumptions about life, which are formed and shaped by their culture, environment, and history, are simply different from our own. So the next time you are tempted to look down your nose at someone who seems less sophisticated than yourself, pause and ask, "What assumptions do these people have that are different from mine and that lead them to act in ways that are different from my own ways of living and behaving?"

Culture and the Gospel

What is a Christian attitude toward culture? I believe Christians should have a positive and critical attitude toward culture. We should be positive and affirming of culture as a gift of God's grace. We were created with the capacity to create culture and thereby to glorify God. But we must also be critical because culture can also reflect human sinfulness, greed, power, and oppression. Those who have little cross-cultural experience can tend to be positive about their own culture when they should be more critical, and critical of others' cultures when they should be more charitable.

So, what can we say about the relationship between culture and the gospel? We can make three statements about how the one universal gospel relates to the diversity of human cultures around the world, both in the present age and through time in the past.

1. The gospel *affirms* most of culture.
2. The gospel *confronts* and critiques some of culture.
3. The gospel *transforms* all of culture.

Let's briefly unpack each of these statements.

First, the gospel affirms most of culture. By this we mean that a person does not have to adopt a different culture, learn a different language, or change their lifestyle to that of the cross-cultural witnesses who introduced them to the gospel in order to become a follower of Jesus. In other words, a person doesn't have to deny their birth identity in order to affirm their second-birth identity as a follower of Jesus. In the history of the missionary enterprise, we haven't always understood this. However, all cultures are gifts of God's grace, and people of every culture and language have the capacity to know God through the person of Jesus. As Lamin Sanneh eloquently reminds us in *Translating the Message: The Missionary Impact on Culture*, the message of Jesus demands to be translated into the vernacular language and culture of all peoples (2009, 1).

Does this imply that nothing in the culture will change when people in a given society encounter the gospel? Of course not. Thus, the second statement is that the gospel confronts and critiques some aspect of every culture. Although culture is a gift of God's grace, cultures also reflect the fallenness of humanity and the sinful nature of human beings, which can be expressed in oppressive social structures and values that are contrary to the gospel. I remember once doing some teaching with Maasai pastors in Samburu, Kenya. I asked them to break into small groups and compile a list of the things in their culture that were affirmed by the gospel. They came up with a long list, which included the controversial practice of female circumcision. After we discussed the things in their culture that they believed were affirmed and supported by the gospel, I asked them to return to their discussion groups and develop another list of the elements of Maasai culture that were incompatible with the gospel and needed to be confronted and critiqued. Perhaps not surprisingly, they returned to the assembled gathering rather quickly, and this time they had a much shorter list.

One of the major challenges in cross-cultural ministry is that it is easy to point out aspects of culture that are different from our own and call them evil but not see elements in our own culture that need radical change. Jesus had something to say about that when he declared, "You hypocrite! First take the log out of your own eye, and then you'll be able to see clearly to take the speck out of your brother's eye" (Matt. 7:5). We need the insights and wisdom of the entire global body of Christ so that we can learn from each other what it means to be a disciple of Christ.

While the gospel affirms most of culture and confronts and critiques some of culture, it transforms all of culture. I once visited the Methodist church in Suva, Fiji, and noticed an unusual baptismal font. I learned that the stone font had a fascinating history and told a story of cultural transformation. Before the gospel came to Fiji in 1835, cannibalism was widespread throughout the islands. The stone structure that I observed in the Methodist church had previously been used to catch the blood of deposed enemies. In light of the gospel, it had been redeemed and transformed, symbolizing new life in Christ. Australian missiological anthropologist Alan Tippett has chronicled the transformation of Fiji from a society focused on warfare and cannibalism to an indigenous expression of Christianity, and he has given us a stunning account of the power of the gospel to affirm most, critique some, and transform all of culture (1980).

CHAPTER SUMMARY

We began this chapter with the story of the Tzeltal to illustrate how culture functions as a system and that a change in one part of the culture will result in changes in other parts, for good or for bad. Culture is not static but dynamic and always changing to one degree or another. We noted that we can divide a culture into three porous categories of ideology, economy and technology, and social relations. The way we proclaim and live out the gospel should touch all three areas of society. This is why the age-old debate between the social aspects and the spiritual dimensions of the gospel is bogus. Jesus never divided the two, and neither should we. The whole gospel relates to the whole culture.

Figure 3.7
GOSPEL + CULTURE + FAITH produce CHRISTIANITY

GOSPEL	CULTURE
God-given	Man-made, makes man culturally
One, unique, holy	Many local and regional forms, good, evil, natural elements
Universal—for all	Universal—in all societies
Eternal, revealed in history	Historical, changing, temporal, transitory
Makes new creation in Christ	Conditions people and reachable areas of creation

Towards culture:
    G. traverses C.
        judges and saves C.
        dedicates, sanctifies C.
        beautifies C.
        exorcises demons in C.

Towards the gospel:
    C. receives (or rejects) G.
        communicates G.
        conditions people for faith in G.

        brings glory to G.

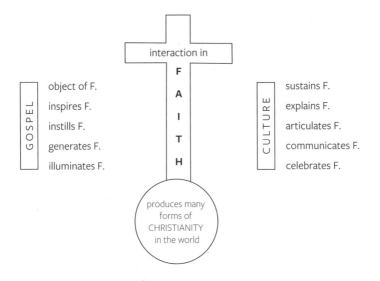

interaction in

F
A
I
T
H

GOSPEL		CULTURE
object of F.		sustains F.
inspires F.		explains F.
instills F.		articulates F.
generates F.		communicates F.
illuminates F.		celebrates F.

produces many
forms of
CHRISTIANITY
in the world

Mbiti 1979, 20.

We noted that in every society the ideal cultural pattern is taught to each generation but that the actual behavior practiced by individuals can and often does vary from the ideal. The closer the actual behavior is to the ideal that is taught, the more stable the society is. The further the actual behavior deviates from the cultural ideal, the more unstable the society becomes. Many cultural ideals are similar to the Ten Commandments, but people in every culture fall short of their cultural ideals. Becoming a follower of Jesus enables people to live up to the majority of their cultural ideals.

Next, we discussed a model for analyzing the four ways in which individuals participate in their culture. Every culture has a fluid zone and a core culture. The core culture is where values and beliefs reside and is the most difficult to change, and yet this is the area where discipleship needs to bring deep change as we confess that Jesus is Lord over all of life.

We next discussed the impact of culture on the individual and noted that we are thoroughly immersed in and totally influenced by our culture. We also distinguished between human nature, which we have in common with all humanity, and cultural nature, which varies from society to society and even within societies among different individuals.

After a brief but difficult discussion on why the image of a "primitive" society still lurks in our consciousness and shapes our attitudes toward others, we concluded the chapter by discussing how the gospel relates to culture: it affirms most of culture, it confronts and critiques some of culture, and it transforms all of culture. Figure 3.7, from the late African theologian John Mbiti (1931–2019), captures much of what we discussed in this chapter on the relationship between the gospel, culture, and faith.

CONCLUSION TO PART 1

Cross-cultural witnesses must understand the concept of culture in order to successfully cross cultural boundaries with the gospel. According to Louis Luzbetak, if one does not understand the concept of culture, then one does not understand the nature of ministry (1970, 59). When cross-cultural witnesses don't take the time to master the language and culture of the people among whom they are living and serving, their ministry suffers. So let me summarize what we need to do in regard to the concept of culture to successfully minister cross-culturally.

First, we need to be aware of the influence of culture on ourselves. Harvard anthropologist Clyde Kluckhohn once wrote, "It would hardly be fish who discovered the existence of water" (1949, 11). We have been "swimming" in our own cultural water for years, and so we are unaware that our human nature has been shaped by our culture. We assume they are the same. It is only when we leave the comfort and confines of our own culture that we can more vividly "see" our own culture. We need to experience other cultures in order to understand our own. We have to remove our cultural blinders in order to understand their impact on us. Once we are able to do that, we'll be surprised by how many things that we thought were biblical are simply cultural.

Second, we must be aware of the impact of culture on others if we are going to understand and appreciate them. This is why we need to enter other cultures as a learner and discover the mental maps of the people among whom we are living and serving. If we don't understand how culture impacts others, then we won't have an appreciation for what it means to be a follower of Jesus in their society.

Finally, we need to ask the question "How does God interact with and relate to human beings in the cultures in which they are immersed?" The Bible is a sacred book of case studies of how God interacted with people in different times and places over a long span of history. For example, God interacted differently with the wandering nomad Abraham than God did one thousand years later with King David, because the cultural context was so different. In the Gospels, we see how Jesus interacted with the Jewish people in Roman-occupied Palestine one thousand years later. Paul's letters to the New Testament churches in Corinth, Ephesus, Philippi, Colossae, and Thessalonica deal with various kinds of issues related to following Christ because the cultural context was different from one city to the next.[3]

With a solid understanding of the importance of culture, we are now ready to consider a method by which we can enter another culture, share the gospel across cultures, and live out the gospel authentically in another culture. I call this method incarnational identification. This is the topic of part 2.

---

3. Study Bibles such as John Walton and Craig Keener's *NIV Cultural Backgrounds Study Bible* (2016) and books such as Kenneth Bailey's *Paul through Mediterranean Eyes: Cultural Studies in 1 Corinthians* (2011) and *Jesus through Middle Eastern Eyes: Cultural Studies in the Gospels* (2008) are so helpful in enabling us to enter the biblical world and understand what is happening through the lens of culture instead of interpreting Scripture only theologically.

PART 2

Incarnational Ministry

4

The Incarnational Model

Wonder! God is coming among humanity;
he who cannot be contained is contained in a womb;
the timeless enters time, and great mystery:
his conception is without seed,
his emptying without telling.

John the Monk[1]

My husband is dead because of your teaching," my student said, silencing the room.

My feet felt stapled to the floor, my heart picking up speed as I tried to keep the sweat from bristling through my shirt.

She went on: "Five or six years ago, my husband and I were sitting in this very room in your missionary training course. You really pushed us beyond our comfort zone as you talked about the importance of cultural immersion and incarnational identification in cross-cultural ministry. We didn't like you very much at the time because you were calling us to a lifestyle that was unlike that of most missionaries in our mission organization. Nevertheless, we felt God's presence in the room that day. We knew the Holy Spirit was speaking directly to us about how we should live and relate to the people in the country in West Africa where we were headed.

"A few months later, our family boarded a plane bound for Africa. As the plane dipped through the clouds, my stomach clenched tight with the uncertainty of

1. Arthur A. Just Jr., ed., *Luke: Ancient Christian Commentary on Scripture*, New Testament 3 (Downers Grove, IL: IVP, 2003), 17.

the unknown. We held fast to your teachings, as they gave us confidence that we were on the right path.

"We said goodbye to French fries and instead filled our stomachs with groundnut soup. We stopped wearing most of our clothes from Kohl's and wore local fabrics sewn by a seamstress in the village. We tossed aside hopes of streetlights and paved sidewalks and adjusted to living next to neighboring mud huts. We traveled to market on our bikes instead of driving, just to journey next to our local friends and hear their stories. Even the African names we were given began to feel natural and comfortable. We were at home."

She stopped, swallowing what seemed like a painful memory, and continued, "One day, my husband visited a village church and accepted water from local people. Accepting water is a local custom that's extremely important in their culture because it symbolizes acceptance of hospitality.

"That night, my husband was in cold sweats, his body burning with fever. I woke up the next morning to find my husband's eyes empty. He was only a shell of the man I loved. The local hospital doctor pronounced him dead upon arrival.

"I was bewildered. Nothing in my training could have prepared me for this. No one told us that waterborne diseases circulated through this part of the country every year during May. Because we listened to you," she said, "because we became incarnational in our ministry, my husband is dead."

She looked down at her shoes, gathering her thoughts. No one in the class moved, and for once—I was speechless. Her words hung in the air, clouding my heart in sadness, regret, panic.

What had I done?

Then she said something that shocked us all: "I'm standing here today because I wanted to say this in front of all these people preparing for missionary service. If we had it to do over again, we would do it exactly the same way. Yes, my husband lost his physical life and my children lost their father, but what followed my husband's death was a community revitalization. Upon seeing the sacrifice and dedication of my husband, many in the village began their pilgrimage of redemption in Christ. More was accomplished for the sake of God's kingdom by my husband's death than through his life." She concluded by saying, "The pain I went through was almost unbearable, but God was there beside me every step of the way. I'm here with my new husband, and call us crazy—but we're going back to Africa!"

I wondered, *Was there any way in my teaching that I could have prevented this tragedy?* They certainly practiced with passion the model of incarnational identification that I taught. I was not able to warn her about waterborne diseases at a certain time of year in that part of Africa because I didn't know. In fact, in training people for cross-cultural ministry, I couldn't give anyone enough knowledge, content, or facts to be prepared for every contingency. However, I could have given more attention to basic anthropological tools that would have prepared these missionaries to discover local culture,[2] master the local language, analyze society, ask informed questions, and make relevant observations. Thus, they may have been better prepared for contingencies.

The Incarnation: More than a Theological Doctrine

The story above illustrates the power of an incarnational way of relating to people. But we have not often thought of the incarnation as a model for ministry. Instead, we have often limited our understanding of the incarnation to an important theological doctrine over which the early church fathers vigorously debated. I submit that without God becoming a human being in the person of Jesus of Nazareth, there is no basis for our faith as Christians. John Donne (1572–1631), in his *Holy Sonnet* 15, captures the importance of this cosmic breakthrough:

> 'Twas much, that man was made like God before,
> But, that God should be made like man, much more. (2014, 31)

Donne is reminding us that as important as creation is, the incarnation is even more important and significant. If the incarnation is only a myth, then we are still lost.

But as important as the incarnation is as a theological doctrine, it is just as important as a metaphor, if not a model, for how to do ministry, especially cross-cultural ministry. Darrell Guder notes how the incarnation is a model for the church's witness in the West and beyond. He notes, "Incarnational witness is, therefore, a way of describing Christian vocation in terms of Jesus Christ as the messenger, the message, and the model for all who follow after him. To speak of the incarnation missionally is to link who Jesus was, with what Jesus did, and how he did it, in one great event that defines all that it means to be Christian" (2004, 9).

Some theologians may push back against this idea of the incarnation as a model for ministry, arguing that the incarnation happened only once when God in a unique divine act chose to enter earth as a human being in the person of Jesus of Nazareth.[3] Australian missiologists Michael Frost and Alan Hirsch, in

2. In this culture, there is actually a culturally appropriate way to hand the water bowl to the person sitting next to you and ask, "Can you drink this water for me?" This keeps you safe if you believe the water is unsafe, and it doesn't culturally offend your host. Later in this chapter, I'll discuss balancing incarnational identification with sustainability.

3. J. Todd Billings (2004, 2012) and John Starke (2011) raise objections from a Reformed theological position. Sherwood Lingenfelter decided to remove the phrase "an incarnational model for

their groundbreaking book *The Shaping of Things to Come: Innovation and Mission for the 21st-Century Church*, respond that "the Incarnation is an absolutely fundamental doctrine, not just as an irreducible part of the Christian confession, but also as a theological prism through which we view our entire missional task in the world" (2003, 35). They spell out five significant ways the incarnation is a model for mission (35–40) and then conclude that "the greatest argument for the case of incarnational mission in the end is the undeniable fact that it was the missional mode in which God himself engaged the world; it should be no less ours!" (41).[4]

The incarnation as a model for mission is radical. If we choose to live incarnationally, there's not an area of our life that won't be challenged and affected—our relationships, how we spend our time and money, our priorities, and so on. Because of my strong commitment to the incarnation as a model for mission, I have occasionally been known as the "prophet of doom and gloom" when it comes to missionary lifestyles. I remember at a retreat center where I was speaking, overhearing a couple in the room next door talking about my radical teaching. The walls of that spartan facility were so thin that I could hear everything they said, including, "If we had listened to Whiteman, we would be sleeping on the floor." Whatever sacrifice we may make to live like and among the people we serve, though, will be more than repaid in huge dividends of deep personal relationships, a sense of fulfillment, and lasting ministry.

The opening story may cause you to wonder how far you are willing to go in identifying with others. For some people, like myself, incarnational identification seems to come naturally. They are as much at home in their host culture as they are in their own. Sometimes more so. For others, incarnational identification is not easy and seems like a huge sacrifice to make without any guarantee of reward. On the scale of lifestyle decisions, the weight of sacrifice outweighs the potential joy of reward that comes with developing deep relationships across cultures. And so, they choose to set limits on how much they are willing to identify with others. This is understandable.

What do I mean when I say the incarnation is a model for cross-cultural ministry? When God became human, God became fully a Jew at a particular time and a specific place on earth. Jesus identified with and was shaped by his

---

personal relationships" from the third edition of his and Marvin Mayers's bestselling *Ministering Cross-Culturally* after he received feedback from theologians. Instead, he substituted the phrase "a model for effective personal relationships" (2016, xii–xiii).

4. Alan Hirsch (2006) and Michael Frost (2014) have both continued with this theme of incarnation as a model for mission in separate books. See especially chapter 5, "Missional-Incarnational Impulse," in Hirsch, and chapter 12, "Adopting an Incarnational Posture," in Frost. The theme of incarnational identification also shows up in Frost and Rice 2017. For an in-depth study of the concept of incarnation and its application to missiology, see Langmead 2004.

Jewish culture in Roman-occupied Palestine in the first century CE. John 1:18 reminds us that "no one has ever seen God," but we know a lot about God because of Jesus, for as S. D. Gordon says, "Jesus is God spelled out in language that [human beings] can understand" (1906, 13). The preface to the book *The Conspiracy of God: The Holy Spirit in Us* by John C. Haughey states, "With justification, the author points out that in the past we have given in to the tendency to present the mystery of Jesus in terms of a Divine Theophany—God coming *to* us under human appearance rather than *from among* us in the mystery of the Incarnation. We must meet the authentic Jesus, a man among men, conditioned by the relativity of time and space as men always are" (1973, 7).

Why did God choose to enter the world as a Jew? It is difficult for our small minds and shriveled-up hearts to comprehend the vastness of God. It is easier for us to understand who Jesus is. Jesus was a Jew, born in Bethlehem but raised in the poor town of Nazareth. In other words, God did not become a generic human being in Jesus; rather, God became a very specific person shaped by the possibilities and limitations of his time and his culture. Jesus was a first-century Jew shaped by a Jewish worldview.

What is the significance of this? For starters, it means that Jesus probably spoke Aramaic with what we Americans would today call a hillbilly accent—that is, he spoke Aramaic with the low-prestige accent spoken around Galilee instead of the higher-prestige accent spoken in Jerusalem. We can conclude this based on the Gospels' account of Peter's denial of Jesus. Peter was found out by his accent. Matthew 26:73–74 says, "After a little while, those standing there went up to Peter and said, 'Surely you are one of them; your accent gives you away.' Then he began to call down curses and he swore to them, 'I don't know the man!'" (NIV; cf. Mark 14:70; Luke 22:59; John 18:25–27).

This revelation of an Aramaic Galilean accent has profound meaning for those in cross-cultural ministry. If Jesus was willing to identify with people to the point that he spoke their language with their low-prestige accent, is it too much for God to ask us to learn the language of the people to whom God has called us and to speak their language without an American or Korean or Hindi accent? This insight means, for example, that if a youth pastor wants to be effective in connecting with a youth group, then it is imperative that the pastor speak the kids' "language," which, of course, refers to far more than just words. A youth pastor must recognize that vocabulary constantly changes and must be attuned to the subtle nuances in the way young people use language differently than their parents do.[5]

---

5. See Hull and Mays 2022 for a discussion of the concept of incarnational identification in youth ministry.

Jesus was immersed in Jewish culture. He entered the synagogue; knew how to properly read from a scroll; took his seat, which was the cultural posture of a teacher; and explained the meaning of Scripture, which he had probably memorized. His parables drew on familiar agricultural lore in a peasant society, which Kenneth Bailey has helped us understand through the lens of the cultural context of the Middle East (2005, 2008). Jesus understood the social structure of his time, knew his place in it, and observed boundaries, except when they were the result of oppressive, sinful systems that were counter to the kingdom of God. Then he chose to cross them, often to the consternation of those in power. The Gospels, especially the Gospel of Mark, portray Jesus healing many people of diseases. The theory of germs being the cause of disease would not be discovered until 1861 by Louis Pasteur. Jewish society of the first century lacked our scientific understanding, but Jesus worked within the narrow confines of the cultural knowledge of his day.

When we emphasize the humanity of Jesus and the role culture and social structure played in shaping who he became, it may appear to some people that we are demeaning Jesus, who after all is God. But in fact, the incarnation demonstrates that God is willing to be present in any culture in every period of human history. In other words, Jesus's humanity does not dilute his divinity; it enhances it. The incarnation as a model for cross-cultural ministry means we must be willing to work within whatever condition a culture is in, regardless of how unsophisticated or corrupt it may appear to be. We must start where people are, embedded in their culture, because this is where Jesus started. Jesus starts where we are in order to transform us into what he wants us to become. He doesn't leave us as he finds us; rather, he invites us to grow in our faith to become more like Christ and to have the mind of Christ.

Incarnation and *Kenosis*: Philippians 2

Paul's letter to the church at Philippi gives more depth of understanding to the idea that the incarnation is a model for cross-cultural ministry. The city of Philippi was an important, prosperous Roman colony in Macedonia located on the main highway leading from the eastern provinces to Rome. The Philippian followers of Jesus had been having some "denominational squabbles" among themselves since false teaching had entered the church. Paul writes from his prison cell or under house arrest in Rome to encourage them to get along with each other and to take on the attitude of Christ.

> Your life in Christ makes you strong, and his love comforts you. You have fellowship with the Spirit, and you have kindness and compassion for one another.

I urge you, then, to make me completely happy by having the same thoughts, sharing the same love, and being one in soul and mind. Don't do anything from selfish ambition or from a cheap desire to boast, but be humble toward one another, always considering others better than yourselves. And look out for one another's interests, not just your own. The attitude you should have is the one that Christ Jesus had:

> He always had the nature of God,
>> but he did not think that by force he should try to remain [or become] equal with God.
> Instead of this, of his own free will he gave up all he had,
>> and took the nature of a servant.
> He became like a human being
>> and appeared in human likeness.
> He was humble and walked the path of obedience all the way to death—
>> his death on the cross. (Phil. 2:1–8)

If Jesus is our model for mission, then incarnational identification must become our method of ministry.[6] This Philippian passage reminds us that Jesus emptied himself and gave up his power, position, privilege, and the prestige of being God's Son in order to identify with human beings.[7] Emptying ourselves precedes identifying with others. Relating to people who are different from us is therefore more about our attitude and posture than about our techniques or strategies for reaching them. We must identify with the people among whom we live and serve, and often this means downward mobility, not upward mobility. In the same way that Jesus emptied himself, we must empty ourselves of our pride, our agenda, our ambitions, and all that we hope to accomplish for God. For Jesus, incarnation led to his crucifixion. If we choose to become incarnational in identifying with others, we may have to die to many preferences, such as our lifestyle, prejudices, reputation, understanding, power, wealth, and even the value of rugged individualism. Jesus uses an agricultural image to drive home the idea of incarnational identification: "I am telling you the truth: a grain of wheat remains no more than a single grain unless it is dropped into the ground and dies. If it does die, then it produces many grains" (John 12:24).

I have found that many cross-cultural witnesses seem willing to do what is necessary to identify with local people, but they frequently are very slow to

---

6. See Whiteman 2005 for reflections on Phil. 2:5–8 as a biblical basis for incarnational identification (p. 1946).

7. *Kenosis* refers to the self-emptying of Jesus and is derived from the verb *kenoō*, which appears in Phil. 2:7.

die to their standards of living and to change their lifestyle to one that is more appropriate for the context in which they are ministering.

Dying to More than Ourselves

Sometimes incarnational identification will lead to physical death, as the opening story in this chapter demonstrates. Jesus's incarnation led to his crucifixion, but what followed his crucifixion? Resurrection! The same pattern is available for us. If we are willing to become downwardly mobile, to die to ourselves in order to identify with others, then we will also be "resurrected." We will be "born again" with a new language, a new community, an expanded worldview, and a new and deeper understanding and appreciation of God's mission in the world.

If there is the possibility for resurrection, why do so many missionaries resist becoming incarnational? We are afraid to make ourselves vulnerable, so we hide behind excuses. I have heard many excuses over the years, including the following:

> "I'm willing to become incarnational, but what about my children? I shouldn't have to put them through that. God called my spouse and me, but God didn't call our children."

> "The local people don't really expect me to identify closely with them, so why should I?"

> "If I was incarnational and lived in a house similar to theirs or used local transportation, it wouldn't be as comfortable and therefore not as efficient in my ministry."

> "If I become incarnational and really enter into their world, then who will make sure the church doesn't stray off course into some weird heresy?"

> "I've been sent out to plant churches that align with our denomination, and so I need to control and manage what goes on. I can't do that very well if I become incarnational. Any weird group could pass for a church, and I have to make sure we keep and protect our doctrinal distinctives and high standards."

The excuses and rationalizations for not living incarnationally are endless, but we must see them for what they are: excuses often generated by fear.

The issue of our identity is even more complicated than adopting an appropriate incarnational lifestyle. We don't always get to choose the identity we want to project. Sometimes the people among whom we are living and serving choose it for us, and sometimes it takes a lot of work and time to get beyond it. We must arrive at an identity and a role that are mutually agreeable, and of course our role and our identity change over time and under different circumstances.

I have been observing, studying, and training missionaries for more than forty-five years, and I've seen a clear pattern emerge. When missionaries attempt to become incarnational, their lives are richly rewarding, and their ministry is effective. They develop deep, meaningful relationships with local people. When I ask them to tell me about their friends, they immediately mention local people, not other missionaries or expatriates. However, when missionaries refuse to identify with local people in this way, they often become frustrated, bitter, angry, and burned-out. They don't have close personal relationships with local people, even after thirty-five years of living in the country, and so their ministry is often ineffective. This antipathy for the local culture and people can take a variety of expressions. A missionary I know who worked in Taiwan for many years but never learned to like Chinese food would often say, "The only Chinese food I like are oranges."

In similar but not identical ways, the process of incarnation, of God becoming a human being, occurs every time the gospel crosses a new cultural, linguistic, or religious frontier. If the mission of God was achieved by the incarnation of Jesus, and if Jesus in turn said to his disciples, "As the Father sent me, so I send you" (John 20:21), then what does this mean for a model of mission, of cross-cultural ministry? I think we can assume that we are bound to work within the limitations of the cultural forms of the people to whom we are sent. This is not a rigid or static or monolithic view of culture because culture changes. Because of the impact of globalization and urbanization on a society, it is even more complicated to identify with people who are different from us. Nevertheless, when Jesus invites us to go into the world in the same way he was sent by the Father, we must start within the confines and limitations as well as the opportunities and possibilities that are imposed by a culture. We start where people are because this is where God started with us in order to transform us into what God wants us to become. When we employ the incarnation as a model for mission, it frequently means downward mobility. When we take the incarnation seriously in ministry, it means we bow at the cross in humility before we wave the flag of patriotism. The incarnation as a model for mission means we must give up our own cultural compulsions and preferences. We do not insist that the expression of the gospel in another culture must be the same as it is in our own. This is so hard to do because we truly believe we have the right interpretation of Scripture, the correct theology, and the best way of being church.

Incarnational Identification Is *Not* "Going Native"

Sometimes when people hear me advocating for incarnational identification, they conclude that I mean cross-cultural witnesses should attempt to "go native" and become just like the people among whom they are ministering. I want to stress that becoming incarnational with others does not mean "going native." For one thing, we can't go native successfully because we weren't born native.

William D. Reyburn underscores this point in an illuminating article titled "Identification in the Missionary Task," written in a previous era of missionary work (1978, 751). Making every effort by way of dress, eating habits, and living arrangements to identify with the Quechuas in the Ecuadorean Andes, he was saddened when people referred to him as a *patroncito*, meaning "boss" or "wealthy landowner." He writes:

> I made every effort for a period to avoid the townspeople, but the term *patroncito* seemed to be as permanently fixed as the day we moved into the community.
>
> The men had been required by the local commissioner to repair an impassable road connecting the community and Tabacundo. I joined in this work with the [Quechua] Indians until it was completed two months later. My hands had become hard and calloused. One day I proudly showed my calloused hands to a group of men while they were finishing the last of a jar of fermented *chichi*. "Now, you can't say I don't work like you. Why do you still call me *patroncito*?" This time the truth was near the surface, forced there by uninhibited alcoholic replies. Vicente Cuzco, a leader in the group, stepped up and put his arm around my shoulder and whispered to me. "We call you *patroncito* because you weren't born of an Indian mother." (751)

Second, attempts to go native are seldom understood, appreciated, or respected by the people among whom we are living and ministering. This is because local people know that we are not one of them, and they wonder why we are trying to act as if we are. Try as we might, we can't pull it off.

Third, we should not attempt to go native because identifying with one group or strata of society may very well alienate us from another. Moreover, due to the increased impact of globalization and urbanization and the flows of ideas, people, and things into a society, it is often difficult to decide with whom in the society we should most identify. Should we identify with the wealthy, the poor, the educated, the leaders, or the marginalized?

So, if incarnational identification doesn't mean going native, then what does it mean? It means that we choose to identify as much as we can with local people and that our goal is to become an "acceptable outsider" in their society. We can't become an insider. An acceptable outsider is an ideal role for a cross-cultural witness. It means that we don't compete for limited leadership roles within the culture. It means that we become a cross-cultural bridge, bringing ideas and culture from one society to another.[8]

Samuel Wells has developed a theological foundation for incarnational identification in his book *Incarnational Mission: Being with the World.* He contrasts *being with* people, *working for* people, and *working with* people in the world. He notes, "Working for is where I do things and they make your life better. I do them because thereby I'm financially rewarded, I receive public esteem, I enjoy exercising my skills, I delight to alleviate your need or hardship, I seek your good opinion and gratitude; perhaps all the above. Working for is the established model of social engagement. . . . Working for identifies problems and focuses down on the ones it has the skills and interest to fix" (2018, 10–11). So much mission work has been and unfortunately continues to be *working for* people, which often disempowers people and breeds unhealthy dependence.

Another inadequate model but an improvement over the previous one is *working with* people. Control and power are taken away from the outsider attempting to intervene and put in the hands of those in need, empowering them to act and solve what they identify as problems. Wells says, "Like working for, it gains its energy from problem-solving, identifying targets, overcoming obstacles, and feeding off the bursts of energy that result. But unlike working for, which assumes the concentration of power in the expert and highly skilled, it locates power in coalitions of interests, initially collectives of the like-minded and similarly socially located, but eventually partnerships across conventional divides of religion and class around common causes" (2018, 11). This model of *working with* people, which is often the language of partnership, still falls short.

However, the model of *being with* people, Wells argues, "begins by largely rejecting the problem-solving axis. . . . Its main concern is the predicament that has no solution, the scenario that can't be fixed. It sees the vast majority of life and certainly the most significant moments of life, in these terms: love can't be achieved, death can't be fixed, pregnancy and birth aren't a problem needing a solution" (2018, 11). If Jesus is our model for incarnational identification, then we need to ask, "How did he spend his time? What was his primary mode of

8. In contrast to going native, Donald N. Larson notes that three viable roles for missionaries are sequentially a learner, a trader, and a storyteller, in contrast to roles we have too frequently used in the past of teacher, seller, and accuser (1978). I would suggest that another viable role is that of appreciator. By occupying these viable roles as cross-cultural witnesses, we can indeed become acceptable outsiders living out and proclaiming the gospel. Harriet Hill, a Bible translator in Côte d'Ivoire at the time, demonstrates confusing incarnational identification with going native (1990). Kenneth McElhanon, also a Bible translator with experience in Papua New Guinea, recognizes the challenge of incarnational identification, but he also sees the benefit for more effective ministry (1991).

operation?" It was *being with* more than anything else. Wells asks, "If Jesus was all about working for, how come he spent around 90 percent being with (in Nazareth), 9 percent working with (in Galilee)—and only 1 percent working for (in Jerusalem). Are these percentages significant—and do they provide a template for Christian mission? Surely Jesus knew what he was doing in the way he spent his time; or do we know better?" (2018, 13).[9]

Becoming All Things to All People

Another amazing biblical passage that helps us understand the incarnation as a model for mission is the apostle Paul's first letter to the church at Corinth addressing how Christians should live in a pagan society. How far should we go in identifying with the culture around us? This is a question Christians in every age have had to face. Here's Paul's response to that question:

> I am a free man, nobody's slave; but I make myself everybody's slave in order to win as many people as possible. While working with the Jews, I live like a Jew in order to win them; and even though I myself am not subject to the Law of Moses, I live as though I were when working with those who are, in order to win them. In the same way, when working with Gentiles, I live like a Gentile, outside the Jewish Law, in order to win Gentiles. This does not mean that I don't obey God's law; I am really under Christ's law. Among the weak in faith I become weak like one of them, in order to win them. So I become all things to all people, that I may save some of them by whatever means are possible. All this I do for the gospel's sake, in order to share in its blessings. (1 Cor. 9:19–23)

Let's unpack this passage. Paul begins by saying that although he is not a slave of anyone, he chooses to be everybody's slave. His audience understood exactly what he was talking about, because slaves were practically a household necessity for many in the Roman Empire at this time (cf. Bradley 1994; Hunt 2018; and Yavetz 1988). But why would he do such a thing? "In order to win as many people as possible," he writes. When working with Jews, he lives like a Jew, for the same reason—"in order to win them." He doesn't have to adjust his lifestyle to conform to all the rules and regulations of Jewish religion and culture, but he chooses to do so. In a similar way and for the same reasons—in order to win them—when working with gentiles, he lives like a gentile. But in terms of his identity, he is a Jew and cannot become a gentile. Kenneth Bailey says it well: "As regards *lifestyle* Paul can live as 'one under the Torah' and he can live 'as one not under the Torah.' But in regard to his *identity*, he knows that *he*

---

9. For a review of Wells 2018, see Whiteman 2019, 85.

cannot become a Gentile, and he plays no games with his readers. Only when we are deeply rooted in our own culture can we risk reaching out across a cultural chasm to people on the other side. A bridge must be securely anchored at each end. Only then can the bridge be completed and only then is travel across the bridge possible" (2011, 256–57).

Then Paul provides a shocker: "Among the weak in faith I become weak like one of them" (1 Cor. 9:22). This seems counterintuitive. Aren't we supposed to be strong, especially among those who are weak, in order to set an example? Bailey explains again: "Leaders usually want to appear strong. They are often willing to serve the weak, as long as they are seen by the public as strong. From a position of strength, they will reach out to those in need. In contrast Paul deliberately *becomes weak to* 'win the weak.' His mission from below informs everything he does" (257).

Incarnational identification means we go as far as we can to identify with others without violating our conscience and while maintaining our sanity. For example, when my wife, Laurie, and I went to the Solomon Islands and moved into the village of Gnulahage on the island of Santa Isabel, we lived like the people. However, it was so hot and humid that Laurie was constantly thirsty. After several weeks, she was still struggling, feeling thirsty all the time. I told her that if we couldn't find a solution, I'd get a small kerosene refrigerator for cold water. Shortly after, some villagers told Laurie what they did when they couldn't quench their thirst. A small green lime called a kamansi grows in the tropics, and if you squeeze the juice into a glass of water and drink it, your thirst will be quenched. Sure enough, it worked, and we had a kamansi tree just outside our house. Perhaps knowing that we could get a small refrigerator also helped Laurie psychologically, but in the end, we didn't need it. Even with small caveats, there is still plenty of lifestyle room for identifying with others. Paul's famous line "So I become all things to all people, that I may save some of them by whatever means are possible" (1 Cor. 9:22) is a good guideline for our incarnational identification with others in mission.

A number of years ago, one of my former students who had been transformed by the idea of incarnational identification went with her husband to South America, high up in the Andes Mountains, to work among the Aymara. She and her husband were particularly focused on working with women trapped in prostitution and children living on the streets. In less than a year into their ministry, she became pregnant with their first child. Her family implored her to return to the United States and have the child where it was safe. She was conflicted. Should she listen to her family back home and have her baby there, or should she be incarnational and give birth to her first child among the Aymara at an altitude of thirteen thousand feet? She contacted me to help her think through a culturally appropriate and incarnational approach to this dilemma. I told her I wasn't the kind of doctor who could help, but I advised her to seek medical advice from local doctors to ease her mind that it was safe for her to deliver at that high altitude. Then I added, "If you choose to have this baby among the very women you are working with, it will do more to bond you to them and establish you in that ministry and culture than almost anything else. Having your baby there will be a powerful way of identifying with them." She chose to stay and have her baby at the altitude of thirteen thousand feet, despite some health risks as a non-native. The child has now become a bicultural young man, able to speak multiple languages, a source of pride for both his parents and the Aymara. What a gift God enabled her to give to the local community and to her son.

This story and the one with which we opened this chapter may leave you wondering if you could ever make that kind of sacrifice. Perhaps you're wondering if you are equipped to serve cross-culturally. Many factors contribute to our ability to identify with the people among whom we live and serve. Some people seem to be born for this, and adjusting to life in other cultures comes fairly easily. For others, it is more challenging. We must not lose sight of the ultimate goal, which is to cross cultures with the gospel and through the words we speak and the way we live introduce people to Jesus. So, we need to identify with others as much as possible, but we also need to live a life that is sustainable. Each cross-cultural witness will have to rely on the Holy Spirit to guide them in living a balanced life that enables them to stay for the long term and establish deep, meaningful relationships with others.

CHAPTER SUMMARY

A proverb from Kenya says, "If you cannot explain a proverb in my language, then you don't know me." What would it take to explain a proverb in a language that is not our own? I submit that the approach we have advocated in this chapter to thoroughly identify with the other so that we learn their language, understand their worldview, and plumb the depths of their culture would put us on the path to explain another person's proverb in their language.

The incarnational approach to cross-cultural ministry, through which we identify with those among whom we live and serve and from whom we have much to learn, involves at least the following eight practices:

1. Start with people where they are, embedded in their culture. This frequently requires downward mobility on our part.

2. Take their culture seriously, for this is the context in which life has meaning for them.

3. Become like a child and approach them as if you are a learner, anxious to see the world from their perspective.

4. Be humble, for you have not yet acquired the knowledge to interpret experience and generate social behavior in their culture.

5. Lay aside your own cultural ethnocentrism, your positions of power, prestige, and privilege.

6. Put yourself in a posture of vulnerability; your defenses have to go.

7. Make every effort to identify with people where they are by living among them, loving them, and learning from them.

8. Discover from within their world how Christ can become the answer to the questions they ask and the needs they feel.

Throughout this book, we will continually rely on and refer to the incarnation as a biblical model for all ministry, especially for those engaged in cross-cultural ministry.

5

Incarnational Communication

Go to the people
Live among them
Learn from them
Love them
Start with what they know
Build on what they have

Chinese poem[1]

We begin this chapter with the fascinating story of Bartolomäus Ziegenbalg (1682–1719), a twenty-three-year-old German Lutheran who was sent by the Danish Halle Mission to South India as a missionary in 1706, nearly a century before William Carey wrote his famous tract in 1792, *An Enquiry into the Obligation of Christians to Use Means for the Conversion of the Heathens*, and then set sail for India the next year, in 1793. Ziegenbalg is reputed to be the first Protestant missionary.[2]

When Ziegenbalg arrived at the Danish East India Company in Tranquebar on July 9, 1706, he soon realized that if he was ever going to be able to communicate and live out the gospel effectively and persuasively, he was going to have to learn the Tamil language and the culture of these Tamil-speaking people,

---

1. The quotation in this epigraph was not an ancient Chinese poem as many sources claim. Nor was it from an ancient Chinese scholar, such as Lao Tzu. It was actually from Dr. Y. C. James Yen (1893–1990), who started China's mass education movement and rural development movement. For further details see https://iirr.org/mission-history/.
2. Catholic Jesuit missionaries preceded him in India by a century or more.

whose religion would later be called Hinduism by British Orientalists.[3] Fortunately, he had been sent by King Friedrich IV of Denmark to do exactly that and to ascertain the image of God in the Tamil people in order to lead them to a fuller knowledge of God as revealed in Jesus. Although Ziegenbalg did not master Tamil, he attended a local school, sat among the village children, and quickly learned to read, write, and speak Tamil sufficiently enough to translate the New Testament and the Old Testament from Genesis to Ruth.

Ziegenbalg was a creative visionary, and he set about the task of not only learning to speak and write the Tamil language but also discovering the intricacies of the South Indian culture and customs and understanding their complex religion, believing that this understanding would contribute to a church that was Lutheran in faith and worship but Indian in character (G. Anderson 1998, 761). With the help of Tamil friends, church members, and ethnographic informants, Ziegenbalg was able to compile a large manuscript in 1713 titled "Genealogy of the Malabarian Gods," which he sent to his mission board in Halle, Germany. August Hermann Francke, Ziegenbalg's spiritual mentor and head of the Halle Mission, was not pleased and quickly rebuked him for "wasting his time" studying these silly superstitious beliefs and customs. According to Dr. Germann, Ziegenbalg's biographer, Francke "wrote back to Tranquebar that the printing of the 'Genealogy of the South-Indian Gods' was not to be thought of, inasmuch as the Missionaries were sent to extirpate heathenism, and not to spread heathenish non-sense in Europe" (Germann 1869, xv). The European assumption, but not Ziegenbalg's belief, was that when the Tamil converted to Christianity, they also would become culturally more and more German and would leave their Indian customs and culture behind. The popular but false assumption of Christendom at the time was that the Tamil should become more Europeanized if they wanted to be Christianized. European culture and Christian religion went hand in hand, reinforcing each other.

Fortunately, the Halle Mission didn't trash Ziegenbalg's manuscript. Moreover, Ziegenbalg sent copies of it to various authorities in Germany, Denmark, and England.[4] In the 1860s, Ziegenbalg's manuscript was rediscovered, and it is astonishing what was found. It was full of information, insights, and ideas that

3. British Orientalists included eighteenth- and nineteenth-century figures such as Max Mueller (1823–1900), who founded the Western academic field of Indian studies, including languages, literature, art, religion, and other aspects of Indian society. In Ziegenbalg's day, the religion of these Tamil-speaking Indians would not have been called Hinduism. The term "Hinduism" to describe the diverse system of religious thought, rituals, and practices in India first appeared in Western ethnographic studies in the eighteenth century.

4. I owe a debt of scholarly gratitude to Dr. Daniel Jeyaraj (2005, 2006), the world's foremost authority on Ziegenbalg, for helping me tell the story of Ziegenbalg more accurately. Jeyaraj discovered a copy of Ziegenbalg's 1713 manuscript "Genealogy of the Malabarian Gods" in Copenhagen that was edited and published in German in 2003 and in English in 2005. Jeyaraj's own renowned

could have helped missionaries connect the gospel to Tamil-speaking Hindus. The book was published in 1869 under the title *Genealogy of the South-Indian Gods* and reprinted in 1984 (Ziegenbalg 1984). Today, Ziegenbalg is recognized as a pioneer in the Western study of South Indian culture, society, and religion.

The Halle Mission board had the erroneous idea that the gospel could be preached in a cultural vacuum. Perhaps they didn't believe it was necessary to spend valuable time learning the language and culture of these Tamil-speaking Hindus in South India as Ziegenbalg was doing. They somehow had the idea that if a missionary just preached the gospel, then God would take care of everything else. When I teach about this, I draw two stick figures, admittedly caricatures, on a whiteboard. One, the "missionary communicator," is wearing a pith helmet and carrying a ten-pound Bible under his arm. He is attempting to communicate the gospel to a "non-Christian receptor." Unfortunately, I have known missionaries who have bought into the erroneous assumption that if they could just "spread the Word," then God would take care of the rest, and they wouldn't need to spend valuable time learning the local language and culture and developing relationships with local people.

For example, in Papua New Guinea, where I served, I knew of missionaries who would fly above the jungles and drop tracts printed in English. Their hope and belief was that the Holy Spirit could use those tracts to convict a person of sin and lead them to a new life in Christ. I suppose that is theoretically possible, but it is improbable. The reason it won't happen is because this method is not incarnational. It does not involve personal contact or relationships established with potential converts who either are nonliterate or cannot read English. Of course, the tracts did not go unused. They just weren't used for the purpose the missionaries had in mind. They turned out to be the perfect size for rolling tobacco into cigarettes!

I remember once when I was sharing this story from Papua New Guinea, one of the young participants suddenly got a look of horror on her face. She said, "Now I can better understand what happened last summer when I was on what we called a cruise with a cause. We sailed around the Caribbean passing out tracts in the various ports of call. I remember when we landed in the Bahamas, after we had gone ashore, I noticed on my way back to the ship that the tracts I had passed out a couple hours earlier were now on the ground covered in mud." I asked her if she had a copy of the tracts they were passing out. She reached into her Bible and pulled out a one-million-dollar bill with a picture of former American president Grover Cleveland on it. In every respect—color, texture, and

work on Ziegenbalg in English is Jayaraj 2006. See also William n.d. for excellent background information on Ziegenbalg.

Figure 5.1
**Missionary Tracts Designed to Look
like US and Brazilian Currency**

artwork—it appeared on first glance to be a legitimate one-million-dollar bill, until you turned it over and discovered it was a fake, designed to share the truth of the gospel. Why would anyone hand out tracts that manipulated people into thinking they were receiving American money in an attempt to introduce them to Jesus, who proclaimed that he was the way, the *truth*, and the life (John 14:6)?

A few years later, I was training a large group of Brazilian Methodists for cross-cultural mission and was telling them the story of the young American woman who had passed out gospel tracts disguised as money as a way to share the truth of the gospel. I noticed several of the participants were becoming agitated as I spoke. Then one of them spoke up and said, "We have done the same thing" and pulled from his Bible two tracts that looked very similar to a five-reais and a one-hundred-reais Brazilian monetary note. On the back of the note was a brief message, Bible verses from John 3:16–17 and Romans 10:9, and a place to stamp the name and address of the Methodist church that had made these tracts available (see fig. 5.1).

Knowing the Content and Understanding the Context

To cross cultures with the gospel effectively, one needs to know the *content* of the message one is communicating and to understand the *context* in which that message is communicated and lived out. Many cross-cultural witnesses spend many years preparing for their ministry to other cultures. They may go to seminary or a Bible college and study Scripture, theology, and church history until they have a good grasp of the Christian story. We teach them how to exegete Scripture—that is, to interpret what Scripture is saying. In other words, they learn the biblical and theological *content* of the message they desire to communicate.

Unfortunately, they never learn how to exegete the *context*—that is, to interpret and make sense of the culture of the community in which they are preparing to serve. They may have taken classes in homiletics—how to preach—but they never learned how to listen and observe effectively. In my training sessions, I often ask, "Where do we learn to understand the context of our cross-cultural ministry?" The response is frequently, "We learn it from where we are living and serving." Yes, of course, there is much truth in that, but where do we learn how to ask good questions, how to make accurate observations, how to draw inferences from what we see, and how to make sense of the place where we are living? We don't train surgeons this way. We don't teach them only the theory or content of surgery and then tell them they'll learn the context when they get into an operation. We don't say to them, "Just take a stab at it. You'll figure it out when you get into it." Unfortunately, too much of our training for cross-cultural ministry is like that. Trainees may hear "You'll figure it out when you get there," but we don't provide good anthropological and ethnographic tools for them to know how to learn from the context in which they are serving.[5] Chapter 12 in this book will introduce you to a number of anthropological and ethnographic tools and practices so you'll be better prepared to exegete the cultural context along with your exegesis of Scripture.

Without adequate training, pastors and cross-cultural witnesses don't know how to discover the worldview of Muslim refugees who have moved into their community or of Buddhists living in the country where they want to serve. The cultural differences overwhelm them, frighten them, and confuse them, so they just rely on the promise of Isaiah 55:11 and hope their words will not return to them void. But their words and actions often do not produce a harvest because they do not communicate the content of their message in ways that make sense to the receptors in terms of their context. The message comes across as irrelevant news, bad news, boring news, or unimportant news. Seldom is it heard and seen as good news. Remember, the meaning of what we want to communicate is determined by the listener, not the speaker.

5. Anthropologist Michael Rynkiewich (2020) drives home the idea that because the context where we are engaged in mission is always changing, and sometimes rapidly, instead of focusing on delivering a lot of mission content in our teaching, which may soon be outdated and irrelevant, we should train cross-cultural witnesses in critical analytical skills, both in ethnography and in historical analysis, so they can understand the people and know how the gospel relates to them and their changing culture.

An example of misunderstanding the context can be seen in the work of two American women missionaries in Kenya. They had been in ministry among a particular people group for fifteen years when a pastor and several laypeople went to Kenya to see their work. The visit seemed to be going well, but the visitors were curious why only Kenyan women and children seemed to be involved in and impacted by the ministry of these two American women. It seemed strange to the visitors that the men in the village were completely uninterested. So the visitors asked some of the Kenyan men why they were "boycotting" the ministry of these women missionaries. Much to the surprise of the American visitors, the Kenyan men said, "We have assumed all these years that what these women missionaries were doing and talking about was not very important because they always stand when they talk. In our culture, if you have something important to say, you always sit down when you talk. These two women missionaries never do that, so we dismissed them and their message as not important for us men." For fifteen years, the content of the gospel was not heard by the men in the village because these missionaries did not adequately understand the context in which they were communicating. They had missed a very important cultural cue about communication, and their cultural offense had prevented the Kenyan men from hearing the offense of the gospel.

We need both knowledge of the content and understanding of the context to be successful in cross-cultural ministry. We also need to know and be committed, in both word and deed, to the content of the gospel that we are attempting to communicate. If we don't know the gospel's content, then any kind of false gospel can emerge. And if we don't understand the context in which the gospel is being received, then it won't make much difference how well we know the content of our message, for it will not be understood or received in the way we intended. To learn to relate to people where they are in their culture, we need to use the tools of anthropology and other behavioral sciences to exegete the context.

The Complexity of Incarnational Communication of the Gospel

When we don't understand or take seriously the context of our cross-cultural ministry, we frequently come across like the caricature of the missionary communicator that I described above. Unfortunately, many laypeople in our churches have this misperception of mission work. I propose a model that attempts to take into account the context of both the communicator and the receptor in the communication of the gospel (see fig. 5.2). There are seven parts to this model.

The first part is biblical meanings. This is our starting point. Here we list the essential elements of what it means to be a Christian. Hopefully, the items we list are those on which all Christians can agree, although different Christian

Figure 5.2
Communicating the Gospel

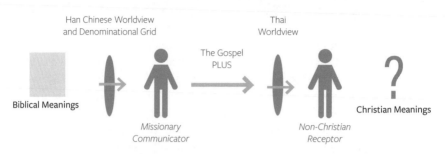

traditions and denominations will put more emphasis on some areas than on others. So, for example, Protestants would be sure to include the importance of Scripture, while Catholics would balance Scripture with magisterium teaching. Wesleyans would emphasize the love of God, while those in the Reformed tradition would perhaps begin with the sinfulness of human beings and the importance of substitutionary atonement—that there is salvation from our sin through the death and blood of Jesus. The elements in the Apostles' Creed would perhaps be a good summary of biblical meanings with which we could begin. Theologians and biblical scholars may debate what is essential as a starting point for communicating the gospel, but that is not our focus here. In any case, the missionary communicator is confident that she or he has a thorough grasp of the basic beliefs and behavior of a follower of Jesus, which compose the category of biblical meanings.

Second, do these biblical meanings go directly into the mind and heart of the missionary communicator? Are they transferred into us like a blood transfusion? No, they are not. They must first pass through a specific worldview (I'll use the Han Chinese worldview as an example) and agree with our denominational grid. And of course, this is where the problem immediately begins. Because cross-cultural witnesses come from all over the globe in this postcolonial world, they are faced with a missiological challenge. Their understanding of biblical meanings from Scripture and tradition are passed through the lens of their worldview and must also pass the "litmus test" of their theological perspective and denominational traditions and requirements.[6] This is the primary reason cross-cultural witnesses emerge with different understandings and interpretations of what the gospel is.

6. This is where you will encounter a wide range of understandings and interpretations, because there are nearly forty-five thousand different Christian denominations worldwide, according to the *World Christian Encyclopedia* (Johnson and Zurlo 2020).

In their groundbreaking book *Misreading Scripture with Western Eyes: Removing Cultural Blinders to Better Understand the Bible* (2012), E. Randolph Richards and Brandon J. O'Brien vividly draw our attention to this challenge of identifying how one's worldview influences the way one reads and interprets the Bible. So, it's not accurate to simply say, "The Bible means what it says and says what it means." Our ability to understand the meaning of the Bible comes through the Holy Spirit, but it is mediated through the language we speak and the culture in which we live. In other words, the worldview we hold and the theological perspectives to which we adhere influence how we perceive and understand the meaning of the Bible. For example, Korean missionaries, who come from one of the most homogeneous societies in the world, have their understanding of biblical meanings filtered through their Korean worldview and their diverse denominational perspectives on Christianity. So naturally their understanding and practice of Christianity is thoroughly Korean.

According to the twenty-sixth edition of the *Ethnologue* of world languages, 7,168 languages are spoken in the world today (Simons 2023). We could safely estimate that there are at least eight thousand to ten thousand distinct worldviews that emerge from the different languages spoken by human beings. In addition, according to the 2020 *World Christian Encyclopedia*, 44,800 different denominations of Christianity exist in the world (Zurlo, Johnson, and Crossing 2020). When we factor in the different genders, social locations, economic statuses, and political perspectives, we can begin to imagine the wide range of possible worldviews.

The third part of the model is the missionary communicator. Because the missionary communicator understands and interprets the biblical meanings based on their worldview and denominational grid, they do not communicate *only* the gospel. They communicate the gospel *plus* assumptions that come from their worldview and the theology and polity of their denominational distinctives. The problem is that most of us are not even *aware* that we have confused the gospel with our culture and our denominational distinctives. This is because we confuse the biblical meanings with the forms we use to communicate and live out those biblical meanings. (In chapter 8, I address the misuse of cultural forms in attempting to convey meaning.)

So, for example, I encountered this problem growing up in the Free Methodist Church, a conservative evangelical church in the Wesleyan/Holiness tradition. I assumed that the way we Free Methodists understood and lived out the gospel *was* the gospel. I didn't believe this just because I was arrogant and narrow-minded. I believed this because of my cultural conditioning. I admitted that some other churches were close to the truth, but I dismissed many others as being far from the truth because they didn't practice their faith the way we

Free Methodists did. I believed that the dominant characteristics and marks of a true Christian were that they did not drink alcohol, smoke tobacco, play cards, dance, or go to movies, and I believed that a person's salvation was in jeopardy if they did. Without realizing it, I grew up confusing my Free Methodist denominational distinctives with the liberating and transforming gospel.

We now come to the fourth part of the model, the gospel message that we proclaim. The missionary communicator in their mind believes they have a firm grasp of the gospel, the whole gospel, and nothing but the gospel. Not only do we proclaim the gospel verbally, but we also live out the gospel behaviorally. As we will learn later in this book, the lion's share of our communication is nonverbal. A saying attributed to Saint Francis of Assisi famously declares, "In everything you do preach the gospel—if necessary, use words." And of course it often is necessary to use words to explain the hope that lies within us (1 Pet. 3:15). The problem is that in both word and deed we often proclaim the gospel *plus*, instead of only the gospel.

Vincent Donovan, after seventeen years of missionary work among the Maasai pastoral tribesmen in Tanzania, East Africa, concluded in his book *Christianity Rediscovered* (1978) that we must present the "naked gospel" to people and let them clothe it with their culture so that it is culturally relevant, makes sense to them, and deals with issues in their context.[7] This is the way an indigenous church can emerge. But unfortunately, we have overloaded the gospel message and lifestyle with so much extra baggage and clothes that don't fit.[8] As a result, it is often hard for us to discover what the naked gospel is and how to distinguish it from our culture and our denominational requirements.

Of course, in reality there can never be a completely naked gospel because every follower of Jesus comes to the gospel from within their own cultural context and historical era. The whole meaning of incarnation is that the gospel does not exist outside culture. It exists only as it enters into and transforms a culture. Nevertheless, the concept of a naked gospel can be a helpful way to begin to understand all the extrabiblical things we have added to the gospel. Eventually, I came to understand that the "five marks of a Free Methodist Christian"—not drinking alcohol, smoking tobacco, playing cards, dancing, and

7. We invited Fr. Donovan on several occasions to speak at Asbury Seminary. He was as engaging in person as he is in his book chronicling his missionary experience among the Maasai. I invited him to speak to students in my large Anthropology for Christian Mission course, and he began by introducing himself, "I am Father Vincent Donovan, a recovering missionary." We all laughed, but his point was profound. The Maasai taught him a new way of understanding and doing mission, and he was recovering from the old colonial ways he had learned over many years.

8. This extra baggage reminds me of the story of King Saul, who tried to clothe the young boy David with his armor, but it didn't fit David. So he took it off and used something familiar in his culture—a sling and five smooth stones—to kill the Philistine giant Goliath (1 Sam. 17:38–40).

going to movies—were not the gospel at all. Imagine my surprise when as an adult I discovered Colossians 2:16: "So let no one make rules about what you eat or drink."

We now arrive at the fifth part of the model, the worldview of the non-Christian receptor. In figure 5.2, the receptor's Thai worldview is different from the worldview of the Han Chinese missionary communicator. For purposes of illustration and simplification, let's call the worldview of the recipient a Thai worldview, even though we recognize, of course, that there are multiple Thai worldviews. When the gospel *plus* passes through the worldview of the recipient, they do not hear or understand exactly what the missionary communicator intended to communicate. Sometimes there is just a subtle difference between what is communicated and what is understood. But often the difference is great and leads to misunderstanding at best or conflict and resistance at worst.

The sixth element in this model of communication is the receptor. When the Thai receptors hear the gospel and interpret it in terms of their worldview, their understanding may not match the biblical meanings at the beginning of the communication process. Let me illustrate this with a story from one of my Thai students, Ubolwan Mejudhon. She began her doctoral research on trying to discover why the Thai people have been so resistant to the gospel after more than 150 years of mission activity. In Thailand, one hears the phrase "To be Thai is to be Buddhist," so the concept of a Thai Christian seems like an oxymoron to many Thai. As she analyzed the Thai worldview and basic values, she discovered that a dominant Thai value was meekness in social interaction. Western and Korean missionaries often came across to the Thai Buddhists as aggressive and domineering, and so their message of "the gospel of peace" was usually rejected (Mejudhon 1994).

The seventh element in the communication process is assessing whether the meanings that are understood by the receptor are anywhere close to the biblical meanings with which the process of communication began. Again, remember that meaning is determined by the listener, not the speaker. It is not always clear whether biblical meanings survive this cross-cultural trip from one context to another. Many times what the missionary communicator thought they were communicating is not what the receptor understood. Something gets lost in translation and transmission. So here is where another element is needed.

Figure 5.3 shows the effort to communicate the naked gospel. Of significance is the arrow pointing from the receptor to the communicator, indicating how important it is for the communicator to understand what the receptor has understood. This requires observing and listening, two ethnographic skills we'll discuss in chapter 12.

Figure 5.3
Communicating the Naked Gospel with Feedback

Let's review the process. We started with biblical meanings as the source of the gospel, but those biblical meanings are immediately filtered through the missionary communicator's worldview and denominational grid. Unaware or unconscious that the gospel has now accumulated some extra baggage, we sally forth, believing we have the gospel, the whole gospel, and nothing but the gospel, so help us God. But, of course, it is now the gospel *plus* that we are communicating. Moreover, it is the receptor, not the communicator, who in the final analysis is the person who determines whether or not this is the gospel. And here is the problem. Unless we can see and understand the world in the same way the receptor understands and sees it, we do not know if what we are communicating is being understood. We may be clear, perhaps even eloquent, in what we are saying, but we will be largely in the dark as far as knowing how it is being heard and interpreted by the receptor. To be incarnational means that we must come into the worldview of the receptor as best we can and from there view what it is that we are attempting to communicate. Until we walk in their shoes, cry and laugh with them, we'll be oblivious as to whether the receptor understands what we are trying to communicate.

The evidence that biblical meanings actually get through this process and survive is mixed. Around the globe, we find that where the Christian message has been proclaimed, there are believers who are truly in a relationship with Christ. There is no doubt about it. God's Spirit has penetrated their culture and gotten their attention, transforming their minds, lifestyles, and even communities. They are disciples of Jesus, and they disciple others. But unfortunately, many others have accepted the forms of Christianity introduced by missionaries without understanding the transforming power and meaning of the gospel. Nominal Christianity and folk Christianity are alive and well all over the world. The *forms* of Christianity are present but not the transforming power to change personal lives and communities that the gospel makes available to believers.

The apostle Paul warned about this problem a long time ago when he said in his second letter to Timothy that in the last days, people "will hold to the outward form of our religion, but reject its real power" (2 Tim. 3:5). Where the gospel has become incarnate in a cultural context, we should expect to discover different kinds of churches, different expressions and interpretations of the gospel. When we find churches that look just like the churches back home— that is, the missionary's home—we should have grave concerns. This problem occurs when the biblical meanings do not survive the communication process from missionary communicator to non-Christian receptor.

My initial reaction to discovering the difficulty (both for the communicator and for the receptor) of the process of communicating the gospel across these cultural barriers is one of despair. There is so much miscommunication from the missionary and misunderstanding by the receptor. It appears that at times we may not even know what the gospel is, let alone how to effectively communicate it in another person's world. However, it is the Holy Spirit who superintends this process of communicating the gospel from one person to another, from one culture to another, from one generation to another. Moreover, this is the plan that God has put in place whereby the gospel traverses time and cultures. God has chosen to use ordinary people empowered by the Holy Spirit as God's vehicles for communicating the good news of the gospel. When we realize that the Holy Spirit is in charge of this process, a burden is lifted from our shoulders. This realization does not give us license to slack off or be culturally insensitive, but it does give us a better perspective of our role as cross-cultural witnesses. It is the work of the Holy Spirit to convict people of sin and lead them to a new life in Christ. Our role is to be clear channels through which God's love flows to others. God calls us to prepare as best we can for cross-cultural ministry and to be faithful followers of Jesus, but it is the work of the Holy Spirit that makes our ministry fruitful. Faithfulness is our responsibility; fruitfulness is the work of the Holy Spirit.

Moreover, when we are aware of the role of the Holy Spirit in the process of communicating the gospel across cultures, we can be confident that God's Spirit is alive and well and working in the culture of the people to whom we are going long before we get there. John Wesley introduced into the theological vocabulary the concept of prevenient grace, the grace that is at work in the life of a person long before they become a Christian. Prevenient grace eventually leads people to saving grace. Although Wesley applied this order of salvation to individuals, I believe it is also applicable to entire societies, as Gerald H. Anderson also argues in his discussion of the role of prevenient grace in world mission. Anderson quotes Max Warren, the longtime general secretary of the Church Missionary Society of the Anglican Church, in a debate with Donald McGavran, saying, "I find God at work everywhere, often working very strangely by my limited human understanding, but working nevertheless. In our mission to the great world outside the Covenant people, we have strong biblical support for a spirit of expectancy as we go to discover in those other faiths the prevenient grace of the uncovenanted Christ" (G. Anderson 2009, 47).

We know from history that there have been times when entire cultures were more responsive and less resistant to the gospel. That is the *kairos* moment when people are open and ready to hear and respond to the good news. This happened in Polynesia (Tippett 1971), in Fiji (Tippett 1980), and in the Solomon Islands (Tippett 1967, 42–43; Whiteman 1983). A large people group responded to the gospel at a propitious moment in their history.

Another example of God's prevenient grace at work in a culture is a story I remember hearing of a nineteenth-century British Church Mission Society missionary who went to minister among the Igbo in what today is southeast Nigeria in West Africa.[9] He had been there about six months, was making progress in learning the Igbo language and understanding the culture, and was beginning to see some positive results of his work. One day he was talking to a group of villagers about Christianity. He told them, "I'm so glad that God sent me from England to you Igbo people so that I could tell you about God, because before I came, you people were ignorant and knew nothing about God." He prattled on for a while until finally an old man sitting in the crowd got up and with a smile on his face said, "My friend, you've got it almost right, but not quite." The British missionary was taken aback because he was not used to being told that he wasn't 100 percent correct. The old Igbo man continued, "We are glad you have come, but it is our Igbo god Chukwu who sent you to us so we could learn more about God, now that you've told us about Jesus."[10]

This is stunning, and what a difference this perspective makes. If we go as cross-cultural witnesses with the expectation that God has left a witness in every culture, that God has been at work in every society at every period of human history, and that God has been present in the lives of people long before we arrived on the scene, it will transform our approach to cross-cultural ministry. For starters, it takes the burden of their salvation off our shoulders. This doesn't mean we should be less passionate about evangelism. Rather, we can become even more passionate, even more committed because we can now be motivated by love and excitement for what God is doing instead of being driven by guilt

9. What follows is a narrative of a historical exchange in the way Christianity was introduced among the Igbo in Nigeria in the early twentieth century. A similar story has been fictionalized by Chinua Achebe in chapter 21 of *Things Fall Apart*.

10. For a fuller story on the Igbo movement to Christianity, see Ekechi 1971.

and fear of hell. This understanding will empower us for a lifetime of ministry and foster resilience in times of difficulty and discouragement.

Some final comments on this model of incarnational communication are appropriate. Many of us have not done the hard work of distinguishing our culture from the gospel. Incarnational communication means that we take our understanding of the gospel, as culturally conditioned as it is, and we develop a relationship with people who are different from us in their culture. We attempt to read the Bible through their eyes and to understand and interpret it from the perspective of their worldview, not just our worldview. When this begins to happen, there will no longer be just a one-way arrow pointing from the missionary communicator to the non-Christian receptor. Now arrows will go both directions because the missionary will learn many new things about God when they view life through the lens of their host culture. Note that the arrow in figure 5.3 pointing from the receptor to the communicator is slightly larger than the arrow pointing from the communicator to the receptor. We may learn more about what God is doing in the world from the receptor than the receptor learns from us.

The Transmission Model and the Constitutive Model of Communication

In the previous discussion of the communication of the gospel from missionary communicator to non-Christian receptor, I employed primarily a transmission model of communication, which holds that communication is "the process of intentionally stimulating meaning in the mind of another" (Haas 2016, 28).

Some scholars today argue that the transmission model of communication is an oversimplification of the communication process and affirm a popular alternative called the constitutive model (Baxter 2004; Nicotera 2009; Pearce and Cronen 1980; Sigman 1992). Instead of portraying communication as merely the transmission of information, the constitutive model posits that communication has power to shape reality itself (Baxter and Montgomery 1996). Jimmie Manning says, "Scholars should [investigate] how relationships, identities and tasks are in the communication [itself] . . . rather than simply continuing our current dominant focus on the communication . . . between two or more people" (2014, 432). To take a constitutive view of communication is to presume that meaning is created in the interaction between communicator and receptor, and of course this is why figure 5.3 contains two arrows instead of just one pointing from the communicator to the receptor. This constitutive approach to communication makes an incarnational approach to communication all the more important.

Lost or Misunderstood in Translation

We will end this discussion of incarnational communication by looking at two examples of what can and often does go wrong when we don't use an incarnational approach to cross-cultural ministry, when the arrow of communication goes only one direction from communicator to receptor, when we see ourselves as only knowers and not learners. The first example comes from a translation of Psalm 23 into the Hmong language from Laos. This is a back-translation into English so that we can understand how the Hmong "heard" the Twenty-Third Psalm. This is a psalm that many English-speaking Christians memorized from the King James Version of the Bible when they were children. Listen to what it sounds like when interpreted and understood through the worldview of the Hmong:

> The Great Boss is the One who takes care of my sheep,
>   I don't want to own anything.
> The Great Boss wants me to lie down in the field.
>   He wants me to go to the lake.
> He makes my good spirit come back.
> Even though I walk through something the missionary
>   calls the valley of the shadow of death,
>   I do not care.
>   You are with me.
> You use a stick and a club to make me comfortable.
> You manufacture a piece of furniture right in
>   Front of my eyes while my enemies watch.
>   You pour car grease on my head.
> My cup has too much water in it and therefore overflows.
>   Goodness and kindness will walk single file
>   Behind me all my life.
> And I will live in the hut of the Great Boss
>   Until I die and am forgotten by the tribe.[11]

My initial response when I read this was to chuckle, but on deeper reflection, a more appropriate response would be to weep. Is there any sense of God as a shepherd coming through this translation? What biblical meanings survived the trip from the biblical text to the Hmong context? I submit that very few did. I would also argue that much of the meaning has been lost in translation. In fact, I doubt we modern-day North Americans understand Psalm 23 as well as the ancient Hebrews did. This is because we don't know very much about

11. From an interview with William Smalley, *Wichita Eagle*, January 7, 1960.

sheep and we aren't sheep herders. Unless we become incarnational and enter into the receptor's context so that we hear how the gospel is being interpreted, these kinds of examples of miscommunication will continue to occur.

Another example of miscommunication of the gospel comes from the Erima people of the Madang Province in Papua New Guinea. Look how they understand the gospel:

> Once upon a time, probably one or two hundred years ago, God sent a spirit man named Jesus to the white men. All lands have their own spirits, and this one was sent to the white men's land. Some men killed the spirit-man Jesus and buried him. While he was dead, Jesus visited the place where dead white men dwell. The ancestors of the white men, in the place of the dead, revealed to Jesus how to make cars, airplanes, radios, pots and pans, etc. What they showed him were secret magical incantations which enable one to make such wonderful things. On the third day, Jesus' spirit rose from the dead, leaving his body in the grave. Having risen in his spirit, he revealed to the white men all the wonderful secret magical incantations he had learned from the dead ancestors of the white men, and showed them how to make all the things the white men now have. After that, Jesus went up in his spirit into the sky to his father. And so now because Jesus died for all our problems, if we get baptized and blessed by a pastor, and if we live good lives, when we die, three days later, just like Jesus our spirits, too, will leave our bodies and go up to heaven. In the meantime, watch the white men carefully! They have not taught us the secret magical incantations for making cargo yet. But maybe someday, one of them will tell us the secret.[12]

This interpretation of the gospel by the Erima people is such a powerful and memorable example of what can and often does go wrong in crossing cultures with the gospel.

CHAPTER SUMMARY

In this chapter on incarnational communication, we stressed the importance of understanding both the content of the gospel and the cultural context in which the gospel is presented in word and deed. Communicating the content without understanding the context will end in the receptor not comprehending the full meaning and not experiencing the transforming power of the gospel.

12. This story is taken from the April 1979 newsletter of Mike and Sandie Colburn, who are Wycliffe Bible Translators in Papua New Guinea and former students in my Anthropology for Christian Mission course. To understand the reference to "making cargo" see John Strelan's 1977 study on the history and theology of cargo cults in Melanesia.

Understanding the context of our host society without being clear on the content of the gospel inevitably means we will communicate the gospel plus a lot of extrabiblical requirements, or perhaps even unbiblical prescriptions. Knowing the content of the gospel and understanding the context in which it is communicated are of equal importance in cross-cultural ministry.

CONCLUSION TO PART 2

The incarnation is more than an important theological doctrine about God becoming a human being. It is also a model for cross-cultural ministry. Being incarnational means we empty ourselves of our pride, prejudices, personal agendas, ambitions, and lifestyle in order to enter deeply into the world of another culture. Incarnation frequently means downward mobility. In the same way that the incarnation led to crucifixion for Jesus, incarnational identification involves a dying to the self to identify with others, but this will be followed by "resurrection" in the host culture, where we are "born again" with a new language, a different worldview, new relationships, and a deeper understanding of God's mission in the world.

In this chapter we discussed incarnational communication, which involves grasping both the content of the gospel and the cultural context in which the gospel is being communicated. When we understand the context, we can communicate the gospel in a way that the receptor can understand.

Even when we strive to communicate incarnationally in a cross-cultural setting, miscommunication is bound to occur. This is the topic of part 3.

Common Communication Problems

6

Worldview Differences

For any of us to be fully conscious intellectually we should not
only be able to detect the worldviews of others but be aware
of our own—why it is ours and why in the light of so many op-
tions we think it is true.

James Sire (2020)

I n 1977–78 my wife and I lived in a small village of 150 people on the island
of Santa Isabel in the Solomon Islands. We were researching the impact of
Anglican Christianity and living with people who only a few generations
earlier had been headhunters. Some of the older men remembered those days
as children and were glad they were gone. Headhunting was now a thing of
the past. Villagers would occasionally talk about how the gospel of peace had
brought an end to headhunting, and they were grateful. Living in the village,
we observed that when the Solomon Islands Anglican priest came to the village
every several months, there was great enthusiasm and interest in the service of
Holy Communion he conducted. It seemed that everyone in the village turned
out. In contrast, only ten to fifteen people attended the daily services of morning prayer and evensong. I wondered why there was such a discrepancy in the
numbers. Why were so many villagers anxious to receive Holy Communion
but so few attending daily prayers?

After observing this pattern many times, I decided to investigate why the
attendance was so much greater when a priest came to the village and offered
Holy Communion. So, I asked villagers, "Why do so many people attend Holy
Communion but so few come to daily prayers?"

"Oh, it's because we get holy food when we take communion," they responded.

"What do you mean by 'holy food'?" I inquired.

"Oh, you know, we receive spiritual power when we eat the bread and drink the wine in communion," they replied.

"Do you mean you acquire *mana* when you partake of Holy Communion?" I asked.

"Yes," they said with a sheepish grin. "We are Christian in name only."

Traditionally, *mana*, or spiritual power, was believed to reside primarily in a person's physical head. The more important a person was in society, the more *mana* it was believed they had. Headhunting was the primary way of gaining *mana*, as they drank the blood and ate the brains of deposed enemies. Now they could get *mana* through Holy Communion instead of headhunting. It was obvious, at least to me, that something was missing, something had been lost in translation in the cross-cultural communication of the biblical meaning of Holy Communion to these Solomon Islanders.

We often misunderstand the people among whom we live and serve, and they frequently misunderstand us and our message. In this part of the book, we are going to try to understand why this happens. The problem is sometimes compounded when we don't realize that we are being misunderstood and that our message is misunderstood as well. One contributing factor, over which we have little control, is the social location our host assigns us. This can result in inaccurate stereotypes, or they may misjudge our motivations and reasons for why we are living among them. To complicate matters further, we are frequently unaware of this problem because the people with whom we live and minister may be hesitant to share their misunderstandings and misgivings with us. Only by building solid bridges of love and trust between us will these kinds of suspicions, mistrust, and misunderstanding subside. This takes time and cannot be accomplished in a seven-to-ten-day mission trip.[1]

I once spent time in Bangladesh with a couple who, at that time, had served there for twenty-eight years. As I hung out with them and observed how they were relating to the Bangladeshi people, it became obvious to me that they were deeply connected with the people among whom they had lived for so long. At dinner one night, I asked them, "How long did it take you to connect with these people at such a deep worldview level?" The man's initial response was, "Oh, you can tell?" I reminded him that I was an anthropologist and that my primary mode of operation was observing people and asking questions. He then continued, "I can almost tell you the day it happened. We had been

1. Today, we see so many examples of cross-cultural misunderstanding and miscommunication in mission. Many short-term mission trips in an attempt to do good may do harm. For examples, see Corbett and Fikkert 2009; Fikkert and Kapic 2019; and Lupton 2012.

serving here for eighteen years, learning the Bangla language, discovering their worldview, religious assumptions, social structure, economy, and beliefs, and I remember the time when interacting with a Bangladeshi man that I realized I had really connected with their language and culture." He then went on to say, "The last ten years we have been five or six times more effective than those first eighteen years because we now understand the Bangladeshi people in ways we never did before." This couple went on to serve in Bangladesh for another seven years for a total of thirty-five years.

Miscommunication on both sides is bound to happen. It is inevitable, but that is no excuse to keep from doing the hard work of discovering the deep underlying assumptions that lead to premature judgments and miscommunication in cross-cultural ministry. It takes time and intentionality.

In this chapter, we will explore the importance of worldview in communicating the meaning of following Jesus to people whose worldview is vastly different from our own. If we don't take worldview into account, miscommunication can occur. We begin by defining worldview, demonstrate how it compares to religion, and conclude with how worldview functions in cross-cultural ministry.

Defining Worldview

What is a worldview? We often hear people talking about a "Christian" or "biblical" worldview. What is that? Many definitions of worldview have been offered, and entire books have been written describing the different dimensions of worldview, how to introduce change to a people's worldview, and why the worldview of the other is so important to understand in cross-cultural ministry.[2]

I define worldview as the central, governing set of concepts, presuppositions, and values that a society lives by. Two caveats are important to note with this definition. First, there can be as much variation among people within a worldview as there is between people with different worldviews. A worldview is not monolithic. Second, a worldview is not static, although it may be very slow to change compared to behavior, which can change more quickly. A worldview is dynamic and changes with time and circumstances, often in response to political, economic, and environmental changes.

The two missiological anthropologists who have written the most about worldview are Paul G. Hiebert and Charles H. Kraft, who served as colleagues for over a dozen years (1977–89) in the School of World Mission at Fuller Theological Seminary in Pasadena, California. Kraft defines worldview as the "totality

---

2. See, for example, T. Anderson et al. 2017; Burnett 1992; Hiebert 2008; Kearney 1984; C. Kraft 2009; M. Kraft 1978; Moon 2017; Opler 1945; and Sire 2015, 2020.

of the culturally structured images and assumptions (including value and com-mitment or allegiance assumptions) in terms of which a people both perceive and respond to reality" (2008, 12). Hiebert defines worldview as the "fundamental cognitive, affective, and evaluative presuppositions a group of people make about the nature of things, and which they use to order their lives" (2008, 15).[3]

There have been attempts, written from a theological and philosophical per-spective, to define a Christian worldview.[4] Renowned biblical scholar N. T. Wright discusses in depth what constitutes a Christian worldview, noting, "Like all worldviews, the Christian worldview is not simply a matter of a private language, a secret or arcane mystery which is of interest only to those who themselves profess Christian faith. All worldviews, the Christian one included, are in principle public statements. They all tell stories which attempt to chal-lenge and perhaps to subvert other worldview-stories. All of them provide a set of answers to the basic questions, which can be called up as required from the subconscious, and discussed. All commit their hearers to a way of being-in-the-world or being-for-the-world" (1992, 135).

Most people are normally not consciously aware of their worldview. Even though our ideas, values, and assumptions underlie our actions and give them meaning, we seldom consciously recognize this. We derive meaning from our worldview, although most of us are not consciously aware that we do so. An example of how we are often unaware of the role of our worldview in help-ing us make sense of the world is the way we read and interpret the Bible. E. Randolph Richards and Brandon J. O'Brien have made this very clear in their book *Misreading Scripture with Western Eyes: Removing Cultural Blinders to Better Understand the Bible* (2012). The fact that we read the Bible through our worldview doesn't negate the truth of the Bible, but we must acknowledge the role worldview plays in understanding and interpreting it. The authors explain that one of the best ways to uncover the hidden assumptions in our worldview is to note when we say or hear others say, "It goes without saying." For example, it went without saying for thousands of years that the earth was flat and that the sun revolved around the earth. Compose a list of all the "it goes without saying" assumptions you hold. You may be surprised how long the list grows.

Let me demonstrate the power of a person's worldview in shaping their perception and understanding of the world around them. An example of the phrase "It goes without saying" is "God helps those who help themselves," which,

---

3. For a comparison of Kraft's and Hiebert's approaches to worldview, see Moreau et al. 2014, 74–75.

4. For the concept of worldview discussed from more of a theological and philosophical per-spective, see T. Anderson, Clark, and Naugle 2017; Huffman 2011; Naugle 2002; and Sire 2015, 2020.

according to George Barna's research, three out of four Americans believe is found in the Bible. This popular saying, however, is from Benjamin Franklin's *Poor Richard's Almanac*, which was a yearly published almanac that appeared continuously from 1732 to 1758. If deep within our worldview is the unconscious assumption that "God helps those who help themselves" and we go to a community where, from our perspective, people don't seem to be making much of an effort to improve their lot, our assumption will influence how we perceive and interact with them. We are likely to surmise that if they are not willing to try to help themselves, then why should we bother or, worse, why should God care and bother to help them. We may unconsciously conclude, "They deserve what they have" or "They made their bed, now let them lie in it." However, if we are able to expose the prejudice and bias that come from our worldview, then we may discover that this is a peasant culture with a subsistence economy. We may see that abject poverty is fueled by structural inequality in which perhaps 2 percent of the population owns or controls 80 percent of the land, as we find in some societies in Central America. Do you see how these subconscious worldview themes that play out in our minds can influence how we perceive poverty, filth, and "laziness" and ultimately affect how we relate to people who are different from us? These worldview themes are not found in Scripture, but they are nevertheless dominant themes in American culture that have spread around the world with urbanization and globalization (Barna and Hatch 2001, 90).[5]

Religion and Worldview

Worldview is even more basic and fundamental than religion, although they both serve similar functions. In other words, many American Christians are more American than they are Christian, but we don't realize it. Many Korean Christians are more Korean than Christian, but they don't know it. This is uncomfortable for us to hear. We would like to believe that we are first and foremost a Christian and that kingdom values permeate our worldview and guide our behavior, but in fact, it is often the other way around. Our national, ethnic, or political identity may be more important to us than our identity as children of God. Our worldview therefore becomes more fundamental and foundational to who we are than our Christian faith. We are more American than Christian. We are more Kikuyu than Christian. We are more Filipino than Christian. We are more Republican than Christian. You get the idea.

5. This data comes from a survey taken between 1997 and 2000 (see Barna and Hatch 2001, 205 [point 2]).

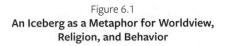

Figure 6.1
**An Iceberg as a Metaphor for Worldview,
Religion, and Behavior**

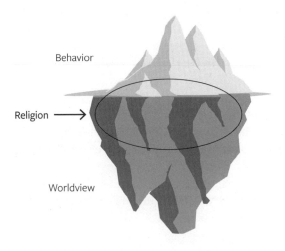

Paul G. Hiebert explains the difference between worldview and religion: "A world view provides people with their basic assumptions about reality. Religion provides them with the specific content of this reality, with the things in the people's model of the universe and with relationships between things" (1983, 371). According to Hiebert, our worldview lies at the deepest part of our existence and identity (2008, 32–33).

One way to think about the relationship between our worldview, religion, and behavior is to see it in terms of an iceberg. According to the United States Coast Guard Navigation Center, nearly 90 percent of an iceberg is found below the waterline, and that's why an iceberg is an appropriate metaphor (see fig. 6.1).

Let's start at the top of the iceberg and discuss all three dimensions. First, behavior is what we can see in others and to a lesser degree in ourselves. We evaluate, judge, condemn, criticize, and ridicule behavior when it doesn't conform to what we believe is correct and proper according to our worldview. Or we may approve of, accept, appreciate, even model behavior that is compatible with what we believe is correct behavior. In too much of cross-cultural ministry around the globe and down through the ages, we have emphasized the need for people to change their behavior if they want to become Christians. We want them to organize their churches and practice their faith in the same ways we do. We may criticize their marriage patterns, their leadership structures, and their political systems if they appear to be too different from our own. We may even call them sinful, disgusting, or degrading. However, conversion to following Jesus is more about changing the unseen dimensions of who we are—our values, our beliefs, and our worldview—than changing our behavior, although sometimes changing both is required if we are to be a true follower of Jesus. So, focusing on trying to convince people to change their behavior without the Holy Spirit fostering a deeper change in their values, beliefs, and worldview at best is superficial and at worst leads to nominal Christianity and hypocrisy. As the Solomon Islanders, who several generations earlier had ceased headhunting to acquire *mana*, confessed to me one day, they now partook of Holy Communion to acquire *mana*, which of course was a lot less hazardous to their health.

In figure 6.1, religion lies both above the waterline and just below it. It lies above it because so much of religion is expressed in symbols, ceremonies, and rituals that we can observe. Religion also lies just below the waterline and is unseen. This is the knowledge that people have about their religion. For some Christians, the Apostles' Creed is a good summary of what they believe, and in some denominations, they recite it every week in church. Once again in cross-cultural ministry, we too often implore non-Christians to merely abandon their religion and adopt ours. But if they merely adopt the knowledge of Christianity without an inward transformation, this too is superficial.

For too many centuries, the standard missionary approach to Muslim evangelism has been attacking and extracting. We have attacked their holy book and religious behavior and have extracted them from their families and communities to join ours. Our not-so-subtle message has been "If you want to become a Christian, then you have to change your religion to ours." Change will certainly occur, but it must be change that the Holy Spirit brings about through conviction. It must not be engineered by outsiders.[6] Today, a fresh wind of the Holy Spirit is blowing in the Islamic world.[7] Many Muslim followers of Isa (Jesus) are discovering they don't have to abandon their birth identity in order to affirm their second-birth identity as followers of Jesus. The phenomenon of insider movements, as they are frequently called, is a controversial topic, sometimes hotly debated among missiologists. To date, the definitive collection of essays on the topic is *Understanding Insider Movements: Disciples of Jesus within Diverse Religious Communities* (2015), edited by Harley Talman and John Travis.

Evangelism that attempts to persuade people to change their religious behavior without changing their worldview falls short of a true biblical conversion. It's like the proverbial rearranging of deck chairs on the sinking *Titanic* after it

---

6. For fascinating stories of Muslim women becoming followers of Jesus, see missiological anthropologist Miriam Adeney's *Daughters of Islam: Building Bridges with Muslim Women* (Adeney 2002).

7. See, for example, Garrison 2014.

collided with an iceberg. A person's religion may change in terms of behavior and some beliefs, but their worldview remains stubbornly resistant to change. When there is only a superficial change in religion and not a corresponding deep change of worldview, then in times of crisis, people will often revert to previous patterns of belief and behavior. Jaime Bulatao, a Filipino Catholic priest and psychologist, in an illuminating book written two generations ago, identified this problem as "split-level Christianity" (1966). He describes split-level Christianity as the coexistence within the same person of two or more thought-and-behavior systems that are inconsistent with each other. At the level of ultimate concerns, such as the creation of the cosmos, eternal destiny, what happens when we die, and a host of other ultimate questions, Christianity provides answers. But at the everyday level of dealing with why tragedies strike, why people become sick, why accidents occur, Christianity as communicated through foreign missionaries doesn't seem to have the answers, and so, according to Bulatao, Filipinos resort to traditional pre-Christian answers to explain what happens. This phenomenon of split-level Christianity doesn't exist only in the Philippines or the Solomon Islands; it exists everywhere, including the scientific and technologically sophisticated West.

In our metaphor, the bottom of the iceberg is worldview, mostly hidden and unconscious, yet it is the central control system within us that affects our religion and influences our behavior. Our sense of who we are, our self-concept, and our perception of where we fit in the world are greatly influenced by our worldview.

Because the language we first learn shapes the vast portion of our worldview, our worldview is developed primarily in the first five years of life, by which time our mother tongue is firmly in place. Not only do we acquire our worldview early in life, but it is also very resistant to change for the remainder of our life. Anthropologists have shown that the things we learn earliest in life are the most resistant to change later in life (Bruner 1956). Similarly, Proverbs 22:6 reminds us, "Teach children how they should live, and they will remember it all their life." So when we send our children off on their first day of school, we may "kiss them goodbye" in more ways than one. This is because the culture in our home and our values have already significantly shaped their worldview. According to the George Barna Research Group, "A person's worldview is primarily shaped and is firmly in place by the time someone reaches the age of 13; it is refined through experience during the teen and early adult years; and then it is passed on to others during their adult life" (Barna 2009).

This shaping of worldview comes through the first language we learn as children. The language we speak shapes our worldview because it gives us grammatical categories and ways of organizing and classifying both the unseen and the visible world around us. Language draws our attention to certain things in the social, political, economic, religious, and even physical environment, while it blocks and hides other things that may be equally important. The powerful influence of language can be seen in the fact that it appears to be easier to abuse, enslave, or even kill people if they are called by names that erode their humanity. In Hitler's Germany, Jews were called "vermin," and this made it culturally more palatable for the Nazis to exterminate them. In the Rwanda genocide of 1994, in which eight hundred thousand Tutsis were killed, the ethnic majority Hutus who carried out this slaughter called the Tutsi minority "cockroaches" (History.com 2022).

The great linguist Edward Sapir (1921) and his student Benjamin Lee Whorf (Carroll 1956) advanced the Sapir-Whorf hypothesis, arguing that the language we speak greatly influences how we perceive and categorize the world around us, and this is the primary shaping force of our worldview. Sapir writes, "No two languages are ever sufficiently similar to be considered as representing the same social reality. The worlds in which different societies live are distinct worlds, not merely the same world with different labels attached" (1929, 209). This is a pretty strong statement and reinforces the notion that in order to communicate the gospel effectively we must understand the worldview of the other.[8]

Our sense of who we are, our self-concept, our perception of where we fit in the world is greatly influenced by our worldview, which is very resistant to change. In fact, it is the hardest thing to change about ourselves.

Figure 6.2
Worldview and Our Perception of Reality

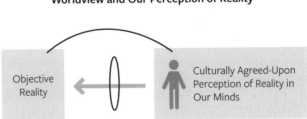

Figure 6.2 attempts to illustrate that we are surrounded by and embedded in a real, objective world. However, different people in different cultures who occupy different social locations, live in different economic circumstances, and

---

8. For a contemporary discussion of the Sapir-Whorf hypothesis, see Guest 2018, 98; and Howell and Paris 2019, 66–68.

hold different political perspectives do not see or experience the same reality. There *is* a real world, but people do not perceive or experience it the same way. Sociologists refer to this phenomenon as the social construction of reality (Berger and Luckmann 1966). People in different cultures, social locations, and economic realities have different worldviews, sometimes dramatically different, and "facts" don't change their perception. They may even create "alternative facts" to support their worldview. Our worldview is what enables us to understand the objective world around us and make sense of it. Our experience of the "real world" makes sense to us in terms of our worldview, which is like a pair of tinted glasses through which we view the world, but we don't realize we are wearing those glasses. They just seem natural. Our worldview also closes the gap between the culturally agreed-upon perception of reality, which is in our minds, and the real world around us.

Let me illustrate. For many people in the world, ancestral spirits are part of their objective reality. Especially in Africa, Asia, and Oceania, there is widespread belief that ancestral spirits are alive and active and can influence the world of the living. In parts of Africa, they are referred to as "the living dead." However, when I ask North American audiences how many of them believe that ancestral spirits are real and not just a form of superstition, frequently no one admits to such a belief. The reason so few North Americans believe in this reality is because our culturally agreed-upon perception of reality, shaped by science and the Enlightenment, provides no room for this belief. Despite the postmodern critique of modernity, our worldview has been shaped and influenced more by science and the Enlightenment than by the Bible in the last three hundred years. Our Enlightenment and scientific worldview assumes that when we die, that is the end of our earthly existence. There is no more. Our spirits cannot influence or communicate with the living. Western Christians have the hope of someday seeing their ancestors in heaven, but they have little anticipation of encountering them here on earth.

My father died shortly after telling me on my twelfth birthday that he wouldn't be alive much longer. That is a difficult age to lose your dad, and I remember how tough my teenage years were without a father. I received some comfort, however, when I would dream about my dad. In my dreams, I would talk to him about the struggles I was having as a teenage boy growing up in America, and it was always comforting to talk with him. But then I would wake up and realize it was only a dream. I have the hope of being reunited with my dad in heaven but little hope of seeing him before that.

Meanwhile, my friends in Melanesia have a very different view of the world and of the place of ancestral spirits within it. Many of them believe that when a person dies, their spirit is released and free to roam, for it is no longer encumbered and bound by time and space. Rather, it is free to move about, interact with the living, and influence the life of their village as long as the person is remembered. When Solomon Islanders would talk with me about their encounters with ancestral spirits, it was clear that they were talking about a real phenomenon, an objective, concrete reality, not a superstition or a vision. One day the villagers with whom we lived shared with me that their ancestral spirits told them to follow the ways of the church and the Bible. The spirits described to the living that when Christianity came to their island, it was as if light had come into darkness. And then the ancestors asked the living, "Why did it take so long for Christianity to come to our island? Why didn't it come when we were still alive?"

What do Westernized people or those who have been trained in or influenced by the West do with that reality? Our culturally agreed-upon perception of reality (i.e., our worldview) says, "That is not possible. The dead can't communicate with the living. It's just superstition, and as soon as these people get some formal education, they will no longer believe such foolishness." But to many Melanesians, ancestral spirits are very real. Belief in them is not foolish at all. One of the reasons that the belief in ancestral spirits is so important to them is because when they come to faith in Christ, one of the first things they ask is, "What about my ancestors? Does God care about them?" Very few if any Westernized missionaries have ever had a course on theology of the ancestors, so they are ill-equipped to respond to Melanesians' questions about ancestral spirits and the spirit world. And yet, when one reads the Bible through the lens of a worldview that is more in harmony with the worldviews found in the Bible—and believes that ancestral spirits are real as do many of my Melanesian friends, and not merely a form of superstition as most Westerners believe—then one finds all kinds of supporting biblical evidence for the Melanesian position.

For example, Hebrews 12:1 says, "We are surrounded by such a great cloud of witnesses" (NIV). Who is in that large cloud of witnesses? All those who had faith in God, and I would include my father. When the disciples are in a boat crossing the Sea of Galilee, Jesus comes to them walking on the water, and they are frightened because they think he is a ghost (Matt. 14:25–27; Mark 6:49–50). But Jesus assures them he is not a ghost; he's not an ancestral spirit. In the episode of the transfiguration, Jesus takes Peter, James, and John up a high mountain, and there they see Moses and Elijah talking with Jesus (Matt. 17:1–9; Mark 9:2–9; Luke 9:28–36). But how could that be? Moses and Elijah had been dead for hundreds of years. Finally, when Jesus, following his resurrection from the dead, suddenly appears in the room where the frightened disciples are huddled together behind locked doors, he essentially says to them, "Don't be afraid. I'm not a ghost. I'm not an ancestral spirit" (see Luke 24:36–39). In one example from the Old Testament, King Saul encounters the dead prophet Samuel through the medium known as the witch of Endor (1 Sam. 28). So there seems to be plenty of biblical evidence that ancestral spirits do exist. The teaching of the Bible on ancestral spirits is not that they don't exist. The biblical teaching is that the living must not rely on the spirits of the dead for guidance. They must rely on God alone (Lev. 19:31; Deut. 18:11; Isa. 8:19–20).

As it turns out, we in the West are the ones who appear to be out of step with reality when it comes to belief in ancestral spirits. Most of the rest of the world, for most of human history, has known that they do exist. People in the West also believed that ancestral spirits were real until the age of the Enlightenment, when that belief was dismissed as uneducated superstition. Craig Keener, in his two-volume treatise *Miracles: The Credibility of the New Testament Accounts* (2011), argues that it is the scientific Western worldview that is out of sync with much of the non-Western world and that we are missing the "reality" of the supernatural and spirit world.

Worldview and Cross-Cultural Ministry

It is our worldview that we want to see changed and transformed when we become followers of Jesus. Living like Jesus with a kingdom orientation is what we want to happen in our own lives and in the lives of those we encounter in cross-cultural ministry.

We cannot assume that others see the world as we do, and therefore we must work hard to understand how others think. We may feel that because we are better educated and because we "know" we are "right," it is foolish to do this, but being incarnational means we enter their world, with all its assumptions, and attempt to see the world through their eyes. When we engage in incarnational identification, we do not have to accept the worldview assumptions of those we are trying to reach with the gospel, but we must take their worldview seriously and try to understand it in order to present the gospel in a way that engages their worldview. Instead of glibly saying, "Christ is the answer," we must first ask, "What is the question?" What are the questions that emerge from the worldview of the people among whom we are living and serving, especially in times of crisis?

An example of the importance of connecting the gospel to a people's worldview is the story of the Binumarien people in Papua New Guinea. They were a beleaguered tribe, decimated by warfare and driven from their land by other tribes. By the time Wycliffe Bible Translators Des and Jenn Oats moved into their village, their population had declined from an estimated 3,000 people to only 111. Wycliffe Bible Translators nearly always begin their translations with the New Testament book of Matthew. When I've read the Gospel of Matthew, I have frequently skipped past the first seventeen verses dealing with the genealogy of Jesus, but when the Binumarien heard those seventeen verses, they realized that Jesus must have been a real person who cared about his ancestors. And then came the big question they asked the translator: "Does that mean that God cares about our ancestors?" When they discovered that God did indeed care, it gave them a whole new sense of who they were and who Jesus was, and that was the turning point in the life of the Binumarien, taking them from near extinction to a people group who became followers of Jesus (Oates 1992).

As we begin to see the world through the perspectives of those who are different from us, we may discover things in the Bible that we never knew before or that we misunderstood because of the limits of our own worldview. Remember, the Bible was written over many years, over two thousand years ago, from the perspective of many different cultures spread out geographically around the ancient Near East. It is unrealistic to think we understand everything perfectly. And it is unrealistic to think our worldview does not affect our interpretation. Although in the world of biblical scholarship this awareness is now commonplace, we seldom take worldview into consideration when we read and interpret the Bible and then try to explain it to someone whose worldview contrasts greatly with our own. In Robert McAfee Brown's *Unexpected News: Reading the Bible with Third World Eyes* (1984), the Bible is read through the eyes of the poor, and they see things differently than the rich. So understanding the Bible is not as simple as "The Bible says what it means and means what it says." The recognition that our worldview affects our interpretation of the Bible does not erode the truth of Scripture. Rather, when Scripture is read from the perspectives of different worldviews, a deeper and more comprehensive truth is revealed. Reading and interpreting the Bible through multiple worldviews reveals things we never saw before. This is one reason why we need four Gospels to get a holistic understanding of Jesus and his ministry.

I once learned from a student about a study comparing in broad terms the way Chinese Christians pray compared to the way North American Christians pray. According to this study, Americans tend to pray for God's blessings for wealth and health and for God to change things in their favor, everything from praying to be healed of cancer to finding a parking spot. The North American worldview assumes that with enough resources and hard work, we can change anything—including sending human beings to the moon. So we pray for God to intervene on our behalf. In contrast, Chinese Christians typically do not pray that God will change their situation or circumstances, such as stopping the persecution they experience for their faith. Their prayers center less on God changing things for them and more on helping them to remain faithful amid adversity. Two different worldviews are expressed in two different ways of praying. Which one is correct? They both are. James 4:2 reminds us that we have not because we ask not, but we must ask in accordance with God's will.

Unless a person's encounter with the gospel transforms their worldview, their conversion is only superficial. Unfortunately, many cross-cultural witnesses do not understand the concept of worldview or the role worldview plays in sharing the gospel. We focus too much on changing people's behavior and their religion. This is the work of the Holy Spirit, not the job of the missionary.

When the gospel challenges our worldview, the gospel will begin to change our worldview, which is what occurs when we take on the mind of Christ. Paul addresses this issue in Romans 12:2 when he writes, "Do not conform yourselves to the standards of this world, but let God transform you inwardly by a complete change of your mind [worldview]. Then you will be able to know the will of God—what is good and is pleasing to him and is perfect." Paul is arguing that unless we undergo a significant conversion of our worldview, through the power of the Holy Spirit, we cannot and will not know the will of God. Paul calls for a transformation of our worldview, not just a change of religion or even a change of behavior. Those changes will follow in time under the guidance of the Holy Spirit after we have experienced a deep change in our worldview. The late missiological historian Andrew F. Walls (1928–2021) notes similarly when he writes:

> Not only does God in Christ take people as they are: He takes them in order to transform them into what He wants them to be. Along with the indigenizing principle which makes his faith a place to feel at home, the Christian inherits the pilgrim principle, which whispers to him that he has no abiding city and warns him that to be faithful to Christ will put him out of step with his society; for that society never existed, in East or West, ancient time or modern, which could absorb the word of Christ painlessly into its system. Jesus within Jewish culture, Paul within Hellenistic culture, take it for granted that there will be rubs and frictions—not from the adoption of a new culture, but from the transformation of the mind towards that of Christ. (1996, 8)

So how do we bring about change to worldview? Over the years, I have become convinced that there are no shortcuts or quick and easy ways. Change takes time, sometimes a lifetime. Worldview change that is consistent with biblical values comes through the process of discipleship. And by discipleship, I don't mean filling in the blanks of a discipleship notebook. That exercise is more about discipleship *information* than long-lasting *transformation* and *formation* into Christlikeness. W. Jay Moon, in his comprehensive book *Intercultural Discipleship: Learning from Global Approaches to Spiritual Formation* (2017), and

A. H. Mathias Zahniser, in *Symbol and Ceremony: Making Disciples across Cultures* (1997), discuss the many genres that can be used in cross-cultural ministry to bring about change in people's worldviews in their pilgrimage of becoming more Christlike.

When people in different cultures embrace the gospel and their worldview is transformed, the way they express their life in Christ is going to be different, sometimes radically different, from that of followers of Jesus in other cultures. Yet despite this difference, two followers of Jesus will have more in common with each other than they do with nonbelievers in their respective cultures. For example, a Chinese follower of Jesus will have more in common with a North American follower of Jesus than either of them will have with those who are not yet Christians in their own society. In other words, the Spirit of Christ in one person greets the Spirit of Christ in the other person and closes the cultural distance between them.

CHAPTER SUMMARY

In this first chapter in part 3, which focuses on common communication problems, we discussed the importance of understanding our own worldview and the worldview of others to communicate the gospel from one culture to another. We noted that our worldview, which is mostly unconscious, is more fundamental than religion. We acquire our worldview early in life, and it remains resistant to change for the rest of our life. Because our unconscious worldview appears to be so natural, we believe we see and understand the world as it really is, without realizing that we encounter the "real world" through our culturally agreed-upon perception of the world. Thus, we don't all see the world the same way. And yet we believe that the universal gospel is for all people at all times and in every culture. This tension between the universal gospel and the particularities of worldview can cause us to incorrectly assume that our task in cross-cultural ministry is to lead people to follow Jesus, organize their churches, and read and interpret the Bible in much the same ways we do. To counter this tendency, we need to incarnationally enter into the worldview of others, attempt to see and understand the world through their cultural lens, and then discover where the gospel can respond to their needs and bring lasting transformational change.

7

Unintended Paramessages

Fearing the firefly's fire, you walk into the witch's fire. (If you try to dodge one problem, you may enter into another one that is worse.)

Builsa proverb, Ghana

It was a packed crowd, hot and humid in the Indonesian night air, and the evangelistic service was drawing to a close. Saeed, a Muslim man in the crowd, had been moved by the preacher from America who told remarkable stories of Jesus, some of which he was familiar with because they were in the Qur'an and others he had heard about from the Injil, known as the Gospels to Christians. The preacher talked about the miracles Jesus performed and of his love for marginalized people, outcasts, women, and children. The picture of Jesus that the preacher was drawing through his descriptive and compelling words was drawing Saeed to want to be closer to Jesus, whom he knew from the Qur'an as Isa. Saeed wanted to know more.

The service came to a close as the preacher began praying while he walked back and forth across the stage with one hand in his jacket pocket and the other waving his huge Bible in the air. Saeed, watching this sacrilegious scene unfold before his very eyes, was aghast. What was happening? No Muslim would ever address Allah in such a casual manner. This preacher must be a fraud, a religious huckster. He certainly was not a man of God. Saeed quickly moved through the crowd to the exit and left, confused, bewildered, wondering what had just happened. Jesus? Yes! The preacher? No!

Figure 7.1
The Problem of Paramessages

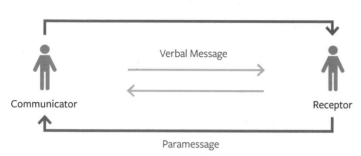

This story, told to me by a colleague, illustrates the power of the many non-verbal ways we communicate, often unconsciously, which can confirm or detract from the verbal message we wish to communicate. When two people interact with each other, there is a communicator and a receptor (see fig. 7.1). These two people communicate back and forth, with give-and-take. Consciously they are using words. The conscious, verbal message is what they concentrate on, making sure they get their message across clearly and correctly. But unconsciously, they are sending and receiving messages without uttering a word. We call these nonverbal forms of communication "paramessages." In fact, communication studies reveal that by far the majority of communication between two people is nonverbal.[1] A person's social location, ethnic identity, gender, attire, body language, and worldview all contribute to the unspoken messages they send. The challenge of paramessages is heightened when we attempt to communicate the gospel to people who are culturally different from us, people with different worldviews and different forms of body language. Charles Kraft, in his book *Communication Theory for Christian Witness*, notes that "*when we communicate, we always send multiple messages.* Or, rather, receivers regularly pick up multiple messages when they interpret. Some of these additional messages may distort or even contradict the main message we are trying to send, as when the message of our life communicates something different than what we are trying to get

1. For an overview of the field of nonverbal communication, see Towler 2020. Anthropologist Ray Birdwhistell (1918–94), who founded the field of kinesics, which focuses on human movement in communication, estimates that 65–70 percent of communication is nonverbal. Albert Mehrabian is the researcher behind the famous 7/38/55 formula: 7 percent of communication is the words we speak, 38 percent is the tone of our voice, and 55 percent is our body language (1971, 1981, 2008). Subsequent research has called into question that 93 percent of our communication is nonverbal. See also Rosenthal (2009). Scott Moreau, Evvy Hay Campbell, and Susan Greener, from a Christian perspective, devote an entire chapter to nonverbal intercultural communication (2014, 115–28).

across with our words" (1991, 53). When a pastor mounts the pulpit to preach the sermon that she has worked on all week long, it may be disconcerting for her to discover that only a small percentage of her communication with the congregation Sunday morning will be in the words she so carefully chose in crafting her sermon.

Sources of Paramessages

What is the source of these many unconscious paramessages? They come from three major places. First of all, the attitudes we have about ourselves are a key source of our paramessages. How do we feel about ourselves? Are we confident or mousy? Do we doubt our abilities? Do we despise ourselves? Are we comfortable in our own skin? Do we think too highly of ourselves? How we feel about ourselves is communicated through our paramessages whether we recognize it or not. A healthy self-concept is therefore an important pre-requisite for effective cross-cultural ministry. If we are not comfortable with ourselves, then we are likely to have difficulty getting along with others, especially in cross-cultural ministry situations. So how should we feel about ourselves? I think we should feel about ourselves as God feels about us. We are not a pile of worthless junk. We are redeemed sinners on God's way. We are precious and beloved because we are created in God's image, just a little lower than the angels (Ps. 8:5). So we should accept who we are and become comfortable with ourselves so that others can be comfortable around us. For some of us, this may require a significant amount of psychological counseling, especially if we were raised in a context in which we did not feel safe and loved.

How we perceive and feel about ourselves is a crucial factor in our ability to develop deep personal relationships with others, both those we serve and other cross-cultural witnesses we work with. I submit that one of the biggest problems in cross-cultural ministry is missionaries' inability to get along with each other. International mission teams with multiple cultures at play increase this challenge (Lingenfelter and Green 2022).

Second, the attitude we have toward others is another source of these para-messages. Do we see others as less than us because we are better educated or better off financially? Do we see others as mere babes in Christ because they have not been walking with Jesus for decades like we have? If we have a paternalistic or maternalistic attitude, then we can more easily rationalize and subconsciously tell ourselves, "The people with whom we are living and min-istering are really like children in the faith. They don't know the Bible or have sufficient theological grounding, and they really need our help, our insights, and our money." Of course, this attitude is picked up immediately by the receptor and damages the relationship between the two.

What if you tend to feel superior to the people among whom you have come to live and serve, even though you know you shouldn't feel that way? Should you try to fake it? Can we fake it? No, of course not. Our paramessages will reveal how we truly feel. What if we simply don't like the people or the culture to which we have been sent? Can we glibly say, "God loves you and has a wonderful plan for your life," all the while thinking, *But I can't stand you.* No, we can't believe one thing and attempt to communicate something different. The paramessages we send will reveal to the receptor how we truly feel about them, despite our verbal efforts to the contrary. Unless we believe at the deepest level of our being that we are equal with others as children of God and that we are equal as sinners who have been redeemed by God's grace, then we are going to send paramessages that say, "You are inferior to me. I am better than you."

I often tell cross-cultural witnesses that if they arrive at the place where they have been sent by their church or mission and discover that they just don't like the people, they should do one of two things immediately. First, they should request a transfer to some other location because they will not have an effective ministry. This may seem extreme, but why stay with people you don't like when you know your feelings will sabotage your ministry? Second, and perhaps more importantly, they should literally and attitudinally fall on their knees and ask God to break their heart and enable them to see the people from God's perspective. Often, we must confess our ethnocentrism, biases, and prejudices that we carry deep within us. Sometimes the first twelve thousand miles are the easiest part of the cross-cultural journey. The last twelve feet may be the most challenging when we live close to people and regularly interact with them instead of ministering from a distance.

One of my sad failures in training people for effective cross-cultural ministry is a woman from the Deep South in the United States who sat under my teaching and was appointed by her mission organization to serve in South Africa. When she arrived, she confided in one of her missionary colleagues her surprise at the number of Black people involved in the ministry. Within a few weeks, she was back on a plane heading home. The deep-seated and perhaps even unconscious racism that resided within her prevented her from connecting with the Black South Africans as her equals, as also beloved and precious children of God.

The third source of these paramessages is the attitudes and beliefs we have about the message we are trying to communicate and about life in general. Do we believe in what we are communicating, or has it become so commonplace that we are simply mouthing empty words without any conviction behind them?

Have we lost our passion, and are we simply going through the motions? Are we optimistic or pessimistic? Do we see the glass of water of life as half full or half empty? Our basic attitude and orientation toward life will be expressed over and over again in the paramessages we send.

Here is the problem. Many of these paramessages lie below the level of conscious awareness for both the communicator and the receptor. This is indeed frightening because we could easily be communicating the very opposite of what we want to say. In other words, these paramessages are largely unconscious, and yet they will often become far more important to the receptor than anything we say verbally. No wonder our communication fails over and over again: we have not paid sufficient attention to some of these paramessages.

After one of my training sessions with missionary candidates, a pastor quickly approached me about my teaching on the power of paramessages in communicating the gospel. He said that he loved to go to Southeast Asia and hold evangelistic crusades because the people were so receptive to his preaching. On one of those occasions, he told his interpreter that he was going to preach against smoking because he saw so many young boys smoking cigarettes. To him, their smoking was sinful, and he thought he should address the problem head-on. His translator advised him not to preach against smoking even though it was a health problem. When the evangelist asked why he shouldn't be preaching about smoking, his translator said, "Look at your feet. You have been here four days, and you are wearing your third pair of expensive designer shoes. Have you noticed that these young boys are barefoot? The people in this area feel you have been flaunting your affluence by the shoes you are wearing, and you have lost all credibility. We can hardly stand to listen to you anymore." As the pastor who was now a missionary candidate was sharing this story with me, tears streamed down his face, and he said, "That was all about the paramessages I was sending, wasn't it? Why did I not learn that before?" He pledged not to make the same mistake again.

Lifestyle as a Paramessage

What are some of the unconscious paramessages that get in the way of our attempts to communicate? In cross-cultural ministry, such things as our lifestyle, the cars we drive, the homes we live in, and the clothes we wear either get in the way of or help facilitate what we really want to communicate. Let's consider the difficult topic of missionary lifestyle as an important paramessage we send.

I have often run into a general reluctance on the part of missionaries to adjust their lifestyle to one that is more appropriate for the cultural context in which they are living. Missionaries are often willing to go halfway around the world for Jesus, but don't ask them to change their lifestyle when they get there. They often rationalize that their lifestyle is their personal choice, their business, and does not affect or interfere with their ministry. In fact, many times I have heard it argued that continuing their lifestyle from back home in their host society makes it easier for them to adjust to the difficult living conditions where they are serving. Many missionaries have said to me, "The local people expect us to live differently because we're not a part of their culture, so it's okay that we continue the lifestyle that we lived back home." One missionary family serving in Southeast Asia went so far as to have a separate room in their home that they called their "Wisconsin room." When they entered that air-conditioned room with all its Wisconsin paraphernalia, they felt "at home." It was an escape from all the unfamiliar sounds, sights, and smells of their host society. It was a cultural respite to be sure, but it also hampered their ability to connect and live with the people they had come to serve.

The key lifestyle issue is not what kind of house you live in or how much stuff you pack into your crate from back home but rather whether your lifestyle enables you to develop deep personal relationships with local people or whether it becomes a barrier to that happening.

In Kenya, Bible translators were working and living in a local context and doing everything they knew to do to identify with the people and live incarnationally. They bought local furniture, lived in a local house, used local transportation, and ate local food. What more could they have done? After they had been there for several years, they discovered by accident one day that local people referred to their house as the "Canadian house." This news really disappointed the Bible translators, because they had tried so hard to fit in with a lifestyle that seemed appropriate for the context. What had gone wrong with their attempt to identify with local people and their culture? When they investigated why their house was considered a "Canadian house," they discovered that it was so perceived because they had filled it to overflowing with African furniture and had arranged the furniture in a typical North American pattern. In local homes, there was very little furniture, and the arrangement was very different.

Effective cross-cultural communication of the gospel is connected to close interpersonal relationships. If our closest friends are not local people but rather other missionaries or other expatriates, then something has gone wrong. In interviewing hundreds of American missionaries in Asia, I asked them, "Who are your best friends here?" The majority named other Americans as their best friends, and many had no friends among local people. They confessed that this was a cultural struggle and an emotional hurdle for them to overcome. They knew they should have close personal relationships with local people, but it was just too difficult. Most of them did not realize that their lifestyle was the major impediment that kept them in a social prison of their own making.

We need to evaluate our lifestyle to see if it is harming or facilitating the development of close personal relationships with local people. This is easier to do than drawing up long lists of things we should pack in our proverbial missionary barrels or crates and decide what we should leave at home. Undoubtedly, missionaries who choose to live like the local people will often experience pressure from other missionaries and from the expatriate community who often encourage them to live more like they did back home. In all my many years of researching and studying missionaries, I have yet to discover anyone who overidentified with the local people, though the children in the following story may have come close.

At a time when missionaries sailed to their destinations in passenger ships instead of flying in airplanes, a missionary family with four children was coming home from Africa. On previous furloughs in the United States, the four children had been teased for wearing out-of-date "missionary clothes." The parents planned well in advance for their reentry to America and bought clothes for their children from the latest catalog. As their ship sailed into the harbor, the children excitedly changed into their new clothes. But as the family disembarked from the ship and walked down the gangplank, they noticed people pointing, snickering, and laughing at them. They were crestfallen, and they wondered what in the world had gone wrong. The parents had purchased new, fashionable clothes just so this kind of embarrassment would not happen. Unfortunately, they had forgotten to tell their children not to balance their suitcases on their heads as they walked down the gangplank!

A Powerful Paramessage

The saying "Actions speak louder than words" captures the power of paramessages in cross-cultural communication. One very powerful paramessage we can send that will facilitate rather than thwart what we want to communicate is to enter a culture as a learner—to listen more and talk less, to observe, inquire, be curious, and explore the surroundings of our host culture.

Entering a new culture as a learner instead of as a teacher who has all the answers is the best kind of paramessage we can send to those we want to influence with the gospel. Our temptation, however, is to think that because we are bearers of the good news, we must go as teachers. But when we enter a culture as a teacher or some other kind of expert, we often close the door to learning about the people and their culture. Through our attitudes of superiority, we also make it difficult for the people to accept us and our message. Eugene Nida, in his classic text *Customs and Cultures: Anthropology for Christian Missions*, speaks truthfully when he says, "It is not primarily the message but the messenger of Christianity that provides the greatest problems for the average non-Christian" (1954, 251). We cannot disregard or extinguish the knowledge and experience we have, for all that we have done is a part of us. But we *can* enter into cross-cultural ministry with a spirit of humility and the attitude of a learner.

I'm reminded of a young missionary who went on furlough after a four-year term in Zambia, where he had taught at a Bible school to train pastors and church workers for his denomination. He decided to audit my "Anthropology for Christian Mission" course, where the dominant theme throughout the semester was entering another culture as a learner and not as a know-it-all with all the answers. He did well in the course and took to heart what he had learned, even though it ran counter to everything his denomination had taught him before. He returned to Zambia for a second term and continued teaching in the same Bible school. Six months after he had returned to Zambia, he wrote me saying that even though he was teaching in the same school as before, it all seemed like a new place to him and the students were like new and different people. But they weren't; they were the same. What had changed was him. He went back to the Bible school as a learner instead of as a theological teacher who had all the answers to questions they weren't asking. He was amazed at how much he had learned from these students about their social world, about the spirit world with which they had to contend as Christians, and about the ordinary struggles of life to which Christ was the answer. Now for the first time, he discovered the urgent questions they were asking, and it made all the difference in his teaching.

When my wife and I went to the Solomon Islands to conduct research on the impact of Anglican Christianity, the village leaders asked us, "Why are you here?" I responded, "I've come to live among you and to learn from you about how Christianity functions in the life of your village." They nodded with approval as if they understood what I was saying. However, the next day they asked the same question, and I responded with the same answer. This seemed to go on for many days. It just didn't make any sense to them why we would choose to come and live with them and like them in this rather isolated village. Finally, one day when I said again that we were there to learn from them, they responded, "You have come to live and learn from *us*? We have never met a white man who came to learn anything from us. Whether they were British patrol officers or missionaries, they always told us what to do." Then with blunt honesty they said, "Well, if you are here to learn from us, then we better get busy teaching you because you don't know anything." They were so right.

They then took their role seriously and began to teach us the many layers of their animistic religion and their Anglican Christianity. Often when we would be walking in the jungle together, they would stop and say, "Take out your paper and pencil and write this down. This is important." They became my teachers, and what I learned from them would later be published in the book *Melanesians and Missionaries* (1983).

The Need for Epistemological Humility

In communicating the gospel across cultures, we need to relinquish our need for certainty in exchange for our quest for understanding. This is epistemological humility. In other words, how can we maintain full confidence in the gospel that we have come to proclaim and live out without also feeling superior about everything else we do? Can you see the tension? When we come with a superior attitude, it closes the door to a lot of communication. You may protest, "We have a gospel to proclaim that will change their culture for the good, and isn't that the main reason we are sent out as missionaries—to change their culture?" No, it is not! Our task is to introduce people to Jesus, who is the most incredible transforming agent in any society the world has ever known. Our task is not to change their culture. That's the work of the Holy Spirit.

My recommendation for most places is that cross-cultural witnesses devote the first two years of their ministry in a new culture to full-time language and culture learning and then continue that learning for the remainder of their time there, whether it be two more years or twenty-two more years. What is happening when we devote a couple years to intentional language learning and to trying to understand their culture? Are we doing ministry then? Were we sent out as missionaries with the primary task being to learn the language and culture of the people to whom we were sent? Our tendency is to think that we need to learn a language and understand a culture so that we can get to the *real* work of ministry. So if we are serious about language and culture learning, then we tend to bracket out that time and see it as only preparation for ministry. Jon Kirby, a Catholic missionary in Ghana for many years with the Society of the Divine Word, reminds us that language and culture learning *is* conversion, *is* ministry in its own right. It is not simply preparation for cross-cultural ministry. He notes, "Language and culture learning stretches and deepens our faith, demands the humble posture of one who has much to learn from the new fount of knowledge in open dialogue, and, by the discovery of a new reality through our new culturally attuned preceptors, the missioner both experiences a genuine conversion and sows the seeds for future conversions" (1995, 137).

I submit that we are involved in ministry from the moment we arrive, even before we can speak the language or make sense of the culture. How is that possible? While we can't even speak a word of their language, people are watching our lives, watching our attitude, observing how we relate to our children, how we interact with our spouse, how we relate to other missionaries, and whether we have any non-Christian friends. During this time, as they observe us, they are deciding whether we are worth listening to when we finally are able to speak their language and live appropriately in their culture. In other words, our paramessages have been communicating the entire time. If ministry is about building relationships and not just verbal exchange, then we are ministering right from the beginning when we arrive as guests in their society. But so many of us don't think that way. We believe we have an urgent message to share and that's why we have to learn their language, but I submit that this is the wrong approach to effective cross-cultural ministry.

If only a small percentage of our communication takes place through the words we use, then the lion's share of evangelism is what is "spoken" nonverbally. The tone of our voice, our lifestyle, and our behavior are all communicating volumes of information. But until we understand what people are actually "hearing" when we are speaking, we won't know if people are accepting or rejecting the gospel for the wrong reasons. Remember, meaning is determined by the listener, not by the speaker. So if we don't know what people are hearing, then we won't be able to tell whether the gospel is offensive or whether we are offending them culturally.[2]

What do I mean by the offense of the gospel? The good news is as challenging to other cultures as it is to our own. Paul reminds us that the gospel was a stumbling block to the Jews and foolishness to the Greeks (1 Cor. 1:23). How is it that the gospel is both good news and offensive? Richard Osmer addresses this paradox. "God's call comes through the gospel. The gospel is the good news of God's salvation of the world in Jesus Christ. It is the message of salvation. Evangelism always must give pride of place to the 'Yes' of God. Divine judgment—God's 'No!'—is in the service of God's grace. In evangelism we are inviting people to respond to the story of God's love of the world in Jesus Christ. We are not shaming, berating them, or threatening them [culturally offending them] in the name of God" (2021, 15).

2. Elsewhere (Whiteman 1997, 3-4), I describe what I mean by the offence of the gospel and that one of the functions of good contextualization is to sharpen the focus of the gospel (which is indeed good news, but it confronts our sinfulness and evil structures in society). Lesslie Newbigin (1986) in his groundbreaking book *Foolishness to the Greeks: The Gospel and Western Culture* makes a similar point and a convincing argument about the gospel's critique of much of Western culture.

The gospel is always offensive, in every culture, so we can't remove the offense of the gospel, but what we can do is remove the offensive way in which we communicate and live it out. Unfortunately, we often offend people culturally, so they never hear the offense of the gospel. Our goal in the cross-cultural communication of the gospel is to reduce our cultural offense so that the offense of the gospel is stronger and penetrates to the very core of the culture. Jesus often offended people, frequently the religious leaders, but he offended them for the right reason, for kingdom purposes.

CHAPTER SUMMARY

This chapter could be summarized by the simple saying "Actions speak louder than words." In crossing cultures with the gospel, we often put so much emphasis on verbal communication without realizing that the many nonverbal or unconscious paramessages we send often speak louder and are even more important than the verbal message we intend to communicate. We therefore need to uncover the unconscious paramessages that influence our communication. These paramessages have three sources: the attitude we have about ourselves, the attitude we have toward others, and the attitude we have about the message we are trying to communicate and about life in general. A powerful paramessage is to enter another culture as a learner. Then we need to step into the shoes of our listeners and discover what they are hearing and interpreting as we attempt to communicate and live out the gospel in their culture.

8

Misusing Cultural Forms and Space

If you cannot explain a proverb in my language, then you don't know me. (When we know a culture thoroughly, we can explain their deeper proverbs.)

Lubya proverb, Kenya

Cultural Forms

Like different worldviews and unintended paramessages, cultural forms can pose a problem in cross-cultural ministry. An example comes from my family's experience in Melanesia. In the ritual of Holy Communion, we frequently say, "Jesus is the Lamb of God who takes away the sins of the world." Although modern-day North Americans can repeat those words, I doubt the words have the depth of meaning for most of us that they had two thousand years ago in the early church. One reason these words may not resonate as deeply for us as they did for the disciples and early Christians is because we no longer live in a culture that kills animals to atone for our sins. But how would one communicate the concept of Jesus as the Lamb of God in a culture where there are no sheep (Whiteman 1993, 2–3)? How would one communicate the meaning of the sacrificial death of Jesus when the conventional form of a sacrificial lamb makes no sense to the people because they have never seen sheep? Such is the case in Papua New Guinea and the entire region of Melanesia. On the other hand, Melanesians are perhaps better prepared conceptually to understand the sacrificial death of Jesus because they do live in a sacrificial world. Traditionally, they killed animals, just like the ancient Hebrews sacrificed lambs, for the sake of appeasing the spirits and for rituals of reconciliation between two warring clans. But they didn't use sheep. They used pigs.

Local church leaders recognize that the perfect sacrificial animal is already in place in their culture, but it is a pig, not a lamb. So, to communicate the meaning of Jesus as the Lamb of God who takes away the sins of the world, would it be better to begin by referring to Jesus as the "Pig of God" who takes away the sins of the world and brings healing and reconciliation to broken people and communities? This idea strikes most Westerners as absolutely blasphemous, repellant, absurd. (And of course, we'll have all kinds of theological arguments as to why only the form of a spotless lamb can be used to communicate the important meaning of Jesus as the sacrifice in place of an animal sacrifice.) When I have raised this possibility with students or missionaries in training, they have often gasped at such a heretical idea. I then reassure them that the idea of Jesus as the "Pig of God" is a starting point, and once the true meaning of Jesus is conveyed by using the familiar form of a pig, then it becomes a bridge to talking about the ancient Hebrews, who used lambs instead of pigs for their sacrifices. When the meaning comes through, because an appropriate form (pigs) has been used, then Melanesians will say, "Oh, this is very good news indeed. This means we don't have to keep sacrificing pigs anymore to appease the spirits. Because Jesus is the 'Pig of God,' his sacrifice makes our pig sacrifices no longer necessary." By changing the form from lamb to pig, the true meaning can now be communicated. Lest one get too anxious that church leaders have altered the Bible in their translations, I know of nowhere that "pig" has been substituted for "lamb." But notes connecting the equivalence of the sacrificial lamb of the Israelites with the pig of Melanesians have aided in understanding the common meaning to which these different forms point. In summary, what is sacred is the meaning, not the form used to communicate the meaning. This is why cultural forms need to be updated and changed through time and across cultures so that the true meaning they are meant to convey will live on.[1]

What are cultural forms? Cultural forms are the obvious parts of a culture, the things that we can see, touch, hear, taste, and smell. They include behaviors, rituals, gestures, ceremonies, material artifacts, language, and food. Cultural forms are very important because they are the vehicles for conveying meaning.

---

1. The distinction between cultural forms and the meanings they convey is foundational to understanding contextualization. See Paul G. Hiebert's in-depth discussion (1978). I have written in a number of places connecting the discussion of form and meaning with contextualization. See Whiteman 2010, 2021, 2023a.

Figure 8.1
Form and Meaning from One Culture to Another

The only way we can communicate meaning is by using cultural forms. Even God uses our cultural forms to communicate with us.

There are very few if any universal cultural forms because cultural forms are nearly always specific to a particular culture. They do not communicate the same meaning from one culture to another. What does this mean? It means that a form used in one culture to communicate a particular meaning will not communicate the identical meaning in a different culture.

Figure 8.1 shows the relationship between form and meaning from one culture to another. Let's say I want to communicate something in my own culture A, and so I use an appropriate and familiar form to do so. But now I want to communicate the same thing in culture B. What happens if I use the same form from culture A to communicate my meaning in culture B? Will the form I use communicate the same meaning? More than likely it will not, because cultural forms do not carry universal meanings across cultural boundaries.

For example, African men holding hands among the Babembe of the Congo is a normal cultural form that expresses friendship between two human beings. In North America, that same form (two men holding hands) carries a very different meaning—they are homosexual. In North America, we signal "okay" by forming a circle with our index finger touching our thumb. But if we use that same gesture in Brazil, it is obscene, similar to the middle-finger gesture in North America.

What about a smile? Isn't a smile a universal form that communicates a sense of happiness across every culture? No, it can be a sign of embarrassment in some Asian cultures or communicate too much familiarity in others. What about music? Isn't music a universal form? No, music doesn't communicate the same thing from one generation to another in my own culture, let alone from one culture to another.

The reason cultural forms present such a serious problem for cross-cultural witnesses of the gospel is that we have a message—the gospel—that we believe is universal and lifesaving for all people, but we must present this universal message in cultural forms, which are culture specific. And we need to use the correct cultural forms that communicate the meaning we want to convey.

Bible translators Eunice Pike and Florence Cowan (1959) spent many years translating the New Testament into the language of the Mazatecos, who lived in the Oaxaca Valley in southern Mexico. When the time came for it to be published, they chose a local term to convey the meaning of the Bible as "God's Word." These Mazateco Indians believed that by eating hallucinogenic mushrooms filled with the chemical mescaline, they could have a supernatural experience and receive a message from God. Therefore, the term used for "God's Word" communicated to the Mazatecos "eating the sacred mushroom." At first, this may not appear to be a serious problem. One could talk about "getting high on Jesus" or "devouring the Word of God," but in fact, it was a serious problem, and the Mazatecos did not read or pay any attention to the newly translated Bible in their language.

The problem came from the fact that there were many ritual precautions and taboos that surrounded the use of the mushroom. People had to ritually purify themselves by abstaining from sex four or five days before eating the sacred mushrooms and four or five days afterward. Because "God's Word" was in the same cognitive category as "eating the sacred mushroom," people were afraid to read the Bible for fear that they would casually break the same taboos imposed on eating the sacred mushrooms. They feared that if they violated the sacred taboos, something terrible would happen to them—they might go crazy, their children might die, their gardens might dry up. The result was that no one read "God's Word." It was just too much work to ritually purify oneself every time before one would dare to open the pages and begin to read the Bible.

A year went by, and the Bible translators were crestfallen. After spending all those years learning the Mazateco language, putting it into writing, and then translating the Bible into it, they discovered that very few Mazatecos were reading the Bible. Fortunately, in addition to their linguistic training, they were also anthropologically aware, and so they began looking for the meaning that was attached to the term they had used for "God's Word." When they discovered the meaning the term was communicating to the Mazatecos, they realized they needed to change the term for the correct meaning of "God's Word" to come through. They came up with a different term, which carried the meaning "this book teaches us about God."

"Oh well, that's different," cried the Mazatecos. "We want to know about God. Our whole lives have been in pursuit of trying to discover who God is and what God is doing in the world. That is why we eat the sacred mushrooms. This Bible is going to teach us something about God?"

"Yes, of course it will," the Bible translators responded. The form—that is, the term for "God's Word"—had to be changed for the true meaning of the Bible to come through.

Now, I want to pose a question that is relevant to our efforts to communicate Christian meanings across cultural boundaries. How much of our Christian life and behavior is caught up in forms that work quite fine for us in our culture or in our denominational subculture but don't communicate much of anything or miscommunicate what we intend to say to people in cultures different from our own? For example, why for so many years have North Americans worshiped at 11:00 on Sunday mornings? The 11:00 a.m. worship hour is an artifact from agrarian America a century or more ago.[2] If you were a farmer, you had to milk the cows in the early morning and in the late afternoon. That gave you plenty of time to spend with your church community in the middle of the day. You socialized, ate together, worshiped together, and strengthened the community. After three or four hours, you would head home to milk the cows. But now we have spread the 11:00 Sunday morning worship hour all over the world, including places where they don't even have cows.

Eugene Nida said to me on one occasion, "I have been able to travel around the world and sit in worship services and take notes on what is happening. Nine times out of ten, I'm able to correctly guess what denomination planted the church I'm attending." How is that possible? Because the cultural forms used are the same in the host country as they are back home in the missionary's church. This is a sad commentary, because it means that people are not encouraged to use their own culturally appropriate forms to worship God. Instead, they borrow the music, the church organization/polity, the worship style, and even the time of day they meet from the missionary's culture. In September 2022, I was in the Philippines doing training for Filipino missionaries, pastors, and church workers. Melba Maggay, of the Institute for Studies in Asian Church and Culture, said to me, "I am actually worried that our eager missionaries who go abroad are simply conduits of what my Japanese friend feels is merely 'an American gospel.'"[3]

Here is the problem. We can end up worshiping the cultural forms and thinking they are sacred and lose the meaning these forms are trying to communicate. In fact, a good characterization of nominal Christianity is when forms continue

---

2. In 1900, according to data from the U.S. Department of Agriculture, approximately 38 percent of the United States population lived on farms, and another 11 percent lived in rural areas but did not farm. By 2000, the percentage of the population living on farms had dropped to less than 2 percent, and the percentage living in rural nonfarm areas had dropped to around 17 percent (USDA 2022).

3. She told me this on September 28, 2022.

but meaning is lost. I submit that there are no sacred forms; there are only sacred meanings. The forms are simply vehicles for conveying sacred meanings.

My former colleague George Hunter at Asbury Seminary's E. Stanley Jones School of World Mission and Evangelism suggested that churches in America have raised stained glass barriers that effectively keep unchurched people from coming to church and feeling comfortable there. These are the many human-constructed cultural barriers that keep people away from church and turn them off to Christianity. They are cultural, not spiritual, obstacles. He told me, "American Christianity has not been spared its own version of the 'culture barrier' problem. I call it the 'stained glass' barrier, but the issue is wider than windows. Our churches are called to reach 'pre-Christian' people in the fastest-growing mission field on earth. But most of our churches speak an insider language that seekers do not understand and feature a musical style they are not culturally shaped to resonate to, and, in many ways, their visit to a church is a culturally alienating experience."[4] If this is a problem in one particular culture, imagine the difficulty in trying to take the gospel from one culture to another.

Two areas of church life give us the most difficulty in communicating what it means to be a Christian in cultures different from our own. These are baptism and Holy Communion. Without adequate teaching about what these forms represent, we have spread them around the world, but the meaning has not always been fully communicated. Those with a strong sacramental theology may believe that the elements of bread and wine are crucial, even in environments where wheat and grapes do not grow.

In the 1960s, the controversial Episcopalian bishop James Pike (1913–69) is purported to have realized that the young people in his San Francisco diocese were not understanding the meaning of the Christian ritual of Holy Communion, or the Eucharist, in the Episcopal Church. So he introduced potato chips and Coca-Cola for the elements used in Holy Communion in the hope that the true meaning of communion would come through better for the teenagers. What is your immediate reaction to this? Perhaps his action is not as revolting or sacrilegious today as it may have been fifty years ago. In my teaching and training of cross-cultural witnesses, I have shared this story, and here are some of the responses I have received:

"It is sacrilegious because it changes the biblical forms of communion."

"Those elements are so ordinary and common, not sacred and special."

---

4. He mentioned this to me on October 3, 2022. Hunter 2000 deals extensively with the way the gospel was communicated effectively through appropriate cultural forms to reach the Irish.

"Potato chips and Coca-Cola are junk food and shouldn't be used for communion."

"Using potato chips and coke cheapens the sacred act of communion."

"Coke is not the color of blood."

In response to these objections, first, I must point out that many Christians have already changed the forms used for communion by substituting grape juice and yeast bread for wine and unleavened bread. Second, in light of the complaint that potato chips and Coca-Cola are so ordinary and common, we need to be reminded that Jesus used the ordinary, common staff of life to commemorate this sacred event.

Now, who are the ones who should judge whether potato chips and Coca-Cola are appropriate elements for the Eucharist? The bishop? The church council? No, the best judges are the teenagers themselves. They are the ones who can tell us what meaning they experienced by using these common forms instead of bread and wine. And what was the result of this "experiment"? These teenagers told the bishop that they now understood Holy Communion much better than before because the new elements remind them that Jesus took the ordinary, the everyday, and made it special, and they realized that he could do that in their lives as well. A powerful message, the true and sacred meaning of communion, came through the mundane forms of potato chips and Coca-Cola.

Space

A fourth problem we encounter when we work cross-culturally is how different cultures understand and use space in communicating. Anthropologist Edward T. Hall, beginning with his book *The Silent Language* (1959), helps us understand that space is a silent language. And it is a language, or paramessage, that is commonly misunderstood in cross-cultural situations because it deals largely with implicit communication. To understand what is happening in our communication that can lead to misunderstanding, we need to make the implicit explicit, and we need to make what is often unconscious conscious.

Hall divides the space between two people communicating into four zones (see fig. 8.2). Hall notes that every culture has these four zones of space in communication, but the way they define these zones can be vastly different from one culture to another. For example, how do North Americans understand the use of space in communication? They normally stand four to five feet apart during casual conversations. Topics of conversation at this distance include politics, local news, recent vacations, the weather, or any other topic in

Figure 8.2
Four Zones of Communication Space

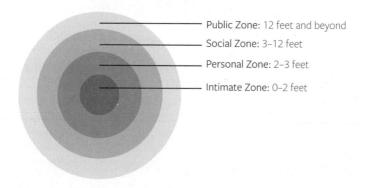

Public Zone: 12 feet and beyond
Social Zone: 3–12 feet
Personal Zone: 2–3 feet
Intimate Zone: 0–2 feet

which anyone can take part. This is their social zone, and it ranges from three to twelve feet. Outside this social zone is their public zone. People in this zone can be ignored because they are too far away for normal conversation. For example, if they come into an occupied room and there are a few people off in the corner talking with one another, they normally won't feel uncomfortable until they come within approximately twelve feet of the group. If they continue to come closer, they feel increasingly uncomfortable until someone turns and acknowledges them and invites them into the conversation. They have moved from their public zone (where it is permissible to be ignored) to within their social zone where, unless they are acknowledged, they will begin to feel very uncomfortable.

If teachers and preachers understood this better, they would alter where they stand when they talk and preach. Most parishioners are at least twelve feet away from the preacher on Sunday morning, and that may be one reason why it is so easy to fall asleep in the middle of a sermon. The preacher can be politely ignored. But if the preacher were to come down from the platform and stand closer than twelve feet, then the parishioners would have to sit up and take notice, because now the preacher is within their social zone, and he or she should not be ignored. Ignoring them would be impolite and would probably cause tension between the preacher and the parishioner.

When Americans want to communicate more intimately, they drop their voice and move closer to the other person, to within two or three feet. This is their personal zone, and topics of conversation at this distance are of a rather personal nature, not intended for public consumption. They also have an intimate zone that extends from physical contact to one or two feet. They use this distance for very personal and intimate communication.

Even though all cultures have similar zones, the proper use of space within these zones is defined quite differently. For example, Latin Americans tend to have smaller zones than do Anglo-Americans. Let's say I'm having a conversation with a man from Brazil, and it's one that is appropriate for my social zone. It's just a friendly, casual conversation, nothing really intimate or particularly personal. As I am talking to this person, before I know it, he's moved closer to me and is in my face. What do I do? I back up to feel comfortable again in my social zone, but as I back up, he comes closer, and this continues as we move all the way across the room. Meanwhile, I am starting to feel like this Brazilian is a bit pushy, but my Brazilian friend is wondering why this man from the United States is so cold and distant. Each of us is feeling uncomfortable, but we are probably not consciously aware of what is happening. We are trying to have a meaningful but not necessarily deep conversation, but our understanding of appropriate space is getting in the way, making communication difficult.

I was training a large group of missionary candidates going to various cultures around the world. I asked how many men in the audience were going to Russia. Several raised their hands. I asked the class, "Do you know how Russian men greet each other?"

One of them said, "We've heard rumors."

"Well, let me show you," I responded. I approached one of the men, held him by the shoulders, and planted a kiss on one cheek, then the other, and before I realized what I was doing, I kissed him directly on the mouth, just like Russian men would do. The whole class erupted with laughter, and I turned as red as a beet. Later, I spoke to this man and his wife about their discomfort with what had taken place. I told them I hoped they could view it as a chance to talk about the challenges they would face when communicating with people in other cultures. I went on to say that our use of space may be a test of the limits of our incarnational identification and one of the sacrifices we may have to make when we cross cultures with the gospel. As cross-cultural witnesses, we have to consciously figure out how people in a culture unconsciously use space so that our communication with them can be fruitful rather than offensive.

CHAPTER SUMMARY

The saying "There are no sacred forms, only sacred meanings" captures the main theme of this chapter. I have tried to demonstrate how cultural forms used in one culture to convey important and even sacred meanings often do not communicate the identical meaning in another culture. This is a problem in crossing cultures with the gospel because we assume that the forms we are using—worship, lifestyle, language, theology—in our own culture will communicate an identical meaning in another. But they seldom do, so we have to be willing to change and adjust the cultural forms to fit the culture of our host society in order for the true meaning to be communicated. In a similar way we often misunderstand and misuse space in communication. The way we use space is a silent language that communicates volumes without ever saying a word. In order to increase our effectiveness as cross-cultural witnesses, we must understand our host culture sufficiently so that the cultural forms we use to convey important meanings and our use of space are appropriate to their context. This will help us avoid inadvertently offending them for the wrong reasons, which would inhibit them from hearing and understanding the offense of the gospel.

CONCLUSION TO PART 3

In part 3, we have addressed four major problems that cross-cultural witnesses encounter when they attempt to communicate and live out the gospel in cultures and subcultures different from their own. Each of these challenges—different worldviews, unintended paramessages, cultural forms, and use of space—deal largely with implicit, unconscious communication. And herein lies the challenge. We are often unaware that our worldview is different from those in cultures different from our own. We don't realize that our paramessages in the form of behaviors and a lifestyle that seem so "natural" to us can often send a message at variance with the verbal message we intend to communicate. Confusing cultural forms with the meanings they are meant to convey can cause enormous misunderstanding in cross-cultural communication. And finally, how we use physical space in communicating with others may feel "right and natural" in our own context but in contexts different from our own may communicate something we do not intend or of which we are not even aware. If we desire to become more resilient and effective cross-cultural witnesses, then we must understand the roots of problems in communication. An anthropological and missiological approach gives us a helpful perspective from which to begin to discover and remove these many "blind spots."

PART 4

Overcoming Culture Shock

9

Understanding Culture Shock

A stranger does not know that the millet water offered him was meant for sowing. (The outsider does not know the secrets of the family.)

Buisla proverb, Ghana

Where were you my freshman year of college?" a thirty-eight-year-old missionary candidate exploded after she participated in the four-hour training session I had just concluded on the topic of identifying and overcoming culture shock. She went on to explain that she had been a child of American missionaries in Latin America and had returned to the United States to attend college. Her first year at the university was an emotional, spiritual, and even physical crisis as she sank deeper and deeper into depression, nearly to the point of taking her own life. All she wanted to do was go "home" to her host country and be with her family and friends. She missed the food, sounds, smells, and rhythms of life there. American culture seemed strange and at times unintelligible to her. She felt like an alien, out of place in the very place she thought she should "feel at home." After all, she was an American! But her fellow American classmates seemed to her so parochial and provincial, ignorant of other cultures and what was happening elsewhere in the world. She hated it.

She went on to say that my teaching on culture shock as an occupational disease, the symptoms one experiences, and the stages one goes through on the way from initial shock to eventual recovery were just what she had experienced. Until that day in my class, she said she had never heard an explanation of what had caused her such turmoil. She was now happily married and with her husband and family was preparing for a life of cross-cultural ministry. But now she knew what to expect when she went to live in a different culture.

Defining Culture Shock

The concept of culture shock was first introduced and developed by Canadian anthropologist Kalervo Oberg (1901–73). He first articulated the concept in a talk he gave to the Women's Club of Rio de Janeiro, Brazil, on August 3, 1954, explaining feelings common to those facing their first cross-cultural experience. His eleven-page talk was published in the *Technical Assistance Quarterly Bulletin* and reprinted in *Practical Anthropology* in 1960. Titled "Culture Shock: Adjustment to New Cultural Environments," his article introduced the concept to the mission world and beyond and has been cited over four thousand times. The concept of culture shock has generated a substantial amount of research and has become a familiar term among cross-cultural sojourners.[1]

"Culture shock," according to Oberg, "tends to be an occupational disease of people who have been suddenly transplanted abroad" and "is precipitated by the anxiety that results from losing all our familiar signs and symbols of social intercourse. These signs or cues include the thousand and one ways in which we orient ourselves to the situations of daily life" (1960, 177).

Oberg identifies four stages of culture shock: (1) a stage of fascination with everything that appears new and different, sometimes referred to as the honeymoon or tourist phase; (2) a period of hostile and aggressive attitudes toward the host country, which is the actual phase that we call culture shock; (3) a period of adjustment, reorientation, and gradual recovery when a sense of humor returns; and (4) adaptation to and acceptance of the new culture. We will discuss each of these stages in the next chapter.

How serious is the problem of culture shock? Does culture shock happen only when you leave the comfort and safety of your own society and go to live in another one that is quite different from your own? No, it is more ubiquitous than that. Culture shock can occur even when we move from one region of

---

1. For example, there has been even more research and writing on culture shock as it affects international travel and business. See Feldman and Tompson 1992; Maclachlan 2017; Marx 2001; and Yale 2017. For a thorough treatment of culture shock as it relates to a variety of cross-cultural travelers, including tourists, immigrants, refugees, international students, businesspeople, and cross-cultural workers, see Ward, Bochner, and Furnham 2001. Anthropologist Michael Winkelman has written a description of culture shock and suggests strategies for managing it (1994). For travelers' experience of culture shock, see Stewart and Leggat 1998. A good summary of culture shock written primarily from the perspective of a traveler is Horizon Unknown 2019. See Linda Anderson's (1994) excellent discussion of culture shock in "A New Look at an Old Construct," where she picks up from Oberg and discusses six principles for effective cross-cultural adaptation.

a country to another. I have observed the culture shock that many seminary students experience when they move their family from Texas to Kentucky or when Christians from Kerala in South India go as missionaries and church planters to North India. Culture shock can also occur when people change jobs, because academic institutions, businesses, corporations, and churches all have their unique cultures.

Over the years, I have interviewed hundreds of cross-cultural witnesses, listened to their stories, uncovered the causes of culture shock, documented the symptoms, and analyzed the process of moving through the experience of culture shock, from initial crisis to eventual adjustment in the new culture. I've come to the conclusion that the way missionaries experience and respond to culture shock is one of the most significant factors in their cross-cultural adjustment. And of course, without a positive adjustment to the new culture, it will be difficult, if not impossible, for them to develop long-lasting, effective, and meaningful cross-cultural ministry.

I once interviewed an American missionary who had prepared for a life of cross-cultural ministry. She recalled how initially she was so excited to be living in such an exotic and interesting place, anticipating a rewarding and fulfilling ministry along with her family. However, it didn't take long for the initial thrill of living in a fascinating country to dissipate and degenerate into deep depression and daily difficulties and struggles. As she sank deeper and deeper into depression, she wondered what was happening to her. What was happening was that she was experiencing culture shock, but she did not realize it. She wasn't going crazy, but she certainly felt like it.

Why do many ethnocentric North Americans have such a difficult time adjusting cross-culturally, and are they the only ones? Jackie Pullinger, famous for working in Hong Kong for over fifty years among people addicted to drugs, once told me that of all the people who come to Hong Kong to work in her St. Stephens ministry, people from the United States have the most difficulty adjusting to the culture. However, it's not just North Americans who struggle with culture shock. It is a common problem for people from any country who go to live in a different culture. Culture shock happens all over the world, among immigrants, refugees, and those relocating for work and educational opportunities. Everyone struggles with overcoming cross-cultural challenges and dealing with the experience of culture shock. There does seem to be a pattern, however. People like Koreans and Han Chinese, who come from relatively homogeneous societies, appear to struggle with culture shock more than those from culturally heterogeneous societies.

Christians from a large and rather homogeneous Asian society, with great enthusiasm and commitment, were venturing out into cross-cultural ministry.

They were going to minister to minority people groups within their own country and to those beyond their borders, expecting to stay for many years if not for the rest of their lives. They were passionate in following God's call on their lives, and so with their Bible in hand, a minimum of theological training, an abundance of courage, and a one-way ticket to their final destination, they sallied forth into the unknown world of cross-cultural mission. However, within the first eighteen months, 90 percent of them returned home. They came home prematurely, frustrated, discouraged, angry, and feeling abandoned by their church and even by God. What had gone wrong? They were not prepared to deal with the cross-cultural differences they encountered and consequently suffered severe culture shock, which ended their ministry before it had barely begun. I was invited to do some cross-cultural training with them to help them understand what had happened as they had entered a culture different from their own. When I explained the dynamics of culture shock, the causes, symptoms, stages, and cures, many said I described what they had experienced. They wondered why they had not been taught about culture shock sooner, because it certainly would have helped them adjust to the cultures they had encountered.

Research indicates that one out of every three Americans who go overseas intending to work in a career comes home within the first year instead of staying the five or ten years they were initially planning on staying. A substantial number of those who embark on a missionary career intending to stay ten to twenty years come home after their first term and don't return.[2] Gone are the days when most cross-cultural witnesses stay for a lifetime. In fact, the average length of service for a career missionary is now only seven years. Missionary attrition has been the subject of a number of research studies, and as one might surmise, there are many contributing factors, including issues of cross-cultural adjustment and culture shock.[3]

Our success or failure in cross-cultural ministry is greatly shaped by what happens in the first two years. As we will discover in the next chapter, when we discuss the stages of culture shock, it takes around two years for most people in most places to complete the cycle of culture shock and arrive at some semblance of adjustment and adaptation. This is the time when we are attempting to learn the language, beginning to make sense of the culture, establishing social

---

2. See, for example, Black and Gregersen 1999; and V. Elmer 2013.

3. Missionary attrition has been the focus of several important studies, since it has been a growing problem for decades. See Hay et al. 2007; W. Taylor 1997; and Sears 2020. Sears 2020 lists a number of factors, in addition to cross-cultural adjustment and culture shock, that contribute to missionary attrition. For a study on missionary retention, see World Evangelicals 2003. See also Paracletos 2015.

relationships, setting up our daily and weekly routines, establishing our home and ministry, and developing our attitudes toward the people and their culture.

My theory of cross-cultural adjustment is 2 + 2 + 2 + 2 + 2 = 20: the first two hours after arriving in our host country shape the first two days, which affect the first two weeks, which impact the first two months, which determine the first two years, which in turn influence the next twenty years of cross-cultural ministry. My interviews with hundreds of missionaries regarding their cross-cultural adjustment confirm that the first hours, days, and weeks are critical to getting off to the right start in making a new country a home and place of ministry. Chapter 11 addresses some ways to reduce the negative experience of culture shock so that the first two years of cross-cultural ministry can be more positive than frustrating.

The experience of culture shock is inevitable for anyone who lives in a culture that is different from their own. Our primary focus, however, is how culture shock impacts people in cross-cultural ministry. So, let's work our way through an understanding of culture shock. First we will look at the factors that contribute to whether a person has a serious or a mild case of culture shock.

The Severity of Culture Shock

Oberg says that "culture shock tends to be an occupational disease of people who have been suddenly transplanted abroad" (1960, 177). The important thing to remember is that while culture shock is an occupational disease, it is seldom fatal, but it can be very debilitating. I say it is "seldom" fatal because there are a number of known cases, including one I know all too well, of people who fell so deeply into depression in the midst of severe culture shock that they took their own lives. What determines whether we have a severe case of culture shock and lose all sense of normalcy, or we have a mild experience and feel just slightly discouraged and emotionally down or mildly annoyed and irritated with the cultural differences in our host society? Hiebert notes that "the severity [of the disease] depends on the extent of the differences between the cultures, the personality of the individual, and the methods used to cope with the new situations" (1985, 66). In my research on missionaries' experiences of culture shock, I have interviewed hundreds of people and examined each of these variables. Let's briefly address each one.

1. *The extent of the differences between the cultures.* If the difference between cultures is great, then the likelihood of experiencing culture shock increases. The greater the difference, the greater the culture shock is a general rule of thumb. When international students and cross-cultural witnesses come to the United States from non-Western countries, they frequently experience severe

culture shock. Life in the US is so different from life in their homeland that they struggle to find their way, to develop meaningful relationships, and to develop an effective ministry. In contrast, if a North American goes to live and minister in the United Kingdom, they are likely to experience a mild case of culture shock, but if that same American goes to Papua New Guinea, they are likely to experience greater culture shock because the difference in cultures is greater.

However, one must be careful not to assume that greater differences always mean greater culture shock. For example, where do you think an American would likely experience more culture shock, in the Philippines or in Thailand? At first blush, it would seem that Thailand is the answer because the Philippines appears on the surface to be more similar to the United States, such as in the widespread use of English. But in fact, according to a research study of Peace Corps workers in both countries (Guthrie 1966), those working in the Philippines experienced more severe culture shock than those working in Thailand. How is that possible? Apparently, because observable elements in the US and Thailand, like food and dress and behavior, look very different, Peace Corp workers were better prepared emotionally and cognitively to deal with the differences. In the Philippines, however, the culture looked and "felt" more American on the surface, and so Peace Corp workers tended to let their guard down and were not as intentional in paying attention to those differences. The result was greater culture shock for those working in the Philippines compared to those serving in Thailand.

2. The personality of the individual. Are you a type A or a type B person? People with a type A personality tend to be competitive, ambitious, and time urgent, and they can become hostile and aggressive in stressful situations. They are the go-getters who take on more tasks than normal and often accomplish them well. In contrast, those with a type B personality are characterized as more laid-back, relaxed, patient, and easygoing. Type B persons are more likely to go with the flow and can more easily tolerate ambiguity in cross-cultural situations. Therefore, type A people tend to have a more severe case of culture shock than those who are type B (van der Zee and van Oudenhoven 2013; and Ward, Bochner, and Furnham 2001).

In research I did in Asia on missionary cross-cultural adjustment, I looked to see if there were any correlations between Myers-Briggs type and missionary cross-cultural adjustment. I found that many types of personalities can handle cross-cultural adjustment, but some do so more easily than others. Those whose personality profile was ENFP (extrovert, intuitive, feeling, perceiving) appeared to have less culture shock and to adjust more readily than those who were ISTJ (introvert, sensing, thinking, judging). The reason I believe ENFPs deal better with culture shock is because they are extroverts, and therefore they derive energy from being with people. Also, a high P (perceiving) score in contrast to a strong J (judging) score indicates that they can handle ambivalence more easily. It is easier for them to go with the flow and to be more comfortable with cultural ambiguity. The missionaries I interviewed who were ENFPs were more likely to go with the flow and adapt to the ambivalence of living in a new culture, and they turned out to be better at adjusting to cultural differences and so had less culture shock. They were not as goal driven or task oriented and may not have accomplished as much as other personality types, but they were sure having a good time doing what they were doing.

The "standard" missionary Myers-Briggs personality type for Southern Baptist missionaries in the 1990s was ESFJ (extrovert, sensing, feeling, judging), which has some significant strength for cross-cultural adjustment and enables one to be a productive and effective missionary.[4] In a 2019 study, "Personality Types and Intercultural Competence of Foreign Language Learners in Education Context," Shiva Azadipour found that those with the Myers-Briggs personality type ESTJ (extrovert, sensing, thinking, judging) adjusted best to cross-cultural differences.

3. *The methods one uses to cope with new situations.* We often think that the best method for coping with culture shock is to withdraw from the people and situations that are causing the uncomfortable feelings and anxiety. However, isolating oneself from the local people and their culture by staying in the presumed safety and comfort of a mission compound or similar situation and hanging out with other expatriates will only increase our culture shock and prolong it. The best method for coping with new situations is to jump into the deep water and learn how to swim. However, the pain of culture shock often invites us to withdraw more than to engage with a people and culture different from our own.

I contacted a former American student and cross-cultural witness in South Asia who for nearly twenty years has seen people come and go in their work with her ministry. Drawing on her extensive experience, she provided a list of how *not* to respond to culture shock:

1. When uncomfortable or challenged, retreat, rest, and withdraw.
2. Recognize that you and your children need to be around other expats as much as possible.
3. To help yourself feel better, cook Western food more often and go out to eat at Westernized places more often.

---

4. See Whelchel 1996 for a comprehensive study of 2,630 Southern Baptist Missionaries' Myers-Briggs personality profiles.

4. Skype, Zoom, and FaceTime with friends and family back home as much as possible during feelings of discomfort.

5. Stay connected as much as possible on social media. The more the better.

6. When it comes to household chores and daily tasks, make sure you find a way to do them just like you did back home. For example, don't hang your clothes out on a line; instead, buy a dryer. Or buy an expensive imported broom to sweep your house instead of using the smaller local ones that you have to bend over to use. Or find someone who can install a Western commode in your bathroom instead of using the squatty potty that came with the rental house.

7. Make shallow friendships with people, especially those who work for you or are somehow indebted to you.

8. Do not ask for help. Figure it out yourself. Be independent. You are an American/Brazilian/Korean, and you came to help, not to be served. Your main job is to serve and help others, not to put yourself in a vulnerable position to be helped by local people.

9. Throw in the towel and give up when things get rough. God probably has something better for you, somewhere else that might be a better fit.

10. Build a false narrative of what your life looks like, especially when sharing about your journey with others, such as financial supporters.[5]

Initial Responses to Culture Shock: Rejection and Regression

The primary cause of culture shock is the anxiety that comes from losing all our familiar signs and symbols of social interaction—all the familiar ways we pick up on how to talk to each other, how to interact with one another, how to behave appropriately, what to think, what to say. Suddenly these familiar ways of interacting disappear and that creates an incredible amount of anxiety within us. These are what we call cultural cues. These cultural cues include words, gestures, facial expressions, customs, and norms of behavior. These often-unconscious cultural cues are so natural that we don't even think about them in our own culture. Suddenly, in a new and different culture, they are missing; they are gone. Oberg says, "All of us depend for our peace of mind and our efficiency on hundreds of these cues, most of which we do not carry on the level of conscious awareness" (1960, 177). So here is the problem. Many of these cultural cues are unconscious, but when we enter a new culture, they are not there. What

5. She sent me the list in an email on June 10, 2020.

happens? This leaves us feeling confused, afraid, and maybe even angry, but we don't know why we feel that way. We can't put our finger on the problem. What we need to do is to recognize why we are feeling confused, afraid, and angry and then name it. Once we do that, we can then better understand what is causing this unsettled feeling and move beyond it in order to grow and adjust to the new culture instead of simply being overwhelmed by it.

Oberg, in his research in Brazil, observed that "when an individual enters a strange culture, all or most of these familiar cues are removed. He or she is like a fish out of water. No matter how broadminded or full of good will you may be, a series of props have been knocked from under you, followed by a feeling of frustration and anxiety. People react to the frustration in much the same way. First, they *reject* the environment which causes the discomfort. But they also experience regression. The home environment suddenly assumes a tremendous importance" (1960, 177–78). To an American, everything American becomes irrationally glorified. All the difficulties and problems of home are forgotten, and only the good things are remembered.

People who experience culture shock typically respond by doing these two things at the same time: they tend to *reject* and *regress*. What do we reject? We reject the new and different culture. And who are the most obvious carriers or sources of this new culture that is causing us all this pain? Our host society, the people we've come to live among, work with, serve and minister with. They are the symbolic source of all our frustration and anger. So we tend to reject the people, their culture, their language, their food, and so on. We end up thinking, if not verbally expressing, *This isn't the way it was back home!*

Moreover, while we are rejecting the people and their culture, we also tend to regress. To what or to whom do we regress? We regress to our own culture and to people who are like us. If we are Americans, we want to hang around with fellow Americans. If we are Koreans, we tend to cluster if not cloister with other Koreans. This is what I call the "back to the womb" phase of culture shock. We regress and just want to withdraw to find a place where we are comfortable again. I have observed this problem of people regressing to their own kind among Brazilians, South Indians from Kerala, Koreans, and people from nearly every other culture in which I have worked and studied. It is a common if not universal response to culture shock.

The problem with both rejection and regression is that they are terrible modes for effective cross-cultural ministry. Because we reject the people we came to serve and we regress to our own culture and its familiar ways, it makes the possibility of being incarnational in this new setting even more unlikely. Nevertheless, these are the two tendencies we will have to overcome if we want to become effective cross-cultural witnesses.

I'll never forget our first (and *last*) Fourth of July party we had with other American missionaries in Papua New Guinea. Even though we were living in the Highlands of Papua New Guinea, all the typical foods one would expect at an American Fourth of July celebration were present—watermelon, hot dogs and hamburgers, potato salad, and homemade ice cream. The food was great, but the conversations were terrible. These American missionaries were mostly complaining about life in Papua New Guinea and how much they missed being back home in the United States. The conversations degenerated more as people drew negative stereotypes of local Melanesians, told derogatory jokes, and demeaned the very people they had come to work among. I was so shaken and upset by this experience that I didn't get over it for days. As I began to investigate who these missionaries were, I discovered that the majority of them had been there from six to twelve months and so were probably deep into the crisis stage of culture shock. They responded by rejecting Melanesian culture and people and regressing to thinking that anything American was better than what they had to put up with living in Papua New Guinea.

The Challenges That Contribute to Culture Shock

We now turn our attention to some specific factors and events that cause a person to experience culture shock.[6] According to anthropologist Michael Winkelman, who directed the Arizona State University Ethnographic Field School in Ensenada, Baja California, Mexico, "Culture shock is caused in part by cognitive overload and behavioral inadequacies, and because intercultural effectiveness is based on understanding and behavioral adaptation, culture shock is best resolved by a social learning approach in which new attitudes and cognitive information are integrated into behavioral strategies for overcoming cultural shock" (1994, 121).

I will use Oberg's idea of culture shock as a disease, for it truly is a dis-ease, as the framework for diagnosing culture shock. As with every disease or illness, there are causes, there are symptoms and stages, and there are things we can do to lessen the severity. In this chapter we are discussing seven challenges that contribute to culture shock:

1. The challenge of developing our personal and social identity and finding meaning in our work

6. In this section on the causes of culture shock, I have drawn heavily on Hiebert's discussion in *Anthropological Insights for Missionaries* (1985, 64–89) and Loss's *Culture Shock* (1983). Additional discussion of culture shock as it relates to cross-cultural ministry can be found in Mayers 1974, 185–90; and Smalley 1963.

2. The challenge of communicating effectively
3. The challenge of confronting different values and beliefs
4. The challenge of working through misunderstanding
5. The challenge of adjusting to new routines and everyday patterns of living
6. The challenge of facing "inefficiency"
7. The challenge of living in a strange environment and climate

If culture shock is an occupational disease, as Oberg suggests, then it has its own etiology, or cause, just like other diseases. As with other diseases, culture shock also has certain symptoms. How do we know when we have it? Sometimes it goes undetected even when we are feeling frustrated, lonely, and depressed. In chapter 10, we will look at several symptoms of culture shock that are telltale signs we are experiencing it. We will also discuss the four typical stages of culture shock that Oberg identifies and that most people go through when experiencing culture shock. In chapter 11, we will discuss some cures for culture shock, or some ways of reducing the trauma of the experience.

First, let's discuss the challenges that contribute to culture shock.

1. *The challenge of developing our personal and social identity and finding meaning in our work.* One of the major challenges we face when we enter another culture is discovering who we are in that different context. Our sense of who we are and who we are becoming has been shaped by the people and culture of our home society. But when we move to another culture, the context changes rapidly, and we can suddenly find ourselves at a loss in knowing who we are. We develop a social sense of who we are through our relationships with others and the positions we occupy in the society. The behavior that accompanies those social positions significantly affects our ability to establish meaningful relationships with others. In cross-cultural settings, the situation is even more complex and difficult, for we often do not have control over the social position in which people in our host society place us. And worse, we are often unaware of how we are being perceived by our host society. We may see ourselves in the role of a missionary—a role that our sending society understands and affirms. But the role of missionary may be perceived very negatively in our host society, or perhaps it doesn't even exist there. Consequently, the position we occupy in a society both provides opportunities and establishes limitations regarding with whom we can develop personal relationships and in what way. Because we get so much of our self-worth from our social identity in our home society, it can send us into an emotional tailspin when we enter another culture and we

have to start all over to establish our identity and to become somebody, not only in our own eyes but in the eyes of those with whom we live and serve.

I remember interviewing a missionary in Japan who was assigned by his mission to do church planting. The most difficult aspect of his adjustment to Japanese society was dealing with his personal identity. The reason he had such a difficult time was because the role of church planter did not exist in Japanese society, and so when he identified himself to the Japanese as a church planter, he just got blank stares in response. Because he didn't have a recognizable job, he struggled with an identity crisis. Because of the work schedule of Japanese men, he found it almost impossible to develop any relationships with Japanese men, and this was contributing to his culture shock and undercutting his sense of purpose. He told me he finally went and joined some sports clubs to find a basis for developing relationships and for developing an identity in that society to which other Japanese men could relate.

The challenge of developing identity is especially great for Americans because they base so much of their identity and worth on what they do. Too often they assume busy is better, wealthy is worthy. If they are busy doing a lot of things, this communicates to people in their home culture that they must be important. However, a more kingdom value is focusing on being who we are in Christ, not doing what we do. Unfortunately, in our American culture, we focus so much on doing and so little on being. But God calls us to conform to God's image by the renewing of our worldview (Rom. 12:2), which is more about being than about doing.[7] One of the paradoxes of cross-cultural ministry is that mission-sending agencies employ us for what we do, not for who we are. But if we concern ourselves less with doing and focus more on being, then it will come more naturally to us to do God's will and we will have more than enough to do to keep us busy and fulfilled. But if our identity is tied too closely to what we do, then culture shock will become a very serious illness for us.[8]

2. The challenge of communicating effectively. Another significant factor that contributes to culture shock is our inability to communicate effectively, both verbally and nonverbally. Some people are more gifted than others at learning different languages, and some languages are much more difficult to learn as a foreign language than others. We also know that the younger a person is, the easier it is to learn a second, third, and even fourth language, but when we as adults come up against another language that sounds like a cacophony of jumbled sounds, we wonder if we will ever be able to decipher actual words and

7. See Whiteman 2006 for a discussion of the role of ethnicity and culture in shaping the identity of Western mission organizations, where there is tension between our social identity and our spiritual identity.

8. See Cupsa 2018 for an exploration of the impact of culture shock on individual identity.

sentences out of all this noise. It can be truly frightening, and we may begin to doubt if we'll ever be able to make sense out of this language, let alone speak it fluently and understand it deeply. We are social beings, and language is one of the primary modes through which we interact with others. Hiebert says, "Ever since our early childhood, we have talked, gestured, written, and talked some more—until we are no longer aware of the communication processes themselves. They have become almost automatic. Suddenly, as strangers in a new world, we are stripped of our primary means of interacting with other people. Like children, we struggle to say even the simplest things, and we constantly make mistakes" (1985, 66).

The problem is that we are *not* children, and so this can be very unsettling for adults, especially for adults who are highly trained and specialized. I found this to be the case especially among American missionary men working in Korea. Many of them would break down and cry in their language classes because language learning was so frustrating, and they thought they were so stupid. They felt like children again, and this was very unnerving. They would say, "Who I am as a man is being stripped away, and I feel like a little child, a stupid little child." The challenge is that we are like little children, and we are going to have to come to grips with feeling like little children and not allow ourselves to become embarrassed about looking and acting like such. Even though we may be sophisticated and highly trained adults, the more we can take on the attitude of childlike wonder, the better we are going to be able to deal with the shock of learning a new language.

3. *The challenge of confronting different values and beliefs.* When we enter to serve in another culture and observe the way people live and interact with one another, it doesn't take long for us to see that we are confronting values and beliefs very different from our own. Sometimes they are rather minor and just annoying, such as a different understanding and use of time so that "meetings never start on time" from an American's point of view.[9] At other times, the values and beliefs are diametrically opposed to our own and assault our most treasured values and beliefs. As cross-cultural witnesses who have come to join God's mission in this society, we often have deeply held values and strong beliefs that we can't imagine living without. When we are challenged with such different values and beliefs, it creates evaluative confusion, which is a major source of culture shock. Hiebert notes, "On the level of values, we are incensed at what appears to be a lack of morality: the lack of proper dress, the insensitivity to the poor, and what to us is obviously stealing, cheating, and bribing. We are even

9. For an excellent discussion of value differences as they relate to cross-cultural ministry, see B. Adeney 1995; and Lingenfelter and Mayers 2016.

more shocked to learn that the people consider *our* behavior just as immoral" (1985, 70). How is it possible that we who are cross-cultural witnesses of the gospel could be accused of being immoral? Talk about evaluative confusion! We see people acting "immorally," and they in turn see *us* acting "immorally."

For example, when we lived in the Solomon Islands, we discovered that we were being perceived as less than moral because we didn't share our food. Melanesians share their food; it is a sign of equivalence between people to do so. Once we realized this and began sharing what we had, we received back much more food than we could possibly eat. The exchange of food in many cultures is one of the most important symbols for developing and sustaining relationships between people. It communicates that we are fellow human beings walking together in this pilgrimage called life.

It is critical that we are in touch with how our behavior is perceived by others, because if it is perceived as immoral, then we are going to be in trouble. In the Philippines, for example, I know of a missionary who was perceived to be acting immorally because he spoke to his dog. He was accused of incest. In the worldview of the Filipinos, talking to your dog is an unnatural act, a nonhuman act, because dogs don't talk. Incest is also perceived as an unnatural act, an abomination of what it means to be human. In the cognitive categories of these Filipinos, talking to your dog and incest are similar if not the same. So while this missionary thought he was just having a conversation with Fido, guess what kind of effect it had on his ministry!

The challenge of interacting with people who have sometimes dramatically different values and beliefs can impinge on our daily life and create enormous stress and anxiety. This contributes initially to culture shock and over time to culture stress[10] until we learn to "be at home" in this different culture.

4. The challenge of working through misunderstanding. The fourth challenge we face that contributes to culture shock is frequent misunderstanding between ourselves and those who are culturally different from us. All the information we learned as children and all the knowledge we bring from our home culture do not always work in our new setting, which often leads to embarrassment and confusion. Similarly, when we first enter a culture, we don't know the things we need to know in order to act in an acceptable manner. For example, William Smalley writes about his experience learning French in France as part of his preparation to become a missionary in what was then called French Indochina. He says:

10. Culture stress comes from changing to a new and different way of living in a different cultural context. It can last for many more years than the two years it typically takes to recover from culture shock, which is characterized by cultural confusion caused by the complete loss of cultural cues in our host society. On culture stress see Dye (1974) and Spradley and Phillips (1972).

When I first went to Paris to study French, I and many other Americans like me, found it difficult to know when and where to shake hands. French people seemed to us to be shaking hands all the time, and very unnecessarily so from our point of view. We felt silly shaking hands so much, and we passed around among us the stories that we heard, such as one about French children shaking hands with their parents before going to bed every night. These stories emphasized the "queerness" of such French customs. This small and inconsequential difference of habit in shaking hands was enough to bring uneasiness, and combined with hundreds of other uncertainties brought culture shock to many. (1963, 49)

When we enter another culture, we often "see everything" and assume nothing. In time, as we become acculturated to the society, the reverse happens—we "see nothing" because it is now all so familiar that it doesn't stand out, but then we also assume everything. An assumption is the lowest form of knowledge. One of the contributing factors to much misunderstanding, even within our own culture, is making assumptions we believe to be true and correct but in fact are false and incorrect.

5. *The challenge of adjusting to new routines and everyday patterns of living.* In our home culture, daily routines do not take much effort and do not cause anxiety. In the new culture, it seems like our daily routine is disrupted continually. Hiebert notes, "In our home culture we carry out efficiently such tasks as shopping, cooking, banking, laundering, mailing, going to the dentist, and getting a Christmas tree, leaving ourselves time for work and leisure. In a new setting, even simple jobs take a great deal of psychic energy and more time, much more time" (1985, 67).

When my wife, Laurie, and I first went to the Solomon Islands, we had no electricity, but we did have running water—just as fast as I could carry it up in two buckets from the river! I remember after about three or four weeks of this new routine, I started complaining, "This just takes so much time to do all this stuff to survive." For example, even the "simple" task of washing our clothes in the river would take hours. Food preparation was such a chore that we cooked only one meal a day, like others in the village. Laurie responded to my complaints by saying, "Honey, it also takes everyone else in the village this much time. After all, why are we here?" We were there to live among the people and to learn from them, and the only way to do that was to live like them, including taking hours to wash our clothes in the river. I just had to slow myself down and get in sync with the routines of village life, but it seemed like we spent an enormous amount of time doing what normally would have been done quickly and easily. No doubt having to adjust to a different routine contributed to our culture shock.

In the first several months, if not the first year, of cross-cultural ministry, we can become frustrated because our daily routines have changed, sometimes uncomfortably so. When that happens, it may seem like we don't have any time left over to do the "real work" that we came to do. It's all survival, and there is little time for ministry. Sometimes we increase the frustration of a change in our daily routine because we try to reproduce the lifestyle we had back home in our new setting. I know of one North American missionary who got so frustrated because she couldn't find the same spaghetti sauce that she was used to back home. She preferred Ragú, but all she could find in the shops was Prego. She told me she spent practically an entire day going from one store to another in her new city in search of the "right" spaghetti sauce.

6. *The challenge of facing "inefficiency."* Americans place a high value on efficiency. We manufacture labor-saving devices and time-saving gadgets to become more efficient in our work and daily chores. We often evaluate the success or failure of an activity based on the ROI (return on investment). We calculate, sometimes unconsciously, how much time, money, resources, and energy were spent to achieve a goal. This concern with efficiency can lead us to become more task oriented than person oriented (Lingenfelter and Mayers 2016, 67–79). This penchant for efficiency causes us to become frustrated when living in another country because we are not able to function nearly as efficiently as we did "back home," and so many activities take more time and are emotionally exhausting. On the other hand, we can easily become very critical of the "inefficient" way some people in our host society go about their work and conduct their personal lives.

7. *The challenge of living in a strange environment and climate.* Cross-cultural witnesses who grow up in more rural areas may find living in large foreign cities to be very challenging. However, today cross-cultural ministry is increasingly occurring in megacities, in contrast to a couple generations ago when most cross-cultural ministry was centered in rural missionary compounds. I remember an older couple who were new to metro Manila, and in their first year they struggled with the hot, humid climate and congested traffic. In my interview with them, I commented on the colorful red, blue, and yellow flag of the Philippines. The woman shot back with a large dose of frustration in her voice: "The only color I see in Manila is concrete gray." She was spiraling down into the second stage of culture shock, emoting her hostility and disenchantment with the environment.

In my research in many Asian megacities, such as metro Manila or Bangkok, a major source of frustration for Americans is the congested traffic. Their daily routine is determined primarily by how long it will take them to get from one part of the city to another to accomplish a task. It was in Taiwan where I heard an American missionary, frustrated with congested traffic, say that "a stop light is only a suggestion."

CHAPTER SUMMARY

Let's return to the story that opened this chapter. For nearly twenty years, the missionary woman had wondered what had happened to her in her freshman year of university. She didn't fit into the American culture, and the worship service in the church she attended seemed dead by comparison to the lively worship she had had back home, where she grew up as a missionary kid. She felt more than just homesick. As she became more and more depressed, she felt at times like she was going crazy. But by God's grace, she survived that first year and eventually acclimatized to American university life but not completely. Not until that day, when I explained the temporary occupational disease called culture shock, did she understand what had happened to her. How many others experience culture shock after the initial excitement of being in a new country wears off? After considering factors that contribute to culture shock, we're now ready to discover in the following chapter the symptoms and stages of culture shock so you'll be able to identify them in yourself and in others.

10

The Symptoms and Stages of Culture Shock

The sole of the foreigner is narrow. (A foreigner has a restricted freedom of movement and is always unsteady. Also, his/her presence leaves a very limited imprint.)

Lugbara proverb, Uganda and Congo

have to admit," a young missionary doctor said to me, "for the past two years since we arrived, I have not experienced any culture shock at all. It seems like I've been in a perpetual honeymoon, and I just love it here."

I sat patiently as I listened somewhat skeptically to his story about how he had anticipated confronting culture shock, but much to his surprise he hadn't experienced any symptoms. He noted that his life had never been better. Since coming to Southeast Asia, he felt more fulfilled and closer to God than he ever had before. His wife confirmed his story, that so far, unlike the rest of the family, he seemed to be riding high and avoiding the land mines of culture shock. I congratulated him on his achievement, told him how rare it was not to have any symptoms of culture shock in the first two years, and that I hoped he could keep the honeymoon stage going for a long time. Then it happened. He failed the medical board exams that he had to take in the local language. The "honeymoon" was over, and he plunged deeply into the cycle of culture shock.

The Symptoms of Culture Shock

So how do you know if you're experiencing culture shock? What are the symptoms of this occupational disease? To that topic we now turn.

Here is a list of thirteen symptoms that one might experience:

1. Feelings of frustration, loneliness, confusion, melancholy, irritability, insecurity, and helplessness
2. Unaccountable episodes of crying
3. Excessive concern over drinking water, food, dishes, and bedding
4. Fear of physical contact with local people
5. Oversensitivity and overreaction to minor difficulties
6. Changes in eating habits or loss of appetite
7. Changes in sleeping habits, insomnia, or severe sleepiness
8. Loss of humor
9. Fatigue and lethargy
10. Depression, which shows up as loneliness, feeling lost or helpless, feeling especially vulnerable, a lack of motivation to do things you once enjoyed, feeling like you've lost a sense of your identity, and an inability to complete tasks
11. Anxiety expressed as preoccupation with your health; a sense of dread; an excessive fear of being cheated, tricked, or robbed; an inordinate concern over the safety of the food served to you; a preoccupation with overall cleanliness; and doubts about your ability to navigate this new experience
12. Feeling ill, aches and pains, sleep disturbances, resurgence of chronic health issues, and feeling "off" with no apparent explanation
13. Self-doubt and questioning your call

Paul Hiebert notes, "The real problem in culture shock is the psychological distortion that comes undetected while we think we are functioning normally. This twists our perceptions of reality, and wreaks havoc with our bodies" (1985, 71). From this extensive list of symptoms of culture shock, we'll focus on three major symptoms—the stress created from living in a different cultural context, physical illness, and psychological and spiritual depression.

Stress from Living in a Different Cultural Context

How much stress is too much stress? A certain amount is healthy and necessary. We do things every day that are stressful, and we keep doing them because the positive reward is greater than the negative stress we experience. Leaving our culture of origin and moving into a different culture create stress because of all the changes we experience—changes in the language we use every day,

The Holmes-Rahe Stress Inventory

Life Event	Points
1. Death of a spouse	100
2. Divorce	73
3. Marital separation from mate	65
4. Detention in jail or other institution	63
5. Death of a close family member	63
6. Major personal injury or illness	53
7. Marriage	50
8. Being fired at work	47
9. Marital reconciliation with mate	45
10. Retirement from work	45
11. Major change in the health or behavior of a family member	44
12. Pregnancy	40
13. Sexual difficulties	39
14. Gaining a new family member	39
15. Major business readjustment	39
16. Major change in financial state	38
17. Death of a close friend	37
18. Changing to a different line of work	36
19. Major change in the number of arguments with spouse	35
20. Taking on a mortgage	31
21. Foreclosure on a mortgage or loan	30
22. Major change in responsibilities at work	29
23. Son or daughter leaving home	29
24. In-law troubles	29
25. Outstanding personal achievement	28
26. Spouse beginning or ceasing work outside the home	26
27. Beginning or ceasing formal schooling	26
28. Major change in living conditions	25
29. Revision of personal habits	24
30. Troubles with the boss	23
31. Major change in working hours or conditions	20
32. Change in residence	20
33. Change to a new school	20
34. Major change in usual type and/or amount of recreation	19
35. Major change in church activity	19
36. Major change in social activities	18
37. Taking on a loan	17
38. Major change in sleeping habits	16
39. Major change in number of family get-togethers	15
40. Major change in eating habits	15
41. Vacation	13
42. Major holidays	12
43. Minor violations of the law	11

Source: Holmes and Masuda 1974, 52.

changes to our daily routines, and changes to our identity and place in society. How much stress is too much stress is different for each of us. Psychologists have turned their attention to this issue of stress created by changes we experience in life. For example, the American Institute of Stress has posted on their website the Holmes-Rahe Stress Inventory created in 1967 by psychiatrists Thomas Holmes and Richard Rahe.[1] Holmes and Rahe examined the medical records of over five thousand patients as a way to determine whether stressful events might cause illnesses. The scale has been tested with other groups as well as cross-culturally. Their theory states that various experiences in life create stress that can stay with us for up to a year or more after the experience has occurred. Check out the items in this inventory and pay attention to any of these life changes that have occurred in your cross-cultural situation in the last year. Then add up the total points of stress you identified.

How many stress points do you have based on the inventory? The relationship between the total number of points you have and your health is probably different at various phases of your life. Although stress is hard to measure, in an article titled "Life Changes and Illness Susceptibility," Thomas Holmes and Minoru Masuda developed a rough scale by which to estimate the stress created by various life-changing experiences (1974). Holmes and Masuda found that 33 percent of those with 150 points or less were *not likely* to become seriously ill in the following two years. Fifty percent of those with 150 points or more were *likely* to become seriously ill in the next two years, and 80 percent of those with 300 points or more were *likely* to become seriously ill in the next two years (1974, 52). Now, by these measures, most missionaries should be concerned about their health. It is not uncommon for them to have well over 300 points.

This study by Holmes and Masuda did not take into consideration cross-cultural differences, and I think those of us in cross-cultural ministry are even more likely to experience debilitating stress in the first year or two of service. It should be clear by now that cross-cultural ministry is a very stressful vocation. In an article by James Spradley and Mark Phillips titled "Culture and Stress: A Quantitative Analysis" (1972), the authors note that second language learning is very stressful and contributes to culture shock. In addition, they list thirty-three cultural readjustment items that are relevant to one's experience in cross-cultural ministry and may contribute to one's stress:

1. The type of food eaten
2. The type of clothes worn

---

1. You can find the inventory on the American Institute of Stress website: https://www.stress .org/holmes-rahe-stress-inventory.

3. How punctual most people are

4. Ideas about what offends people

5. The language spoken (assume you have only limited ability in that language)

6. How ambitious people are

7. The personal cleanliness of most people

8. The general pace of life

9. The amount of privacy you have

10. Your financial state

11. Type of recreation and leisure time activities

12. How parents treat children

13. The sense of closeness and obligation felt among family members

14. The amount of body contact, such as touching or standing close

15. The subjects that should not be discussed in normal conversation

16. The number of people of your same race

17. The degree of friendliness and intimacy between unmarried men and women

18. How free and independent women seem to be

19. Sleeping practices (amount of time, time of day, and sleeping arrangements)

20. General standard of living

21. Ideas about friendship—the way people feel and act toward friends

22. The number of people of your religious faith

23. How formal or informal people are

24. Your own opportunities for social contacts

25. The degree to which your good intentions are misunderstood by others

26. The number of people who live in the community

27. Ideas about what is funny

28. Ideas about what is sad

29. How much friendliness and hospitality people express

30. The amount of reserve people show in their relationships with others

31. Eating practices (amount of food, time of eating, and ways of eating)

32. Types of transportation used

33. The way people take care of material possessions (1972, 522)

On one of my sabbaticals, I interviewed hundreds of first- and second-term missionaries in East Asia and asked them if they had experienced any unusual or uncharacteristic behavior during their time of going through culture shock. Many of them admitted that they had had fits of unexplained anger. A lot of couples talked about how this was a time of stress and conflict in their marriage. One male missionary said that during the time he was going through culture shock, he started baking bread as a way to relieve the stress. Kneading the dough was better than taking his frustrations out on his family or the local people with whom he was living.

Physical Illness

Another symptom of culture shock is physical illness. I remember when my wife and I, together with our toddler son, first went to the Highlands of Papua New Guinea to serve as cross-cultural witnesses at an ecumenical research institute. It seemed like at least one of us in the family was sick nearly every day for the first six months or more. They were never serious illnesses, but they were aggravating. All kinds of local explanations were offered for why we were sick so often, but I believe we were experiencing one of the symptoms of culture shock. Hiebert notes that a common consequence of high stress is physical illness, especially chronic headaches, ulcers, lower back pain, high blood pressure, heart attack, and chronic fatigue (1985, 72). Getting sick in a foreign setting can often increase our anxiety, and anxiety is a true symptom of culture shock. I mention it here because if we do not deal with anxiety, it often leads to physical illness. Kalervo Oberg, author of the pioneering study on culture shock, offers the following list of symptoms of anxiety:

1. Excessive washing of our hands
2. Excessive concern over drinking water, food, dishes, and bedding
3. Fear of physical contact with local people
4. That absent-minded, faraway stare where you just wander off in your mind to never-never land
5. Feelings of helplessness
6. Desire for dependence on individuals from your home culture who have been there for a while
7. Fits of anger over delays and other minor frustrations
8. Delays and outright refusal to learn the local language
9. Great concern over minor pain and skin problems
10. Excessive fear of being cheated, robbed, or injured
11. Homesickness for the familiar (1960, 178)

Psychological and Spiritual Depression

When missionaries experience psychological and spiritual depression, it is frequently the low point in their cross-cultural adjustment.[2] The most serious consequence of stress is the depression that often follows a sense of failure. The tensions and strains arising from the confusion and problems of living in a new culture make missionaries good candidates for depression. It is a serious problem that many cross-cultural witnesses must face in the early years of their time in a new place. We often compound the problem because we are afraid to share our feelings of failure with other missionaries or national Christians.

I have frequently found in my role as an anthropologist and researcher of cross-cultural adjustment that I have functioned as a pastor for missionaries. This is because I have become a trusted outsider, one with whom they feel free to share their troubles because I'm not a part of their mission organization and they don't have to report to me. I've been amazed at the "stuff" that has been shared with me, but they needed someone to talk to, someone who would be empathetic and could understand their struggles in their cross-cultural situation. Don't be hesitant to seek out counseling and pastoral support, preferably from the people among whom you are living and serving, when you are experiencing culture shock in the form of psychological and spiritual depression.

Now, if it isn't bad enough that we often are afraid to share our feelings of failure, and it seems as if there is no one to be our pastor or counselor, many of us are driven by unrealistic expectations formed from the public image of what a missionary is. The public image may be changing somewhat today because missionaries tend to serve for much shorter periods of time, but when I was growing up, missionaries were perceived to be perched on the pinnacle of the spiritual pyramid. Pastors and laypeople were considered less spiritual than real missionaries. We also have often seen them as a "hearty pioneer who suffers great deprivation, a sanctified saint who never sins, an outstanding preacher, soul winner, doctor or personal worker who overcomes all obstacles" (Hiebert 1985, 73). This is the stuff of missionary biographies. Now, here's the problem. Many of us have the notion that when we leave our home country and fly overseas and land in another place, we will somehow become that person, that paragon of all missionary virtues. But when we arrive at the new place where we've come to make our home and begin our ministry, we realize we are the same person we were when we left. We realize we are falling far short of our idealized, but unrealistic, missionary image.

---

2. Spiritual depression has been described as "a deep sense of sadness or emptiness that results from a disconnect with one's spirituality, sense of purpose, or relationship with God or the divine" (Lewis 2023).

Figure 10.1
Tension between Expectations and Performance

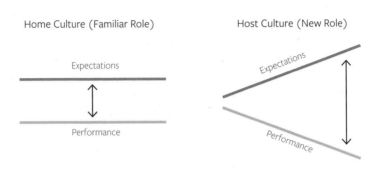

When we come to realize we are not superhuman missionaries but rather ordinary persons and very human, we often face depression, and sometimes it is very severe. Hiebert notes, "Unfortunately, if we think we are failing, we work harder to maintain our self-esteem. But this only multiplies our problems, for the fear of failure itself saps our energies. Defeated, we conclude that we are faulty and not acceptable for God's service" (1985, 74). And when that starts to happen, we're really in trouble.

This issue of being driven by unrealistic expectations in cross-cultural ministry highlights the tension between our expectations and our performance. Figure 10.1 illustrates this tension.

In our home culture most of us live with some tension between our expectations of what we want to accomplish and our actual performance. It seems like we frequently struggle to get everything done on time, or when we do finish a task, it isn't quite as perfect as we would like. I find that I am frequently about a month behind in finishing a writing assignment or preparing for a training or speaking event. The tension we feel between our expectations and our performance only increases when we go to another country as cross-cultural witnesses. Often our expectations of what we want to accomplish are higher because now we are "missionaries," those paragons of virtue who can accomplish virtually anything. But our performance frequently decreases dramatically because we can't yet speak the language fluently, and we don't understand the subtle nuances of the new culture. All the problems of cross-cultural communication just exacerbate these tensions.

I remember well a conversation I had with a young missionary in Africa who was regretting the fact that while he had been in seminary in the United States, he felt he was always too busy to take time to do personal evangelism. In his own mind, he rationalized that he was preparing to do greater things, and so his evangelistic efforts could wait until he was a missionary overseas. Well, now he was overseas and feeling very frustrated with the slow progress he was making in learning the language and connecting with the people so that he could do the evangelistic work he came to do. He was now wondering why he had wasted all those years in seminary, postponing his efforts at evangelism.

Unrealized expectations contribute to a greater amount of culture shock. This can be very discouraging. At least you won't be able to say, "No one told me it would be this way," because I just have. These are some of the experiences many of you will have. Some will have a severe case of culture shock, others a milder attack of the disease. I remember one woman I interviewed who said that her experience of culture shock was like falling into a black hole, and she just kept sinking deeper and deeper. In her utter despair, she found her notes on culture shock from my training session given at her missionary orientation before she left the United States. Rereading those notes helped her to understand that she was perfectly normal and not as crazy as she was beginning to imagine.

Identifying the symptoms of culture shock is an important first step on the road to recovery. This leads us to the next discussion: the stages of culture shock that we typically go through.

The Stages of Culture Shock

If culture shock is an occupational disease, as anthropologist Oberg suggests, and if it has definite causes and visible symptoms, then like most illnesses, it passes through discernible stages until the person is brought to health and wholeness.

Oberg identifies four stages in the process of going through culture shock (1960, 178–79). First is a honeymoon stage, which may last from a few days or weeks up to six months. The second stage is a period of hostility and an aggressive attitude toward the host society; this is the crisis period of the disease. The third stage is one of adjustment, reorientation, and gradual recovery. The final stage is a period of adaptation and acceptance. Drawing on Oberg's model, Hiebert identifies the four stages of culture shock as tourist, disenchantment, resolution, and adjustment (1985, 74–77). Combining these two models, I have designed figure 10.2, which lists the four stages as tourist and honeymoon, hostility and disenchantment, resolution and resolve, and adjustment and adaptation. In what follows, I discuss these stages and also note the length of time we normally spend in each one. Although this model does not account for 100 percent of people's experience, it seems to fit the majority of those who suffer from the disease called culture shock.

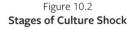

Figure 10.2
Stages of Culture Shock

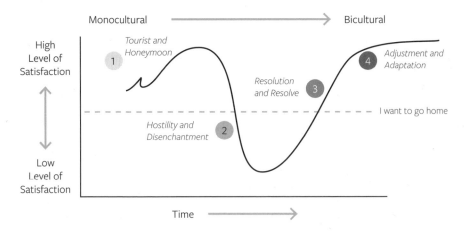

Figure 10.2 shows that we start out as monocultural people, knowing only our own culture. And of course, it's debatable how well we know our own culture at the deepest level of our worldview because those who know only one culture know no culture at all. The long-term goal in cross-cultural adjustment and ministry is to become a bicultural person, which I will discuss in depth in chapter 14. Going through all the stages of culture shock puts us on the path toward becoming a bicultural person.

The figure shows that we enter another culture with a high level of satisfaction, but before long the excitement and fascination of being in a different culture start to wear off, and our level of satisfaction decreases. Notice the brief dip in our level of satisfaction shortly after we enter the new culture. One missionary candidate suggested I make this amendment to the diagram. For him and his family, that short dip occurred when they went through immigration and customs after a long flight. They were momentarily fearful and anxious, wondering if they would have any problem getting through immigration and customs.

You'll notice the dotted line that goes across the figure midway between a high level of satisfaction and a low level. I call this line "I want to go home," because when our level of satisfaction declines and we dip below that line, we would rather be home than trying to survive in our new culture.

When we are going through culture shock and feeling miserable and depressed, it is comforting to know that we are normal human beings and that in time the trauma will end. What we are experiencing is normal, not abnormal.

It would be a good idea to keep a personal journal during this time so that you can later read and understand what you went through. By recognizing that culture shock is normal, we can turn culture shock into a positive experience that prepares us for future ministry. I'm convinced that how we adapt to the culture in the first couple years influences the rest of our ministry in that place, and how we respond to culture shock will in turn shape those first couple of years.

Let us now look at the four stages of culture shock.

Stage 1: Tourist and Honeymoon

We call the first stage the tourist and honeymoon period of cross-cultural adjustment because it is a wonderful, exciting time. It's a stage of fascination with everything new and strange. We are thrilled to be in a new place, and our social media posts and emails to friends and family reflect this. We frequently talk about how we just "love the people" at this stage, and we see only the positive aspects of this new culture.

This tourist stage can last from a few weeks up to about six months. There are of course dramatic exceptions to this rule. One missionary to Japan told me her tourist stage lasted about forty-five minutes, from the Narita airport to downtown Tokyo, and it was all downhill from then on. A family in the Philippines was mildly upset with me because, as they complained, "We never got a tourist stage at all, and, Whiteman, you promised us one." The story of the medical missionary in Southeast Asia who spent two years enjoying the tourist and honeymoon stage clearly demonstrates an exception to the pattern of adjustment.

One of the many problems with short-term mission trips that last for a week to ten days is that participants seldom leave the tourist stage. I've known of people who have made five or six short-term mission trips and now feel they are experts on the dynamics of cross-cultural ministry. Unfortunately, they've never gotten out of the tourist stage, are still monocultural, and are not yet in a learning mode.

For most people, the tourist stage ends in about two to three months, and then they enter the second stage.

Stage 2: Hostility and Disenchantment

The second stage, which we call hostility and disenchantment, is what most people identify as culture shock. During this period, the fascination of the new diminishes or leaves completely. Hiebert notes that this stage begins "when we establish our own homes, take responsibility for ourselves, and start making a contribution to the local community. It is here that frustrations and anxieties arise. We have language problems, shopping trouble, transportation woes, and laundry mix-ups. We are concerned about the cleanliness of drinking water, food, and bedding and afraid of being cheated or robbed. We also feel left alone. Those who welcomed us so warmly have gone back to their work and now seem indifferent to our troubles. The result is disenchantment" (1985, 75).

No longer is the strange culture exciting and interesting. Now it becomes a pain, and a pain in many ways. We seem to be losing control, and we can easily feel insecure and become hostile. It is often the local people and the local environment that are causing this unsettled feeling. We begin complaining about the very people we've come to serve, and we wish we could escape, if only for a brief period of reprieve. We develop stereotypes that caricature the host culture in negative ways. If we're from the United States, we band together with other North Americans. If we are from South Korea, we look for other Koreans and complain with them about local people. We may unconsciously become mired in the negative aspects of culture shock, but we may not realize that this is what's happening to us. As our personal satisfaction declines and we frequently dip below the "I want to go home" line, we may start to question if we made the right decision to move here or if we really did hear God's call correctly. From time to time, we may have some good days during this crisis period when we feel more at home and less like an alien in the new culture, but the overall trend is one of increasing frustration, alienation, tension, and embarrassment. We want to go home, but of course we can't. Too much time, money, and prayer have been invested for us to just give up. It's often thought that the only ways to go home with honor as a missionary are through retirement, death, or illness, and some people actually get sick during this critical stage of culture shock and go home.

This stage of the disease generally lasts from six to twelve months for most people in most parts of the world. However, in my research in East Asia, I discovered that many missionaries were taking much longer to go through the entire culture shock cycle, and for many, the stage of hostility and disenchantment lasted longer than twelve months. Perhaps the difficulty of the languages and the inscrutable nature of Asian cultures make it more difficult for some to adjust compared to a cross-cultural witness working in Latin America, for example.

If you overcome this stage of culture shock, you will stay and most likely have a fulfilling and fruitful ministry. If not, you will leave prematurely and return home before you have a nervous breakdown.[3]

3. For more discussion on the emotional and psychological effects of culture shock, see Ward, Bochner, and Furnham 2001. The authors take a more positive approach and note three major components of culture shock: affect, behavior, and cognition.

Stage 3: Resolution and Resolve

When we start laughing again, it is a good sign that we have come through the transition and are now on the road to recovery. Even while we were feeling miserable, we were learning a few more words in the language. We were getting out and around by ourselves, finding ways of making some sense out of this new culture and language. Problems continue, no doubt about that. But we take on an attitude of "grin and bear it." We resolve to stick it out, stay the course, instead of running away. This is the time when missionaries reach back into their lives and down deep into their call and remember, "God called me here. The Holy Spirit will be my comfort and enable me to survive. Jesus promised to be with us. God did not bring me this far only to abandon me now." In this third stage, we need something that enables us to resolve to stay, to learn, and to grow in this new culture. People who do not have a sense of call or purpose usually don't weather the cross-cultural storm, and they pack up and go home prematurely.

The previous "crisis stage" of culture shock is the one that gets most of our attention, but how we respond in this stage of resolution and resolve is equally important. Hiebert notes, "How we relate to the people and culture at this stage is particularly crucial, for the patterns of adjustment we form here tend to stay with us. If we develop positive attitudes of appreciation and acceptance of the host people, we have laid the foundations for learning their culture and becoming one with them" (1985, 76).

Referencing again figure 10.2, we can see that many people have an experience at the bottom of stage 2 (hostility and disenchantment) that enables them to stop spiraling downward as their level of satisfaction decreases. When this happens, they can begin to crawl out of the pit of despair. The turning-point experience can come from many different events. We may break through the social, cultural, and language barriers to discover a good local friend on the other side. We may be surprised one day when we discover that we are able to get through preaching our first sermon in the local language. We may be called on to do something for which we feel unprepared or ill-equipped and discover that we have more understanding of what's going on in this new culture than we realized. I believe God frequently sends those experiences into our lives just when we are at the end of our psychological and spiritual rope.

In this third stage of resolution and resolve, the negative criticism of people begins to give way to joking about them. And before we know it, we are cracking jokes about ourselves and our own difficulties (cf. Oberg 1960, 179). I've always believed that humor is a good index of mental health in cross-cultural living. When we were living in Melanesia, my wife and I had a working agreement with each other that when we stopped laughing, it was time for us to go home.

That would be an indication that there was no longer any joy in our cross-cultural work and ministry in the place where we were serving. Unfortunately, I have met missionaries all over the world who stopped laughing years ago. And sure enough, they aren't very happy or fulfilled people, and they spread their misery wherever they go, causing trouble with local people, other missionaries, their own sending organization, and dwindling supporters. So, use this idea of laughing as a guide or indicator of your cross-cultural adjustment. Are you laughing yet?

During this third stage of resolution and resolve, we tend to still feel superior to the people and their culture and probably have a touch of ethnocentrism lurking in our minds. Our incarnational identification with local people has not yet happened or borne much fruit, but we are slowly making progress. We are on the road toward becoming one with the people. We are not there yet, because we still have a sense that we are better than the local people among whom we are living and serving. We still haven't come to the place where we discover how much we have to learn from them.

Also, what happens during this third stage is that we often run into newer newcomers than ourselves, and we discover that we are no longer the "new kid on the block." It is great to show someone else the ropes of how to get around in the society because suddenly we discover how much we have learned since arriving here. The best way to learn something is to teach it to others, and that dictum works in cross-cultural situations. Showing a newcomer the way around the society can build our own confidence and increase our sense of beginning to identify with the people and their culture.

This stage generally lasts between six and twelve months. The nice thing about this stage is that as time goes on, living here gets better, not worse. Eventually, we progress and move into the fourth and last stage of adjustment and adaptation.

Stage 4: Adjustment and Adaptation

Eventually, if we progress through the entire culture shock cycle, we will come to the fourth and last stage, that of adjustment and adaptation. How will we know when we are there? We enter this stage when we feel comfortable in the new culture, when we begin to feel at home and know we belong there. Feeling comfortable and at home means we have finally come through the culture shock cycle and are beginning to adjust and adapt our lifestyle to the new culture. However, just because we have come through the culture shock cycle does not mean there are no longer any challenges or difficulties ahead. The crisis of culture shock will often evolve into the experience of cultural stress, which is unlikely to disappear quickly. Consequently, complete adjustment and adaptation to a new culture takes much longer than the average two-year cycle of culture shock. Unfortunately, some people live with cultural stress their entire time of cross-cultural ministry.

Now, in this stage of adjustment and adaptation, we begin accepting the cultural differences as just another way of living in and perceiving the world—sort of a "different strokes for different folks" mentality. We take on a much more tolerant attitude toward others and their cultural differences. The anxiety from living there disappears, although there are still moments of strain. In fact, only when we have a complete grasp of all the cultural cues will the strain disappear, and that will seldom happen in the first year or two of cross-cultural ministry. In many parts of the world, it may not happen in the first three- or four-year term of service.

Stage 4, adjustment and adaptation, is the launching pad for complete incarnational identification and will likely lead to many years of effective and rewarding cross-cultural ministry. Now, with complete adjustment and adaptation, not only do we accept the food and drink and habits and customs of the people, but we actually begin to enjoy them, and we miss them when we return home and leave that culture.

Young Yun Kim discusses how we are designed and equipped as human beings to adjust and adapt to new and different cultural contexts. "Every new experience, particularly the drastic and disorienting one that strangers encounter in a new environment, leads to new learning and growth. The unique character of the human mind, after all, is its plasticity—the capacity to face challenges and, in doing so, acquire new knowledge and insights. Situations of cross-cultural adaptation bring profound and all-encompassing challenges to strangers as they soon realize that many of their previously taken-for-granted assumptions and life tools, such as language and social norms, are no longer relevant or appropriate" (2001, 45–46). It can give us hope to know that, despite how we may feel during the doldrums of the stage of hostility and disenchantment, we have the capacity to adjust and adapt. Some go through this stage more easily than others, but everyone can learn the skills of cross-cultural adjustment and adaptation.

This concludes our discussion of the four stages of culture shock, but let me make a few comments before we look at the cures for culture shock in the next chapter. I'm often asked if children go through the same stages of culture shock as do adults. They do, but because children are often quicker to learn the local language and to understand the culture and perhaps to make friends, they often move through the stages more quickly than adults, and they frequently don't sink as low in their level of satisfaction as their parents do. It is important that we are aware that our children will experience culture shock, and we need to explain to them the process and the stages they will go through.

You may wonder if you will go through culture shock only once. I wish that were the case, but it isn't. If you come home for a year-long home assignment and then return to your host society for another term, you will certainly go through culture shock again. I have occasionally been told by missionaries that sometimes the cultural adjustment in a second term is even more difficult than in the first. When this happens, I think it is because we are not as geared up emotionally and spiritually to deal with the cross-cultural differences because we have already been through that once. This, unfortunately, gives us false confidence, and our lack of preparation can trigger the culture shock cycle. We do tend to go through culture shock again, but we usually move through the cycle more quickly and with less depression and discouragement.

Reverse Culture Shock

There is another type of culture shock about which people forget to tell us. This is the culture shock that occurs when we return home. It suddenly hits us and catches us unaware or unprepared. What has changed while we have been away from home for a few years? Everything! Certainly, our home culture has changed. Clothing styles have undergone a change, our relationships have changed, the churches with whom we have been connected have changed, and so forth. But perhaps even more importantly, we have changed. We have another language to think in, an expanded worldview, new relationships, and probably a shift in our values, hopefully toward more kingdom ones. So we come back home as a changed person to a culture different from what we knew before, and that is a recipe for culture shock.

Frequently when we return home, we are excited to share our experience with friends and family, but five minutes into the conversation, they are anxious to show us the new sofa they bought on sale last month or to discuss some other mundane topic. They don't seem interested in learning about our experiences, or in much of the rest of the world, for that matter. They seem so provincial, so parochial, and it drives us crazy!

R. W. Brislin and H. VanBuren, in an interesting article titled "Can They Go Home Again?" (1974), suggest that individuals who have readily absorbed the host culture's meaning system will have greater difficulty reentering their home culture. In addition, they suggest that readiness to return home also affects the reentry experience, with those most ready to return having the least difficulty. So, our reward for becoming incarnational and adjusting well to our host culture is that when we return home, we'll be miserable, at least for a while. If we haven't adapted to our host culture very well, then we'll probably return home and slip back into our home culture rather easily and without too much trauma.[4]

What causes this reverse culture shock, and why is it often more severe than the culture shock we experience when we go to a new culture for the first time? When we come home, we begin the same process of going through all four stages, beginning with an initial tourist stage of excitement when we step out of the airplane. We're glad to be "home," and we're looking forward to telling our friends and family and supporters about our cross-cultural ministry experience. For some, the tourist stage of being home can last for quite a while, but for others, it comes to an abrupt end when they encounter some aspect of their home culture that now seems repugnant to them. For North Americans, it could be our grocery stores with their overabundance of choices. It could be the worship services that feel comparatively dull and dead. It could occur by reading the newspaper or watching the evening news on television and seeing so little international coverage.

In light of this nearly inevitable problem of reverse culture shock, it may be wise to rethink the standard missionary practice of four years in cross-cultural ministry and then a year on home assignment, or what we used to call furlough. If you're going to come home for a full year, it will be nearly impossible to stay in the tourist stage the entire time. For many people today, the home assignment is a very short period, frequently three months or less. The yearlong furlough is an artifact of the nineteenth century, when missionaries traveled by ship and the trip could take several months. The advantage of this pattern (more frequent and shorter visits to our home culture) over the old one (year-long furloughs) is that it is less disruptive to your work if you leave it for shorter periods of time, and it also reduces the risk of falling into the second stage of culture shock during your time back in your home country. In other words, it is possible to spend your entire home assignment or furlough in the tourist stage. When I was living in Africa, I heard a young missionary kid once say, "When I grow up, I want to be a missionary on furlough!"

It generally takes us a year or two to get over reverse culture shock. We normally pass through all the stages until we reach adjustment, but then we often make an interesting and sometimes unsettling discovery. We are not able to completely adjust to our home culture. There are aspects of it that seem out of sync with our values after our cross-cultural experience. I remember when we left Papua New Guinea to return to the United States, where I began teaching in the E. Stanley Jones School of World Mission at Asbury Theological Seminary in the small college town of Wilmore, Kentucky. I went through all the stages of

---

4. For an in-depth study of reentry, see Greenwood 1992.

reverse culture shock in about two years, but at the end of that period, I realized that I didn't completely belong anywhere. I was no longer 100 percent North American, and I hadn't become Melanesian or African or Asian, even though we had some wonderful experiences in their countries. I had gained a whole new sense of identity from this cross-cultural experience in Melanesia, and I now saw myself more as a citizen of the world and a child of the kingdom of God than as an American Free Methodist. In other words, my American patriotism and denominational loyalty had now taken a back seat to a wider and deeper understanding of who I was as a child of God in the world.

The good news when we are experiencing the painful throes of culture shock is that in time this too will pass and that we are normal human beings, not incompetent freaks, as we might have first assumed. There are also some "cures" and strategies that can shorten the duration of culture shock and lessen its severity. We will turn in the next chapter to discussing four things we can do to reduce the negative impact that culture shock may have on us.

CHAPTER SUMMARY

Cross-cultural witnesses experience culture shock when they live in a place that is different from their home. The problem is that it often catches them by surprise; they wonder what is happening to them and why they are feeling so depressed, irritable, and even hostile toward the very people they have come to serve. When we recognize the symptoms of culture shock and have an awareness of the stages we go through in overcoming it, then we are better prepared to deal with it and take steps to overcome it.

In this chapter I have highlighted three primary symptoms of culture shock: rising stress, physical illness, and psychological and spiritual depression. These symptoms are interrelated in our bodies, but I've focused considerably on an increase in stress when we live cross-culturally because stress contributes to physical illness and depression. A number of lists have been included in this chapter to enable the reader to identify any symptoms they may be experiencing as evidence of culture shock they may have had in the past or are experiencing in the present.

I also noted the four stages that a person suffering from culture shock typically goes through over a two-year period. When we first enter a culture different from our own, it is an exciting and wonderful phase, and we may initially feel like tourists, taking everything in and relishing the new sights and sounds, trying new foods, and having other adventures. It's a wonderful time but usually lasts only a few weeks or perhaps as long as a few months. And then comes the second stage, which is the opposite of the first stage. Now we can become disenchanted with all that is new, and we may sink into depression. This is the stage we usually identify as "culture shock" because it is such a shock to our minds, spirits, and bodies. This stage can last from six to twelve months before we enter the third stage of resolution and resolve. In the third stage our satisfaction with life in our new culture grows over time, and we are reminded that we are going to be able to survive because Jesus promised he would be with us. We begin to learn more of the language, understand the nuances of the culture better, develop local friendships, and gain some cultural competence.[5] Those who are cross-cultural witnesses are reminded that God has called us to this ministry and will not abandon us. This helps us become resilient. Within another year or so most people move to the fourth stage of adjustment and adaptation. We begin to feel at home and know we belong here. We adjust our lifestyle to one that is appropriate for our new context, and over time we become bicultural as well as bilingual. We will know that we have arrived at the fourth stage when we feel comfortable in the new culture.

Finally, this chapter discussed the importance of knowing about and learning how to respond to reverse culture shock, which begins when we leave our host society and return to our home culture. Those who do the best at identifying and relating to their host culture are frequently "rewarded" by having the most difficult time readjusting to their home culture. Nevertheless, with time we can also overcome reverse culture shock as we frequently have similar symptoms and go through stages that we experienced in our initial episode of culture shock in our host society. The good news about culture shock is that we can overcome it. In the next chapter we will discuss how to cope with the occupational disease of culture shock that cross-cultural witnesses experience.

---

5. For helpful suggestions on acquiring cultural competence in cross-cultural situations, see the work of David Livermore (2009, 2015, 2022) on developing cultural intelligence.

11

Cures for Culture Shock

Sitting for a long time will give the opportunity to kill the bush cow. (Patience will be rewarded.)

Builsa proverb, Ghana

If culture shock is an occupational disease, as I have argued, and if it typically progresses through a cycle of four rather clearly defined but sometimes overlapping stages, and if there are identifiable symptoms that one may have, then surely there must be some cures for and ways of managing the culture shock that one experiences in cross-cultural situations. Kalervo Oberg, at the conclusion of his groundbreaking article on culture shock, says, "The question now arises, 'What can you do to get over culture shock as quickly as possible?' The answer is to get to know the people of the host country" (1960, 182). Throughout this book, I have been guided by the concept of incarnational identification as a way to connect with people who are different from us. Incarnational identification is not only a solid biblical model for cross-cultural ministry but also a sound anthropological approach to understanding and living with people who are different from us.

Anthropologist Michael Winkelman notes that "because cultural shock derives from the distress of intercultural contact experiences, those abilities that make an individual effective in intercultural communication and adaptation should also reduce culture shock, especially those aspects that reduce primary aspects of culture shock: stress reactions, communication problems, disrupted interpersonal and social relations" (1994, 125). Intercultural effectiveness is required to overcome the difficulties of culture shock. This includes "the ability to deal with psychological stress, the ability to communicate effectively, the ability to establish interpersonal relationships, the ability to understand and adjust to another culture, and the ability to deal with different social systems" (125).

Although there is no mathematical formula to determine who is more apt to have intercultural effectiveness, there is research that helps give us an idea of a person's likeliness to succeed cross-culturally. Sonja Manz, in "Culture Shock—Causes, Consequences and Solutions: The International Experience," offers eight dimensions that serve as a basis for evaluating a person's aptitude for intercultural effectiveness (2003, 6; Apfelthaler 1999, 111).

1. *Ethnocentrism*: adjustment is endangered by the attitude toward the culture of origin and the rejection of the host culture.
2. *Intercultural experience*: the adjustment process appears to be easier for individuals who have gone through culture shock and adaptation before.
3. *Cognitive flex*: open-mindedness toward foreign attitudes, ideas, and environments lowers the effects of culture shock.
4. *Behavioral flex*: the ability to change one's behavior is a positive factor for acculturation.
5. *General intercultural knowledge*: a general awareness of cultural differences facilitates adjustment.
6. *Specific intercultural knowledge*: specific knowledge about the characteristics of a certain culture decreases culture shock.
7. *Adequate behavior*: the capability to adjust behavior toward the host culture makes adaptation easier.
8. *Interpersonal skills*: skills in verbal and nonverbal communication and the ability to react accordingly support efficient adaptation.

Paul Hiebert suggests four major ways to manage the experience of culture shock and overcome this difficult occupational disease (1985, 80–85). They are:

1. Recognize our anxieties
2. Learn the new culture
3. Build trust
4. Deal with stress

We will discuss each of these in turn.

Recognize Our Anxieties

We need to recognize our anxieties, to identify them and name them. It is perfectly normal for us to be afraid of new situations because of the uncertainties they contain. In the long run, however, fear can turn into anxiety, and this is where the trouble starts. Hiebert says that anxiety is a feeling of uneasiness and dread of some vague unknown danger (1985, 81). It is the anxiety, and not the specific fear, that is the most damaging part of culture shock, because the anxiety can eventually lead to depression. If we can pinpoint our anxieties, if we can recognize them, then we can deal with them. We'll find three things are often true about these anxieties.

First, many of our anxieties are unfounded. There's just no basis in fact for feeling anxious. For example, parents who are preparing to live in another country may have some legitimate concerns about their children's health, education, and safety, but sometimes their concerns evolve into unfounded anxiety. I remember one missionary telling me that they felt anxious after being told there was no toilet paper in Tanzania, so they filled their crate with toilet paper. Imagine their surprise when they got to Dar es Salaam and found toilet paper for sale everywhere. Perhaps it wasn't their favorite brand of soft tissue, but toilet paper was available!

Second, when we learn to live in the new culture and identify with the local people, many of our anxieties will simply disappear. This of course takes time. Many of our anxieties come because of a lack of knowledge, and so we make unfounded assumptions about the place we are going to live. Remember, an assumption is the lowest form of knowledge. When we start to learn the language and figure out how to survive in this new culture, many of the things we were worried about will disappear and our anxiety will dissipate.

Third, when we adjust our lifestyle to one that is more appropriate for the context, even more of our anxieties will disappear. It is amazing how we create so many unnecessary anxieties because of the way we live, the stuff we feel we must have, the house in which we think we need to live, the schools to which we believe we should send our kids, and on and on. I know of a missionary who went to one of the poorest countries in the Western Hemisphere. He took all his stuff with him—his DVD player, television, stereo equipment, laptop computer, microwave, electric can opener, and other electronic gadgets. When he arrived and discovered the abject poverty all around him, he was afraid he would be robbed. So he kept his house closed up and would not let local people enter for fear they would see all his stuff, word would spread about what he had, and before he knew it, he would be robbed. By not living at a level appropriate for that cultural context, he created a situation that increased his anxiety. He was so worried about protecting his stuff that he was not emotionally available for effective ministry. This is one of the biggest problems with taking too many possessions with us into cross-cultural ministry—they end up possessing us. We worry about protecting them, a lot of time and energy go into that activity, and we create a lot of unnecessary anxiety.

Simply knowing what culture shock is and the various stages we will go through will help us know that we are normal and will enable us to deal with our anxieties instead of covering them up. Ultimately, we cannot cover up our anxieties because they will get back at us in the form of illness. We have to raise them to a level of conscious awareness, discuss them, and then deal with them. Cross-cultural counseling can be very helpful in enabling us to do this.

Learn the New Culture

From the beginning of this book, I have stressed the importance of learning the new culture to be effective in cross-cultural ministry. But it turns out that learning the new culture is also a very helpful cure for culture shock. It is important to distinguish between learning the local language and learning the culture. Many mission organizations are more concerned with learning the language than they are with learning the culture. Most don't even give lip service to learning the culture, let alone take it seriously.

I think one reason this happens is because, as cross-cultural witnesses, we believe we have a vital message to communicate, and so our goal is to learn the local language so that we can get our message into the minds and hearts of our hearers. Unfortunately, we seldom recognize the importance of also understanding their culture. Until we really understand their culture, we may be masters at speaking their language, but we'll still miscommunicate. We need to understand the depths of their culture in addition to speaking their language fluently if we are going to be as effective as possible in communicating. Language learning is vital, but it is only the first step.

One of the goals of this book is to foster a positive attitude in those who are preparing for cross-cultural ministry so that when they arrive in a new place, they have a sense of excitement and anticipation regarding all the new things they will learn rather than a fear of the unknown. If our fear is greater than our excitement over learning new things in the culture, then we'll tend to hang out with people who are like us. They will become our friends instead of local people. It is not unusual to have a lot of fear when we first enter a new culture because we have little knowledge of what is happening. However, as we slowly start to learn more and more, our fears will decrease, and before long we will be up and running in the culture. When this happens, we gain confidence, which releases more energy for more involvement in the culture. With more involvement comes more confidence, and a positive reinforcing cycle is initiated.

Now, what is the best way to learn the new language and culture? Before we depart our home culture and arrive in our host's society, it is helpful to learn what we can through formal classes, reading books and articles on the culture and people, and watching videos. However, the best way to learn is to plunge in and get involved with the local people immediately. We learned our first language and culture through involvement with people, and this is how we'll learn a second language and culture. This may not be as easy to do as it first appears, because this is also the time when we will be going through culture shock, and we'll want to withdraw from the culture rather than engage in it.

I remember a missionary who was studying French in France in preparation to serve in a French-speaking country. I spoke with her after three months of French language study to see how she was doing. She was struggling, feeling as if she wasn't learning anything and on the verge of panic. I asked her to walk me through a typical twenty-four-hour period, and minutes into our conversation, it became clear what the major problem was. After language school, she would retreat to the safety and comfort of her apartment. She did not go out and interact with French people because "It was so hard." I told her she would have to break that pattern if she was ever going to get her mind around French to the point where she thought and dreamed in French, but unfortunately, she didn't.

I'll never forget our first days in the village of Gnulahage on Santa Isabel in the Solomon Islands. Because I am such an introvert, it is really hard for me to make small talk. In fact, it's almost impossible. And when you're trying to make small talk in another culture using a language you don't understand well, it can be really stressful and very hard work. I found myself quickly slipping back into my comfort zone and predictable mode of reading books about Solomon Islanders and fieldwork methods instead of actually doing the fieldwork. Fortunately, my wife intervened. She helped me see what I was doing and encouraged (made?) me to get out of our grass hut and to start talking and interacting with the villagers. Doing so was really painful, but slowly I began to make sense out of the culture and learn more of the language. Despite years of training and preparation for doing anthropological fieldwork, it was still a very frightening experience for me. But much to my delight, my involvement increased my confidence, which released more energy for interacting with the villagers. Eventually, I put away my books and began learning directly from the people, and this turned out to be a very helpful cure for dealing with my culture shock.

Build Trust

Building trust is a third cure for culture shock. Hiebert notes that learning the new culture is not enough, as important as it is. We can learn the new culture, but the people may still view us with suspicion (1985, 83). Marvin K. Mayers, in his book *Christianity Confronts Culture*, writes about the importance of building trust in cross-cultural ministry. He discusses what he calls the "PQT," the prior question of trust, which is absolutely crucial to overcoming culture shock and to developing an effective cross-cultural ministry (1974, 31–35). We build trust by becoming vulnerable, by being consistent, by delivering what we promise. One of the ways to build trust is by trusting others with our things, with our money, with our children, with our lives. I believe that we are given opportunities nearly every day to build trust with local people. Sometimes they come to us unexpectedly.

One of those unexpected opportunities came to us one day when we were living in the village of Gnulahage in the Solomon Islands. Our neighbor, who was also the village catechist for the village Anglican Church, came to us and said he and his family would like to take our nearly three-year-old son with them to a day-long church celebration in a village about a two-hour walk away. We asked our son if he wanted to go, and he was delighted. So our neighbor strapped him onto his back and disappeared into the jungle. Our son had the time of his life that day, but what we did not realize is that the experience helped create an incredible amount of trust. By entrusting our son to their safekeeping, we built trust with them. Three weeks later, we were given another opportunity to build trust. Our son came down with a bad case of thrush, a yeast infection in the mouth that he had picked up from playing with other children in the village. As it grew progressively worse, he couldn't eat or drink anything, and the villagers began to worry. After a few days, some men came to us and said, "We have a remedy for this. It is traditional medicine that we make by combining the leaves from three different plants into a potion that cures this problem every time. We'd like to make it and give it to your son." I responded, "Thanks for your concern, but I think he's going to be okay." The next day he was getting worse, but I was still reluctant to trust their "medicine." They offered a second time, and I politely refused. By the third time they offered to help, I realized the Lord was trying to teach us something about trusting these villagers, and so I agreed to accept their medicine. Off they went into the jungle in search of medicinal plants to prepare the medicine. They came back several hours later with their concoction wrapped in a cloth. They squeezed the liquid from the cloth into a spoon and gave our son a spoonful, then a second, and finally a third. I inquired, "Why are you giving him three spoonfuls?" They responded, "Oh, don't you know? One for the Father, one for the Son, and one for the Holy Spirit."

In the end, our son was so sick and weak that even three spoonfuls of their traditional medicine in the name of the Trinity weren't enough to combat the thrush, and it required some modern medicine from a clinic a two-hour walk away. But do you know what that experience did for my wife and me in relation to that village community? It built trust like nothing else could have. I'm convinced that God sent that into our path to test our faith, to build trust, and to deepen our relationship with the community.

Deal with Stress

The experience of culture shock creates enormous stress for us, and so one of the cures and ways to adapt is to recognize that we are under stress and then proceed to deal with it appropriately. We can't ignore it because, if we do, it will more than likely make us sick, physically as well as emotionally. Wayne Dye (1974) has written a helpful article that uncovers the stress-producing factors in cross-cultural ministry and suggests a way to deal with it. His formula shows these factors and how to reduce the resulting stress (see fig. 11.1).

Dye discusses how the factors above the line will increase the stress we experience in cross-cultural living. They are involvement, difference in values, frustration, and difference in temperament. The factors below the line will reduce the amount of stress we experience. Although this formula lacks mathematical precision, it is nevertheless a helpful guide for us to discover those things that are *increasing* our stress and to develop ways to *reduce* stress through acceptance, communication, emotional security, and inner spiritual resources. We'll briefly discuss each of the factors in this formula.

Figure 11.1
Factors Increasing and Decreasing Stress

$$\frac{\text{Involvement} \times \text{Difference in Values} \times \text{Frustration} \times \text{Difference in Temperment}}{\text{Acceptance} \times \text{Communication} \times \text{Emotional Security} \times \text{Inner Spiritual Resources}} \times \text{Unknown Factors} = \text{Amount of Cultural Stress}$$

Dye 1974, 62. Designed by BPG.

Factors That Increase Stress

Involvement. Involvement with people can sometimes be stressful, but involvement with people in another culture, especially when we do not thoroughly understand their language and culture, is even more stressful. In reaction to the stress, it is easy to withdraw and avoid interacting with local people. This may be the primary reason for the creation of what Charles Taber calls "missionary ghettos" (1971). We want to be with people like us and withdraw from those who are culturally and religiously different. However, if we are living in another culture and our goal as cross-cultural witnesses is to live out and proclaim the gospel, then we have no other option than to become involved with *people*. Tom and Betty Brewster have written a very helpful article that underscores the importance of involvement with people and their culture and that offers practical suggestions on how to proceed in learning a culture different from our own (1972).

Difference in values. As the difference in values increases between our own culture and the new culture we are in, the stress we experience also increases. I'm not referring here to central biblical values that may clash with values that are not biblical. The value differences that cause us the most difficulty are cultural values, such as cleanliness, sense of responsibility, use of time, and understanding of privacy.

An excellent source for discovering one's values in relation to those of different cultures is Sherwood Lingenfelter and Marvin Mayers's *Ministering Cross-Culturally: A Model for Effective Personal Relationships* (2016). They discuss the contrast of six value pairs: time orientation versus event orientation, task orientation versus person orientation, dichotomistic thinking versus holistic thinking, status focus versus achievement focus, crisis orientation versus non-crisis orientation, and concealment of vulnerability versus willingness to expose vulnerability. The authors have developed a forty-eight-item basic values questionnaire in the appendix that enables a person to see graphically where they stand on these six different value orientations.

Value differences between cultures can be tricky and can catch us unaware. For example, cultures that are similar in outward appearance, such as the cultures of America and Australia, may have quite different underlying values. So we plunge into the outwardly similar culture expecting the underlying values to be the same, but they are not. And this can create significant stress. If a value, such as punctuality, personal cleanliness, or privacy, is held strongly in our own culture but held lightly in another culture, then this makes our adjustment more difficult and contributes to culture shock.

Frustration. We can experience cultural frustration because we don't know the rules of the game, personal frustration with others, and the frustration of adapting and adjusting to a lifestyle different from our own. We can easily get frustrated when we arrive in a new place of ministry with clearly planned agendas and usually unrealistic goals. Interruptions in our work are normal and misunderstandings occur, but they frustrate our attempts to reach our goals. Many frustrations we bring on ourselves because our lifestyle is not appropriate for the context in which we are living and working. Other frustrations simply come with the territory of cross-cultural ministry. Unfortunately, the more frustrated we become, the more likely we are to develop negative attitudes toward the host culture and its people. This then causes us to resist learning and adapting to the culture. Consequently, we can easily fall into a vicious cycle of frustration with the culture and its people.

Difference in temperament. People with different temperaments, such as type A or type B, and different personality profiles, such as the Myers-Briggs sixteen types, will respond differently to the same cross-cultural situation. The greater the difference between our personality and the basic personality found in the host community, the more difficult our cross-cultural adjustment, which adds to our cultural stress.

Let's now turn to four factors that can reduce stress in cross-cultural ministry.

Factors That Reduce Stress

Acceptance. If we can accept the culture of our hosts as a valid way of life, then stress decreases. If, on the other hand, we believe that people cannot become followers of Jesus within their own culture, then we will probably not adjust to it and our stress will not decrease. As noted above, involvement in a culture increases stress, but if we accept that culture as valid and the people in it as valuable, then stress will be reduced. Acceptance has both a cognitive (or intellectual) dimension and an affective (or emotional) dimension. Intellectual acceptance involves seeing other customs and values as being just as valid in their context as customs and values are in our context. This requires a healthy dose of cultural relativism. This kind of understanding can be taught, and this is an area where cultural anthropology can help significantly. The affective, or emotional, component of acceptance is far more difficult to change. Many of us find it easier to be accepting of others in our minds than in our hearts. We know what it's like when people accept us cognitively but not emotionally.

Communication. If a difference in values increases cultural stress, then communication is a good way to reduce it. Communication helps bring value differences into conscious focus so that we can analyze them and adjust our thinking and behavior in order to cope. People also frequently cite isolation as a cause of stress, but further probing often reveals that they are not isolated from all people. They usually have daily contact with many. However, they may be isolated from those with whom they can relax and be themselves, with whom they share a language, values, and interests that allow them to really communicate. Dye tells of an expatriate in Papua New Guinea who said to a visitor, "You are most welcome as you are the first human being I've talked to in months" (1974, 67). This person taught dozens of national students each day and lived within a mile of ten other Westerners with a religious and cultural background different from his own, but emotionally none of them were "human beings" to him. Without communication, the sense of isolation can become almost unbearable. In addition to easing isolation, communication with our hosts reduces stress by building mutual understanding between us, which aids acceptance and minimizes frustration.

Emotional security. An important, if not crucial, personal attribute for adjusting to cultural differences is a healthy self-concept. With it and the accompanying emotional security, we are free to explore, to take risks, to venture out into the new culture and learn a new language. The greater our emotional security, the more easily we will handle the inevitable frustrations of living in another culture, which in turn will reduce our stress. Most of us derive our self-image from our occupation—what we do, not what kind of people we are. But this is an inadequate foundation on which to build a sense of who we are. The good news is that, as followers of Jesus, our emotional security rests in our identity as children of God created in the image of God.

Inner spiritual resources. The power of Christ and his Spirit is an important factor in reducing stress. We are reminded of this in 2 Peter 1:3: "We have everything we need to live a life that pleases God. It was all given to us by God's own power" (CEV). And Philippians 4:13 says, "Christ gives me the strength to face anything" (CEV). Spiritual resources won't change our personality and temperament, but they will help us deal better with the stress that arises from the differences in temperament between us and those with whom we live and minister.

Dye's formula for assessing the amount of cultural stress we may experience in cross-cultural ministry is a very helpful tool we can use for personal reflection. Dealing with stress is a key "cure" for culture shock.

Final Thoughts on Culture Shock

When we discuss culture shock as one of the inevitable factors in cross-cultural ministry, we nearly always think of it in negative terms. And there are good reasons for that, as we have discussed in looking at the stages and symptoms of culture shock. It can be painful emotionally and even physically, leaving us bewildered and confused at times. However, I think going through culture shock can also be a positive experience for cross-cultural witnesses. How is that possible? For one thing, it reminds us that we are totally dependent on God. The experience also strengthens our resilience to face difficult and challenging times in the future. I have experienced culture shock many times, and when I'm going through it, I know I will arrive at the end of the experience stronger and better prepared for future ministry.

Figure 11.2 captures many of the elements we have discussed in this section on culture shock. I have used it often in my teaching and training of cross-cultural witnesses.

As we observed in chapter 2, we are products of the culture in which we were raised. So when we enter another culture, we take our cultural baggage with us. That baggage includes our lifestyle, identity, values, relationships, and routines, among other factors that give us a sense of who we are and why we are here.

How we approach cultural differences in the culture to which we go and live is critical. Note that we will inevitably experience frustration, confusion, tension, and embarrassment simply because the culture is different from our own. However, if we take the approach of incarnational identification and relate to people with an attitude of openness, acceptance, and trust, then we will more likely choose to observe, listen, and inquire as a coping strategy. These are all good anthropological tools for learning from and relating to people who are different from us. And look at the likely results: rapport and understanding, exactly the outcome we want for effective cross-cultural ministry. With rapport and understanding, we will adjust to the culture and overcome culture shock much more quickly.

Unfortunately, because of our ethnocentrism (believing that our culture and way of life are better than others), we too often approach cultural differences with fear, suspicion, and prejudice. We of course experience frustration, confusion, tension, and embarrassment as the inevitable fact of living cross-culturally. Our "coping strategies" will include criticizing, rationalizing, and withdrawing, and, of course, choosing those strategies will lead to alienation and isolation from the very people we came to serve. How unfortunate, and yet I have observed and interviewed many missionaries who were not able to adjust to the culture, and their ministry has suffered.

In my many years of interviewing and researching missionaries' cross-cultural adjustment, I have found that when these cures for culture shock are put in place, they enable those people experiencing culture shock to move through the cycle more quickly and easily. This in turn builds a foundation for further cross-cultural adjustment and dealing with cultural stress.

Figure 11.2
Crossing Cultural Boundaries

A person grows up looking very much like the cultural background in which he or she was raised. If your cultural background is a "square," as mine was, you turn out to be a square. If it is "round," you are round.

When you leave the safety of your own culture and enter another, you do not leave your cultural baggage behind. You take it with you. And you may feel like the proverbial "square peg in a round hole."

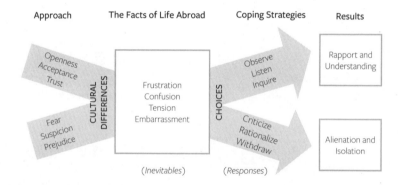

But you can adjust; you can fit in. You can adapt yourself in this new culture. Some make the transition effectively and gradually identify more and more with the people. Some fail to adapt (which means the people must adjust to them).

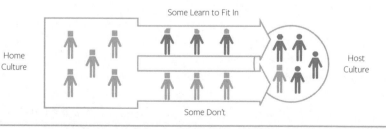

Adapted from D. Elmer 2002, 66, 72. Designed by BPG.

Crossing cultures effectively with the gospel requires us to adjust and adapt to the culture and to cultural differences within our host society. Drawing on Hiebert's work, I want to conclude this chapter by discussing how we can adjust to the culture in which we are living and serving as cross-cultural witnesses (1985, 76).

One way is to physically live in the society but to remain isolated culturally and socially. If we are Americans, one way to "adjust" is to keep our distance, build an American ghetto, and spend most of our time with other Americans. United States military bases all over the world are proof of this. One can spend twenty years in the military, moving from one base to another around the world, and never leave America culturally and socially. We are even transported from one base to another in a culturally "hermetically sealed" airplane or ship and never have to deal with the local culture and its people and language. It is not only North Americans who use this form of cross-cultural adjustment. I have observed it in Koreans and others. Similarly, cross-cultural witnesses can live on a mission compound and make periodic forays into the local culture to do ministry. Although the classic nineteenth- and early twentieth-century missionary compounds do not exist like they used to, missionaries can still create culturally equivalent compounds through social media, spending hours "hanging out" with others who are like them. That, of course, is seldom effective. There are people who still argue about why we should live on missionary compounds separated from the local people, but I think most of those arguments are bogus. If you find that your mission organization has assigned you to live on a compound because there is no other inexpensive housing available, take every opportunity you have to get off the compound and into the lives and homes of local people and their culture. This form of "adjustment"—keeping ourselves isolated from the people—seldom works well, if at all.

A second form of "adjustment" is to do the very opposite and reject our past and who we are and go native. By now you may be thinking that this is the way to become incarnational. I must respond with a resounding no! We seldom find missionaries who try to go native, but occasionally some think they have.

Perhaps the best example is Dr. Charles Fox (1878–1977), a New Zealander who spent seventy years in the Solomon Islands with the Anglican Melanesian Mission. Fox was a missionary's missionary, learning several Melanesian languages fluently, loving the people, and identifying with them. I had read all of Fox's books (1910, 1924, 1958, 1962) before I met him in person and interviewed him in Napier, New Zealand, in February 1977, when he was ninety-eight years old. Fox lived another six months after our interview. He made it to his ninety-ninth birthday on October 1, 1977, and then died twenty-eight days later on Saint Simon and Saint Jude Day. This was an auspicious day for Charles Fox to die, for it was the day of celebrating the founding of the Melanesian Brotherhood, an evangelistic and missionary wing of the Melanesian Mission.[1] Fox was the only European to ever join the Melanesian Brotherhood. His body was brought back to the Solomon Islands, where my wife and I were fortunate to attend his funeral and burial. In our interview, Fox had tried to impress on me how he had become a Solomon Islander, so when I got to the Solomon Islands, following my archival research in New Zealand, I asked around about Dr. Fox. I inquired of Solomon Islanders everywhere I went, "Did Dr. Fox become a Solomon Islander? Did he become one of you?" People would often smile and say, "No, he didn't. He always remained a New Zealander who loved English potatoes and ice cream, but he came closer to identifying with us than any other European missionary, and we loved him for it." Now, if Fox couldn't go native after seventy years of cross-cultural ministry, what is the chance that we can do so after only seven years (the average length of service for a career missionary in 2022) or even after seventeen or twenty-seven years?

In the end, this kind of "adjustment"—trying to go native—doesn't work. If we try to deny who we are, then it takes away from our effectiveness as an outside person and as a bridge to another culture for the people among whom we are living and serving. It is obvious that trying to go native is not a solution to the challenge of cross-cultural adjustment.

A third kind of "adjustment" is compartmentalization. "Compartmentalization" means that we live in different worlds and keep them separate in our minds. So the adage "When in Rome, do as the Romans do" captures this idea. But compartmentalization is just a temporary fix and doesn't lead to the best solution, which is the fourth way of adjusting.

A fourth way of adjusting is to identify with the culture and to work for some type of integration with our own. When this happens, we become bicultural, not culturally schizophrenic. We will deal in depth with the process of becoming bicultural in chapter 14. Meanwhile, figure 11.2 reminds us that if our goal as cross-cultural witnesses is to effectively cross cultural boundaries with the gospel, then we must develop rapport and understanding with those among whom we live and serve. This is more likely to occur if we approach cultural differences with openness, acceptance, and trust. May God help us to do so.

---

1. On the Melanesian Brotherhood as an indigenous evangelist movement in the Melanesian Mission, see Whiteman 1983, 194–98. On Charles Fox as an empathetic missionary, see Whiteman 1983, 214–17.

CHAPTER SUMMARY

Anthropologist Kalervo Oberg reminded us early in this chapter that the best way to get over culture shock is to get to know the people among whom we are living. So I have suggested four cures that will help us overcome the debilitating effects of culture shock and get to know the people we're living among: recognize our anxieties, learn the new culture, build trust with local people, and deal with stress instead of ignoring it or trying to cover it up. I suggested that even though the experience of culture shock is often unpleasant, it nevertheless can ultimately become a positive experience by reminding us that we are totally dependent on God. The experience of culture shock can also strengthen our resilience to face difficult or challenging times in the future. Finally, we looked briefly at four ways cross-cultural witnesses have attempted to adjust to living in a different culture, and we concluded that only incarnational identification with the culture and integrating it with our own will produce a long-lasting "cure" to coping with culture shock.

CONCLUSION TO PART 4

A major challenge for cross-cultural witnesses is dealing with culture shock, which inevitably affects everyone who enters a culture that is different from their own. In my teaching and training through the years, I have given an inordinate amount of time and space to this topic because it is so pervasive and has contributed to many cross-cultural witnesses coming home earlier than they expected. In researching the cross-cultural adjustment of missionaries, I have found that many did not realize that it was primarily culture shock causing their negative attitudes toward their host society and contributing to their psychological and spiritual depression. Over the years I have received many letters and emails from cross-cultural witnesses saying that what they learned about culture shock and how to overcome it saved their first term of service. I therefore felt compelled to give considerable space in this book to discussing culture shock. We are now ready to turn to the last part of this book and focus on how we can become more effective cross-cultural witnesses.

PART 5

Growing into Effective Communicators

12

Discovering Cultural Differences

Small, small, catches the monkey's tail. (Tackle something step by step, and you will accomplish it.)

Builsa proverb, Ghana

I remember the day well. We were walking back from the clinic at the administrative center on the island of Santa Isabel. It was a two-hour walk through the jungle to our village of Gnulahage on a hot and humid day, but no one was in a hurry. We had the rest of the day to get back home. I had accompanied some villagers to the clinic because one of them was quite ill. As we walked, we talked.

As I overheard their conversation, I realized that they held both a medical understanding and a magical interpretation of what had caused the illness. This really surprised me, because these Solomon Islanders had been Anglican Christians for a couple generations, and I erroneously assumed that any belief in or practice of magic had disappeared, along with headhunting, a couple generations earlier. So I ventured to ask, "Do you practice ritual magic for healing?" They were surprised at my rather forthright question. I learned later that this was something people never talked about in church. They answered my question with a question of their own: "Do you believe in magic?"

I knew that my response to their question was critical. If I answered, "Of course not. That's just silly superstition," then I would shut down any further discussion, and I was there to discover how Christianity functioned in the life of their village. I knew I had to answer their question truthfully, but I also had to do it in a way that would enable them to feel free and safe in revealing their understanding of the supernatural world to me. I responded, "I believe magic is real, but I don't practice it. I would like to understand and learn more about how you perceive and practice magic." Then came the surprising retort from one of the villagers as he declared with a bit of nervous laughter, "If you like our magic, then you're really going to like our experience of ancestral spirits."

That brief exchange walking back to their village together opened the door for me to learn much more about their understanding of the spiritual world and how their Anglican Christianity related to it. I had to create a safe and welcoming environment and build a bridge of trust over which they could travel as they revealed more about their life and culture. I have often thanked God for giving me the right attitude and the right words at that propitious moment. That encounter was possible because in my training as an anthropologist, I had learned how to discover cultural differences, the topic of this chapter.

I have argued throughout this book that understanding cultural differences is very important in shaping how we relate to and interact with people. It is often cultural differences that trip us up and render our ministry ineffective. So how can we discover these significant and sometimes subtle cultural differences? To do that we need to learn how to listen well, observe accurately, and inquire insightfully; to make and record accurate observations; to ask good questions; and to draw accurate and reliable conclusions from what we hear and see.

In this chapter, we will discuss the anthropological research method of participant observation as a great way to connect with others in cultures that are so different from our own. We'll introduce the idea of doing ethnographic research and becoming good ethnographers as part of the lifestyle of cross-cultural witnesses. This involves asking good questions and listening well, observing and recording, and writing field notes. Finally, we'll discuss the importance of adopting the perspective and posture of cultural relativism that is necessary to combat our implicit ethnocentrism, which can block us from seeing the world through the eyes of those who are culturally different from us.

An anthropological approach to cross-cultural ministry gives us some helpful tools to discover and analyze our own culture and the culture of others. We must learn to do both. We need to understand our own culture and worldview and its impact on how we view others, read and interpret Scripture, and become followers of Jesus. But we also need to grasp the nature of others' culture and how their social location, gender, economic status, and history have created them to be who they are.

Because cross-cultural witnesses in this era of globalization and urbanization are going from every place to everywhere, the cultures they encounter are always changing, and sometimes rapidly. No longer is mission just from the West to the Rest. Kima Pachuau underscores this reality when he observes,

"It is intriguing to note that around the same time that missions conceptually changed from being a 'foreign' enterprise of the Western churches to the 'world mission' of the global church in the 1960s, Christians from Africa, Asia, and Latin America began to engage actively in missional new efforts" (2018, 150).

It is my fervent hope that this book will be useful in preparing and encouraging cross-cultural witnesses from cultures across the globe. Because mission activity is occurring from every place to everywhere and the context of mission is often changing, preparation for cross-cultural ministry requires more than simply the accumulation of specific knowledge about a people and a place, which may not be relevant for any length of time. Therefore, instead of acquiring a vast array of knowledge, we are further ahead if we teach cross-cultural witnesses how to discover and understand local cultures, probe the depths of the local religion, analyze local society and the interaction of its component parts—ideology, economy and technology, and social relations (discussed previously in chapter 3)—and discover their place within it as a cross-cultural witness.

Anthropologist Michael Rynkiewich argues that teaching and training cross-cultural witnesses in missiological content is necessary but not sufficient preparation (2020). No amount of cultural and historical content learned through formal training can prepare future missionaries for every inevitable challenge they will face or the constantly changing cultural context in which they will serve. He notes, "If I cannot prepare my students for every eventuality in the culture where they are going to be in mission, then I can reduce the content and train people in critical analytical skills, both in ethnography and in historical analysis. That is, teach them to do research so that they can figure it out for themselves" (343).

The field of anthropology provides us with a unique, holistic perspective on humanity and has developed research methods to explore human beings in their various cultural contexts. We begin with the primary method used in anthropology to discover cultural differences: participant observation.

Participant Observation

In the early days of developing the field of anthropology in the mid- to late nineteenth century, anthropologists gathered information primarily from world travelers, such as explorers, missionaries, colonial administrators, and others who would bring back reports of exotic people and places. These "armchair" social theorists wouldn't deign to go and actually live among the people they were studying. However, that aloof approach to research began to change when anthropologist Bronislaw Malinowski went to New Guinea just as World War I was breaking out in 1914. Because he was Polish and not a British citizen, he could not return to Britain, where he was earning his PhD in anthropology. So the Australian government enabled him to live among the Trobriand Islanders in Melanesia for several years, participating in their life while observing and collecting data that would result in an influential ethnography called *Argonauts of the Western Pacific*, published in 1922. Inadvertently, Malinowski introduced the concept of participant observation as an important research method, which involves extended immersion in a culture and participation in its day-to-day activities. In the United States, Franz Boas, who is regarded as the father of academic anthropology in America, sent his students, such as Margaret Mead and Alfred Kroeber, to live among the people they were studying.[1]

Anthropologist Kenneth Guest notes, "The practice of participant observation over time entails building deep relationships with people from another culture and directly engages the ethnographer in the life of the community" (2018, 79). Participant observation enables us to begin to see and understand the world from another's point of view. It is now a well-established anthropological research methodology that is particularly well suited for cross-cultural witnesses, enabling them to come into the lives of others and uncover important cross-cultural differences. Howell and Paris underscore why this is such an important method for understanding cultural differences: "Participant observation and its related methods highlight the extent to which cultural anthropology focuses on small-scale cases—villages, clubs, neighborhoods, congregations, families. The anthropologist draws on many aspects of life to create a holistic understanding of the situation. A holistic understanding assumes that all parts of human life—from birthing practices to the economy to warfare to art—are interconnected" (2019, 13).

Anthropologist Harry Wolcott, in his important book on ethnographic research, notes that "participant observation is founded on firsthand experience in naturally occurring events. Today, we no longer have to pretend to a level of objectivity that was once fashionable; it is sufficient to recognize and reveal our subjectivity as best we can, thus to maximize the potential of fieldwork as personal experience rather than to deny it" (2008, 49). Anthropologists Kathleen DeWalt and Billie DeWalt underscore the naturalness of participant observation when they note that "a good deal of what we learn in the field is tacit. The process of participant observation is, in part, a process of *enculturation*. The researcher gradually absorbs the big picture and some of the details that lead

1. One of the more sophisticated yet practical approaches to participant observation and ethnographic interviewing is the method of componential analysis used by Spradley in his books *The Ethnographic Interview* (2016) and *Participant Observation* (2016). These books are practical, self-teaching handbooks that guide readers step-by-step through the process of making observations and writing an ethnography of the people among whom they are living and serving.

to an understanding of people's daily lives, structure of events, social structure and expectations and values" (2011, 80). Participant observation seems like an ideal and natural way for cross-cultural witnesses to discover cultural differences. Anthropologists have identified several levels of participation in a culture, along with corresponding limitations, in order to understand cultural differences. The range is from nonparticipation to complete participation, as the table below demonstrates.[2]

Participant Observation

Type	Level of Involvement	Limitations
Nonparticipation	Researcher has no contact with the population or field of study.	The researcher is unable to build rapport or ask questions as new information comes up.
Passive Participation	Researcher is only in the bystander role.	This limits the ability to establish rapport and immerse oneself in the field.
Moderate Participation	Researcher maintains a balance between "insider" and "outsider" roles.	This allows a good combination of involvement and necessary detachment to remain objective.
Active Participation	Researcher becomes a member of the group by fully embracing skills and customs for the sake of complete comprehension.	This method permits the researcher to become more involved in the population. There is a risk of going native as the researcher strives for an in-depth understanding of the population studied.
Complete Participation	Researcher is completely integrated in the population of study beforehand (i.e., they are already a member of the particular population being studied).	There is the risk of losing all levels of objectivity, thus risking what is analyzed and presented to the public.

Which of these levels are most appropriate for cross-cultural witnesses as they try to discover cross-cultural differences among the people with whom they are living and serving? Another way of asking the question is, "Which of these levels of participation are the most incarnational?"

Howell and Paris capture well what Laurie and I experienced:

For Christian anthropologists, participant observation can be a spiritual practice. Anthropological research is never distant or detached. Like Jesus's ministry, anthropological research involves being close to people, speaking their language,

2. This table is based on Wikipedia, s.v. "Participant Observation." See also Emerson, Fretz, and Shaw 2001.

eating their food, participating in their weddings and funerals, and caring about their concerns. In a sense, Jesus could even be described as God doing participant observation. In Jesus, God came to live among us and experience our lives as we do. Of course, just as the anthropologist retains elements of her or his own distinctive identities, so Jesus was still Other (divine), even as he shared fully in our humanity. Although an anthropologist never "incarnates" from one context to another, like Jesus anyone can draw closer in understanding and love through participating as fully as possible in another's world. Jesus's life and ministry provide wonderful inspiration for anthropologists doing fieldwork. (2019, 24)

Becoming a Good Ethnographer

Participant observation is the primary method used in the anthropological craft of writing an ethnography, and ethnographic research is indispensable for cross-cultural ministry. Some people seem to be naturally gifted at ethnographic inquiry, but it is a skill that we can all learn. To become effective cross-cultural witnesses and to discover cultural differences, we need to become good ethnographers. When we are functioning as ethnographers, we look for the ordinary, the usual, the normal, and the everyday routines of people. This approach contrasts significantly with the unusual, contrived, or unnatural environment of conducting surveys, responding to questionnaires, and doing experiments. Human beings behave differently when their environment is manipulated, so as ethnographers, we participate in the ordinary, everyday lives of the people among whom we are living and serving.

In his award-winning book *A Public Missiology: How Local Churches Witness to a Complex World*, missiologist Gregg Okesson devotes an entire chapter to "How to Study Congregations" (2020, 147–77). He notes that an ethnographic approach to studying congregations is especially well suited for understanding parishioners' implicit theology used in everyday life. Explicit theology is systematic theology, dealing with doctrines of creation, sin, election, redemption, and eschatology and codified in creeds and statements of belief. It's what we learn in seminary and Bible college. Cross-cultural witnesses also need to understand how people in their host society live out their theology. We discover this best through ethnographic research—living with the people—not from books and lectures. Okesson states, "The fundamental goal of ethnography is to understand a context from within sustained, immersed observation, while allowing people on the ground to provide meanings to any of the data that emerges" (163–64). He goes on to suggest specific areas to research and practical ways to gather information.

An ethnography is a written description of the culture of a particular people in a particular location focusing on as many of the elements of the culture as possible, given the limitations of time and resources. Anthropologists frequently spend a year or two trying to discover and make sense of as much of the culture as possible. As I noted above, when my wife and I lived in the Solomon Islands during my initial fieldwork, I was researching the question of the impact of Christianity and Christian missionaries on Solomon Islanders. We lived in a small village of 150 people. The village was carved out of the jungle at the foot of a mountain, about a mile inland from the coast on the island of Santa Isabel. Even though my research focus was the impact of Anglican Christianity on Solomon Islanders, we were interested in observing everything we could and participating in the life of the village as much as possible. At the end of the day, I would type up my notes of what I had observed and learned that day on a Hermes portable typewriter beneath the light of a kerosene lantern. It was a great experience, and we loved living there, but we didn't learn enough to write a complete ethnography of the village of Gnulahage. However, by taking a holistic approach in observing and recording as much of life as possible, we were able to discover why magic continued to be practiced; how partaking in Holy Communion was understood and interpreted as a way of gaining *mana*, or spiritual power; how and why parents disciplined their children; why ancestral spirits were seen as real and important in the life of the village; and many other aspects of life among these Solomon Islanders.[3]

One of those nights, while I was typing up my notes of the day's observations, the village catechist, who led the Anglican morning and evening prayers in the village chapel, sauntered into our house and began chatting away. After about an hour, he got up and said, "I think it's safe for me to go home now." I asked what he meant. He replied, "My wife's sister is visiting us with her newborn baby. I've just come in from the bush, so there are spirits clinging to me. They like to attack newborn babies, so I decided to drop by your house first and shake off the spirits before going home because they won't bother you." I learned a lot from that episode, because we were practicing participant observation as a way to discover cultural differences in that village.

If we believe that the gospel is relevant to all of life and not just to what we do once a week in a worship service, then we need to understand as much of the society as we possibly can and discover where the gospel connects with life and where it misses engaging people altogether. Conducting ethnographic research as part of our cross-cultural ministry will help us make those discoveries of where the gospel is connecting and where it is not.

Engaging in ethnographic study is as much an art form as it is a scientific technique. Prominent anthropologist Harry Wolcott, in his groundbreaking

---

3. This ethnographic research culminated in my book *Melanesians and Missionaries* (1983).

book *The Art of Fieldwork*, notes that "fieldwork is characterized by personal involvement to achieve a level of understanding that will be shared with others." He goes on to say that sometimes that personal involvement may be very challenging and difficult. "There may be discomfort and hardship aplenty connected with the experience, ranging from the distractions of diarrhea or lost luggage to the despair of personal failure or lost hope, but the extent of one's suffering and sacrifice are not factored into judgments about the worth of the fieldwork as fieldwork" (2005, 58).

Becoming a good ethnographer is a craft we can hone with practice and good guidelines. Cross-cultural witnesses will increase their effectiveness as they become better ethnographers, because doing so will enable them to dig deeper into the culture and better understand the worldview of those people among whom they are living and serving. Travel guides and country profiles, such as the Culture Shock series of fifty-four books that focus on customs, etiquette, how to dress appropriately, and ways of greeting others, are interesting and helpful, but in the end, they are rather superficial. As cross-cultural witnesses, we primarily want to get below the surface-level behavior and discover what is inside people's heads and hearts. This is sometimes difficult to accomplish, and it takes time. Kenneth Guest gives us sage advice when he says, "A good ethnographer must be patient, flexible, and open to the unexpected. Sometimes sitting still in one place is the best research strategy because it offers opportunities to observe and experience unplanned events and unexpected people" (2018, 78).

In an unfamiliar situation where we do not yet know and understand the cultural rules, we have to prioritize and determine what is important and what is not. When we are new to a situation, we tend to see everything and assume nothing. But as we grow to understand and become familiar with the situation, we tend to assume more and see far less because it becomes so familiar. This observation describes a contrast between tourists and ethnographers. Tourists often do not have a clue what local people are thinking and assuming, nor are they interested in finding out, and they frequently don't need to. As tourists, they often set out to take lots of photos and have different "cultural" experiences without necessarily taking the time to learn the meaning behind what they are observing. Their objective as tourists is to see and record as much as they can.

In contrast, one of our objectives as cross-cultural witnesses is to learn the culture well enough so that we understand the local assumptions. At the same time, we want to maintain a keen awareness of what we are seeing. We therefore guard against the tendency of the situation becoming so familiar that it numbs our ability to see everything. A good ethnographer comes to understand what local people are assuming without losing the ability to see things in fresh ways that may have become familiar to local people. When missionaries behave more like tourists than cross-cultural witnesses, it reveals a significant shortcoming in their preparation for and practice of ministry.[4]

As cross-cultural witnesses, we enter a culture as outsiders who know very little, but our goal is to get behind what we see and to understand the assumptions that lie behind or beneath the things we observe. However, even as we come to understand the culture at a deeper and deeper level, we have to guard against making premature judgments and false assumptions. Remember, assumptions are the lowest form of knowledge, even in our own culture, let alone in another.

Finally, the most important attribute in becoming a good ethnographer is an insatiable curiosity. We need to cultivate curiosity and a childlike sense of wonder and awe when we move into a community. Curiosity may kill the cat, but it is indispensable for a good ethnographer.

I remember once taking a three-hour road trip in Indonesia, climbing from Jakarta on the coast to Bandung in West Java, located at twenty-five hundred feet in the lush and beautiful Parahyangan Mountains. I was in the company of American missionaries, and as we traveled along, I was so curious about the landscape, farming patterns, villages, and many other things I was seeing for the first time. I asked my traveling companions dozens of questions and made intuitive connections based on what I was observing. The next day I interviewed the missionary couple on their mission experience and cross-cultural adjustment. They commented on how astounded they were by how I had been asking so many questions, putting together observations, and making connections the day before. They asked, "How did you figure out so many things in such a short time? It has taken us years to discover what you learned in several hours." I remember responding that perhaps it was because I was trained as an anthropologist to observe and because I was curious about everything.

Asking Good Questions and Listening Well

In our effort to understand and uncover cultural differences, we need to learn how to ask good questions in a manner that creates a safe environment for the people we are questioning. Establishing rapport is absolutely critical, and that is as much an art form as it is a technique. The typical questions a reporter asks are who, what, when, where, why, and sometimes how. Notice, these are open-ended questions, for which a yes or no answer is inadequate. As cross-cultural

---

4. This is one of the problems of so many short-term mission adventures when volunteers go without any cross-cultural preparation and understanding and end up behaving more like tourists. To counter this tourist-like approach to short-term missions, Priest has produced the edited volume *Effective Engagement in Short-term Missions* (2008). See also Livermore 2006 for a helpful guide.

witnesses, we're interested in learning about and understanding the cultural differences of others. These six questions can be a good starting point.[5]

Harry Wolcott, in his book *Ethnography: A Way of Seeing*, explains different forms of interviewing that can take place in the process of doing ethnographic research. He includes casual conversation, life history questions, key informant interviewing, semi-structured and structured interviews, and questionnaires (2008, 54–62). He sees casual conversation as the most significant way of gathering information. He developed this typology because, as he notes, "I wanted students to recognize a variety of approaches and to be able to assess the advantages and disadvantages not only for getting certain kinds of information but for the constant vigilance one must exercise in maintaining rapport. Direct questioning always involves a certain risk and tends to emphasize an extractive element in fieldwork. . . . Further, even if you get exactly the information you need, you may damage your chances for learning more" (54–55). Because direct questions can put the informant into a defensive posture, open-ended questions are preferable.

Asking good, open-ended questions is a start to uncovering cultural differences, but perhaps even more important is the ability to listen well. In discovering cultural differences, listening is more important than talking. Anthropologist Kenneth Guest has observed that

> a successful ethnographer must also be a skilled listener. We spend a lot of time in conversation, but much of that time involves listening, not talking. The ability to ask good questions and listen carefully to the responses is essential. A skilled listener hears both what is said and what is not said—something we refer to as zeros or silences. Zeros are elements of a story or a picture that are not told or seen—key details omitted from the conversation or key people absent from the room. Zeros offer insights into issues and topics that may be too sensitive to discuss or display publicly. (2018, 78)

Anthropological research that leads to ethnographic descriptions of a small group, a village, a church, a business, an organization, or another form of social activity involves good conversations. Some people are natural conversationalists, and if we are not, then we have to learn how to make good conversations, which are essential for understanding the cultural differences in others. Celeste Headlee, in a riveting TED Talk, suggests ten basic rules for having a better

---

5. Stan Nussbaum (2007, 75–89) has written a very helpful chapter on asking great field questions in his book *Breakthrough!* He suggests five criteria for the questions we ask: (1) Is it essential for answering the analytical question we are pursuing in our research? (2) Is it clear to the respondent? (3) Is it penetrating and not superficial? (4) Is it unbiased? (5) Is it nonthreatening? His book also provides worksheets and good advice for practicing writing great questions.

conversation. I believe these rules are excellent for good ethnographic research and for uncovering cultural differences.

1. Don't multitask. Be present. Be in the moment. Don't be thinking about other things.
2. Don't pontificate. Enter every conversation assuming you have something to learn. Everyone is an expert in something.
3. Use open-ended questions. Start your questions with who, what, when, where, why, or how. Ask, What was that like? How did that feel?
4. Go with the flow. Stories and ideas will come to you, but you need to let them come and then let them go. Don't get distracted by other thoughts when you're in a conversation.
5. If you don't know, say that you don't know. Err on the side of caution.
6. Don't equate your experience with theirs. For example, if they lost a family member, don't tell them about your experience, because it isn't the same. It's not the same. It is never the same.
7. Try not to repeat yourself. It is condescending and really boring for the listener.
8. Stay out of the weeds. The details, like dates, don't matter to most people. They care about you, not all the details of your story.
9. Listen. This is the most important thing on the list. Listening is the most important skill you can develop.
10. Be brief. Be interested in other people. Have curiosity. Keep your mind open and your mouth shut, and be prepared to be amazed. (Headlee 2015)

When we are asking questions and listening to people in order to understand the cultural and religious differences that lie between us, it is important to suspend judgment. One of our tasks is to search for where God is already at work in the culture where we are living and serving. Another of our tasks is to enable people to redeem their own religious and cultural structures for God's purposes. We will need to develop a hermeneutic of charity toward people embedded in their own culture and religion. This is why cultural relativism is important, a topic we will discuss at the end of this chapter.

Observing and Recording Cultural Differences

While conducting my research in the Solomon Islands, I always carried a pen and a notebook in my back pocket. I would jot down things I saw or comments

I heard. Sometimes I would write down just a word or two, but they would be sufficient to jog my memory later in the evening when I was writing down my observations for the day. The villagers were sometimes intrigued by my notes, but they came to realize that if I was jotting something in my notebook, it must be important. On more than one occasion while I was participating with villagers in an activity, they would say to me, "Whiteman, get out your pen and notepad and write this down. This is important." Something as simple as jotting down observations had the accumulative effect of building rapport and trust and enabled me to learn many things that "we would never discuss in church."

World-renowned Bible translator Eugene Nida, who was involved in over two hundred translation projects around the world, once shared with me how he had written his influential book *Customs and Cultures: Anthropology for Christian Mission* (1954). He said he always carried a pack of 3 x 5 note cards on which he jotted down things he observed about local culture, language, and religion. He was scheduled to conduct two translation workshops for Bible translators in Brazil, but after he arrived, he was told the first workshop was canceled. So he got out his stack of notecards and used the six weeks to write one of the earliest and most important books on the value of anthropology for cross-cultural mission.

Here is a simple formula to follow when observing and recording what you are experiencing:

1. What do I see?
2. What do I hear?
3. What is happening?
4. What do I think?
5. What do I feel?

The concept of reflexivity has come into anthropological research in recent decades. Instead of trying to hide behind a charade of "complete objectivity," which is seldom possible, we should record our own subjective experience along with what we are observing. By doing so, we let our unconscious biases and ethnocentrism come to the fore so that we can more easily deal with them instead of covering them up or ignoring them.

Writing Field Notes

Writing field notes is another part of ethnography and can be useful for cross-cultural witnesses. Field notes are the rough result of the process of turning conversations, observations, and experiences into written text that focuses on the dramatic as well as the mundane in a social setting. They are not polished prose. Emerson and his colleagues note, "Writing [field notes] requires a block of concentrated time. Sometimes, incidents that span a few minutes can take the ethnographer several hours to write up; he tries to recall just who did and said what, in what order, and to put all that into words and coherent paragraphs" (2011, 48). A general rule of thumb is that for every hour of observation, an additional hour is required to write it up. The sooner the field notes are written following the observations and participation, the better. Emerson and his colleagues state, "Over time, people forget and simplify experience; notes composed several days after observation tend to be summarized and stripped of rich, nuanced detail. . . . Writing fieldnotes *immediately* after leaving the setting produces fresher, more detailed recollections that harness the ethnographer's involvement with and excitement about the day's events" (49).

It's important to pay attention to concrete details rather than writing abstract generalizations in field notes. Emerson and his colleagues state, "The ethnographer's central purpose is to describe a social world and its people. But often beginning researchers produce fieldnotes lacking sufficient and lively detail" (2011, 57).[6]

Many early missionaries were excellent observers, and contrary to the popular stereotype, they didn't set out to destroy the culture of their host society. Because they wanted to tell people the story of Jesus, they gave time and attention to discovering and documenting the culture. Some missionaries in the past did this exceedingly well, and in the process, they made significant contributions to ethnography and anthropology as well as enabling their ministry to be more effective and longer lasting. The late Australian missiological anthropologist Alan Tippett compiled a seven-hundred-page volume of ethnographic writing from sixty-two missionaries titled *The Ways of the People: A Reader in Missionary Anthropology* (2013). Some of this early writing contributed to the development of anthropology itself, and these articles demonstrate the value of ethnographic research for cross-cultural ministry.[7]

The Importance of Cultural Relativism

As we seek to discover cultural differences, a certain perspective is important: cultural relativism. Cultural relativism can help us engage with others with honesty and integrity and discover cultural differences without bias and prejudice. Cultural relativism is one of the quintessential perspectives to emerge from the field of anthropology. The pioneers of cultural relativism were working against

6. For further guidance and practice on creating field notes, see Kirner and Mills 2020.
7. See Whiteman 1985 for additional examples of missionary contributions to anthropology and vice versa.

centuries of racist ideas and prejudices that posited that humanity was divided into a set of distinct racial groups that represented different stages in the evolution of civilization. Franz Boas is one of those early pioneers who, along with his students, developed the concept of cultural relativism in the first few decades of the twentieth century. Cultural relativism states that values, beliefs, and behaviors of a particular people must be understood in terms of their cultural context. This is a hedge against perceiving and judging another culture on the basis of one's own culture. Of course, we all naturally do this, and we do it even more if we have not had contact with people in other cultures and religions. Cultural relativism encourages humility and self-reflection rather than hubris and is a helpful antidote to ethnocentrism and unconscious and implicit bias.

The concept of cultural relativism is very helpful to cross-cultural witnesses, although some Christians may have an immediate negative reaction to it, believing that it leads to moral and ethical relativity and erodes confidence in moral absolutes. The perspective of cultural relativism is *not* ethical relativity. Guest underscores the importance of adopting the perspective of cultural relativism in conducting an ethnographic study: "Ethnographers must begin with open-mindedness about the people and places they study. We must be wary of any prejudices we might have formed before our arrival, and we must be reluctant to judge once we are in the field. . . . Can we see the world through the eyes of those we are studying? Can we understand their systems of meaning and internal logic? The tradition of anthropology suggests that cultural relativism must be the starting point if we are to accurately hear and retell the stories of others" (2018, 78). If cultural relativism is an important perspective for anthropologists doing an ethnographic study, then how much more important is it for cross-cultural witnesses to come to understand the people among whom they are living and serving as they communicate and live out the gospel?

In my research on nineteenth-century missionaries in Melanesia, I discovered those who unfortunately did not approach the Melanesians with openness and with an attitude of cultural relativism and the ability to suspend judgment in observing others. For example, Presbyterian missionaries working in the southern New Hebrides described their potential Melanesian converts in very negative terms. In their annual report for 1875, they noted, "We labour among very, very low and fearfully degraded races" (New Hebrides Mission 1875, 19). An even more graphic portrayal of the "natives" is given by the missionary Mrs. Agnus Watt, who in describing her New Hebridean charges notes, "Oh if you were just here and saw heathenism, with the wild savage look of the miserable dirty creatures—in all cases perfectly nude. Yet they are immortal, they have souls to be saved; they are degraded, it is true, but Jesus can save unto the uttermost" (Watt 1896, 90–91).

At the beginning of this chapter, I told of how I was tested early in our time in the Solomon Islands. This testing revealed how well I had integrated the perspective of cultural relativism into my training as an anthropologist and my experience as a cross-cultural witness. When the villagers asked me, "Do you believe in magic?" I knew that my response to their question was critical. I had to answer truthfully, but I also had to answer in such a way that it would further the conversation, not shut it down. I would be tested often during our time of living with the people in this village, but employing my perspective of cultural relativism helped me to affirm that these Anglican Solomon Islanders had a much different perspective than that of my conservative American Christian background. Their perspective was different, but it was not wrong just because it didn't agree with mine. Nevertheless, I had to be gently reminded more than once by my wife, "We are here to observe and understand these people, not make them more like us."

In a brilliant article on the use of cultural relativism in anthropology and mission, Lindy Backues notes, "Given that the internal logic of Christianity is translation (not dissemination), the Gospel takes on the clothing of its proximate surroundings, honoring and esteeming local contexts in the process. Like the Word become flesh, the Gospel 'moves into the neighborhood' and communicates and participates in the local idiom (cf. John 1:14). Thus, by virtue of its own internal logic, Christianity of the variety examined here offers significant space for pluralism as well as for cultural relativity" (2017, 123).

CHAPTER SUMMARY

In this chapter, I have tried to make the case that discovering cultural differences is critically important to our development as cross-cultural communicators of the gospel. I've noted that the research tools of cultural anthropology are well suited to enable cross-cultural witnesses to discover and understand the cultural differences in their host community. The method of participant observation is a natural one in which we live among people, and it involves making observations that are intentional and focused. As we seek to become good ethnographers, we learn how to ask good questions and listen well, observe and record, and write field notes. In all this, I argued that cultural relativism is an important perspective that helps us suspend judgment, avoid premature assumptions, and combat our ethnocentrism as cross-cultural witnesses.

13

Becoming Aware
of Cultural Baggage

Because the baboon cannot see its bald bottom, it laughs at
the defects of others. (People can easily overlook their own
glaring deficiencies and self-righteously criticize others.)

Oromo proverb, Ethiopia

'll never forget the day I discovered the nickname the Rwandans gave me. I
was in the final months of my two-year assignment as a volunteer missionary
to Central Africa. Nicknames are often created to capture the personality,
character, and essence of a person. The Africans called me "Bwana Itsitungu,"
which means "the man who can take care of himself." Now, was that a com-
pliment given to me by the Rwandans, or was that a complaint? As a white,
middle-class, American male, that's the way I was raised, to be independent
and self-sufficient, and because I had lost my father at age twelve, those values
were all the more important to me. To the Rwandans, however, because they
experienced me as self-reliant and self-sufficient, they found it difficult to connect with me on a deeper, personal level. The message I was sending to them
was "I don't need your help."

I broke down and wept. I felt as if my entire time in Central Africa had
been a failure. My cultural baggage had tripped me up. I was only twenty-four
at the time, but I remember praying and asking God to give me another sixty
years of cross-cultural ministry, but never again did I want to be called Bwana
Itsitungu, the man who can take care of himself. From that day to this, I have

attempted, but not always successfully, to cultivate a life of dependence and interdependence with others. The writing of this book is a good example. I couldn't have done it by myself.

Often, the cultural baggage we carry with us is unconscious. One way to discover worldview assumptions and help a person become aware of their cultural baggage is through proverbs. The proverbs of a culture different from ours can give us a window into another person's culture, and proverbs in our own culture can function as a mirror, enabling us to make our implicit worldview assumptions explicit in our conscious behavior.

Stan Nussbaum has written a book that can help Americans become aware of the cultural baggage they carry with them when they enter another culture. In his book *American Cultural Baggage: How to Recognize and Deal with It* (2005), Nussbaum notes that as long as we live in the United States, we get along well without being consciously aware of our worldview and culture. We automatically do things in an American way, and all is well. However, "when you go into another cultural setting, it doesn't work so well. You suddenly discover that you have unconsciously brought a lot of cultural baggage with you, and it is always causing trouble. You get angry with people because they do not measure up to expectations you didn't even know you had. You get laughed at or avoided for doing things in a normal American way without even thinking" (9).

Nussbaum's book provides 235 proverbs that are part and parcel of American life, at least for my generation, and then he identifies what he calls the "Ten Commandments" of American culture. These are worth repeating for those readers who are Americans, and reviewing them is of value for those who are not because it will give them a window through which they can better understand Americans they know and interact with.

1. *You can't argue with success.* Success is a very high value, and every American child learns early in life the importance of being successful in something. Even if success is arrived at in an incorrect or wrong manner, that's okay because achieving success is more important than how a person obtained it.

2. *Live and let live.* Freedom and privacy are important values to Americans, and so we take the attitude that the way a person lives is their business and we shouldn't interfere or criticize. Therefore, tolerance of others is very important.

3. *Time flies when you're having fun.* Having lots of fun is an important ideal for Americans, especially for young people and those who have retired from work. They can give more time to doing things and going

places that are fun. As long as they are having fun, keeping track of time is not so important.

4. *Shop till you drop.* Shopping for some Americans is a form of entertainment, and many go shopping even if there is nothing in particular that they need to purchase. This phrase captures the notion that the United States is perhaps the ultimate consumer society.

5. *Just do it.* This is such an iconic phrase that a shoe manufacturer uses it as their logo. The focus is on action and overcoming obstacles, such as regulations, obtaining permission, and laborious planning.

6. *You are only young once.* Americans put a high premium on youth and emphasize having fun and doing things before adult responsibilities settle in and curb one's freedom.

7. *Enough is enough.* The American focus on human rights and fighting injustice leads them to stand up for their rights. This phrase is often uttered at racial protests, protests against gun violence, and protests against behaviors that trample on their rights.

8. *Rules are made to be broken.* This phrase picks up on themes of individualism and thinking for oneself. If a person has a better idea or plan, they should go for it and not be constrained by "rules" that seem outdated.

9. *Time is money.* Time, like money, is a commodity that shouldn't be wasted. Americans buy time, save time, and sell time and never want to be accused of having idle time.

10. *God helps those who help themselves.* This mantra, lodged deep within the worldview of most Americans, causes them to view a person negatively if that person is not trying to better themselves economically, educationally, and socially. The assumption is that if they aren't trying to improve their lot in life, then neither God nor anyone else should help them.

Know Thy Self . . . before Ministering with Others

Throughout this book, I've stressed the importance of adopting an incarnational lifestyle as the best way to come to know and understand another's way of life, including their values, worldview, and beliefs. However, our own "hidden" values, worldview, and beliefs are often a barrier that keeps us from relating fully with those from other cultures. Whether we are from North America, Kenya, India, France, Korea, or China, we need to uncover our own values, worldview, and beliefs if we are to effectively cross cultures with the gospel. There are five reasons we need to do so.

1. They influence our behavior in other cultures and affect the kinds and quality of relationships we build with other people in cultures that are different from our own.
2. They influence how we perceive the local culture, language, and people.
3. They influence our ability to accept people.
4. They are not necessarily biblical or Christian, but we seldom question them. We feel secure in the myth that we live in a "Christian nation" or a "Christian culture."
5. Being aware of them will help us share a Christian gospel that is not tied up in our national way of life. In other words, the kingdom of God and the American Dream are not always the same!

What Is Cultural Baggage?

Cultural baggage is the behaviors, material things, attitudes, values, and beliefs we take with us unknowingly into another culture. They may be appropriate in our home society, but when we enter our host society as cross-cultural witnesses, they can become a heavy load that thwarts our life and ministry. The problem is that much of the baggage we carry is unconscious, and so we need to bring it to conscious awareness so that we can accept, modify, or change it. I often recommend that people going on a short-term mission trip take two suitcases—one packed with everything they think they will need, and another one completely empty. Why do such a crazy thing? I tell them to take an empty suitcase to remind them of all the new things they will learn and experience in their host culture and to bring it back full—not of souvenirs and trinkets but of new discoveries of where they saw God at work, of budding cross-cultural relationships, and of a new and critical perspective on all the stuff they took with them initially. Only occasionally have people actually taken me up on my challenge, but the "empty suitcase" perspective is important because it will begin to make us aware of all the cultural baggage we take with us.

Why didn't I know I was carrying the cultural baggage of independence and self-sufficiency? And how had this baggage, without me realizing it, kept the Africans at a distance? One reason is that we frequently are unaware of our cultural baggage until we begin interacting with and living among people who are different from us. This story illustrates how our values, worldview, and beliefs can become barriers in communicating and living out the gospel with people who are different from us. Rugged individualism and self-reliance are two dominant American values, but an unexamined strength can become a double weakness in cross-cultural ministry. This is clearly what happened to me. I was carrying a heavy load of cultural baggage and didn't even realize it until it was pointed out to me when I learned my African nickname.

Most of the examples and stories of cultural baggage we are going to discuss necessarily reflect my own North American and Western worldview. But this problem of carrying cultural baggage is one that all cross-cultural witnesses face. People in every culture struggle to come to grips with the values, worldview, and beliefs that influence their behavior in cross-cultural settings. In fact, the less we understand and know our own worldview, the more ethnocentric we are likely to be. And the more homogeneous a society is, the more ethnocentric the people tend to be. So, we sally forth with great intentions of being effective cross-cultural witnesses, but we are burdened with our own cultural baggage. We may have a lot of information about our culture, but we are largely unaware of the assumptions we make about the nature of reality. We are unaware of this because our unconscious worldview has not come to our conscious awareness, and we have no other worldviews with which to compare and contrast it. Therefore, understanding ourselves thoroughly and deeply is an important prerequisite to uncovering the misunderstandings that come with living in another culture.

Gaining self-understanding is one of the primary values of studying anthropology. It is certainly interesting to learn about other cultures and the way people live and think in other parts of the world, but the lasting benefit of anthropology is understanding how our own culture has shaped who we have become. Anthropologists note that a person who knows only one culture actually knows no culture. It is primarily by living in a culture different from our own and building relationships of trust and understanding that we can begin to hold a cultural mirror up to ourselves and uncover our deeply held values, worldview, and beliefs.

Could the cultural baggage of independence and self-reliance that is common among Americans affect our theology and our understanding of our relationship with God? I think so. Ralph Satter, a pastor and former student, wondered why his American congregation struggled to understand God's grace and accept it in their lives, his included. His doctoral research led him to conclude that the three dominant values of individualism, activism, and self-reliance hindered their ability to understand God's grace as a free gift (Satter 1991). It is nothing we can earn or strive for or attempt to achieve. The worldview of his congregation actually got in the way of them fully accepting and understanding the gift of God's grace.

Lifestyle as Cultural Baggage

Whenever we feel the need to perpetuate our lifestyle from back home in a new cultural setting, we bring with us into the new culture a boatload of cultural baggage. I remember an interview I had with Jackie Pullinger in Hong Kong in 1992. Her story of how she came to Hong Kong as a young nineteen-year-old and began working among people addicted to drugs in the infamous Walled City of Kowloon in 1966 is legendary (Jackie's story is told in Pullinger 2007). Jackie founded the St. Stephens Society, and people from all over the world volunteer to help her ministry. She told me in our interview that I wouldn't like to hear this, but from her experience Americans have the most difficulty adjusting to living in Hong Kong and working with her St. Stephens ministry. The people who do the best in adapting to her ministry context in Hong Kong are those who went to boarding schools in Britain and adjusted better to living in community. They seemed to have brought less cultural baggage to Hong Kong.

But it's not just Americans who have this struggle. For example, food is a significant factor in everyone's lifestyle, and when we enter another culture and the foods we had "back home" are no longer there, it becomes cultural baggage and can get in the way of our adapting to our host culture and effectively crossing cultural boundaries with the gospel. For example, Korean missionaries may wonder how will they survive without their daily intake of kimchi. I remember at Asbury Theological Seminary how international students in their first semester would cook their own food in their dormitory rooms. They couldn't stand the American food in the cafeteria and told me they got sick when they ate it. Perhaps their sickness was as much cultural as it was physiological and culinary. Eventually, as they became more acclimatized to the American cultural context of seminary life, they were able to stomach the food in the cafeteria.

Property as Cultural Baggage

In many non-Western cultures, people have a more collectivist approach to owning things such as land and products. David Maranz, in his book *African Friends and Money Matters* (2015), identifies a lot of the cultural baggage Westerners carry that causes misunderstanding with Africans regarding the use of property and money. He notes, "Many [African] people like to think that if something is not in active or current use, it is 'surplus.' If they do not have one, or less, then the owner should give it or some of it, to the one who has none or less. This can apply to anything from personal possessions, money, supplies, buildings, land, and equipment" (80). Maranz goes on to quote an African friend who says, "Everything that is not in actual use is seen as being 'available.' Consequently, if relatives or friends consider that they have immediate need of a thing, they believe they are entitled to take possession of it. Thus, the real Africans, ones who do not have a 'double culture' that is, who have not been overly influenced by Western ideas, and who have not been alienated from African ideals are subject to this custom" (81).

When Americans live in these cultures and are not willing to share their private property, they come across as extremely stingy people. Missiologist Jay Moon noted that when he and his family lived in a Builsa village in Ghana, people were happy for folks to have private property—as long as they were willing to share it. For example, if a person bought a wireless radio, that was great—as long as they played it loud enough for everyone in the village to enjoy the music.[1]

We faced this problem surrounding private ownership when we lived in Papua New Guinea with our three-year-old son. One day we got into a bit of a conflict with our Melanesian neighbors over Geoffrey's Matchbox cars. He took his cars out to play with the neighborhood kids, but within a short time, he came back to the house crying because they had been broken. The wheels had been torn off, and the doors had been ripped off their hinges. There wasn't much left of the cars. We discussed it and decided that maybe the problem was that they did not have their *own* cars. So, thinking like typical Americans and influenced by the value of private property, we decided to give each of the neighborhood kids their *own* Matchbox car. We assumed they would take better care of their own car because it was their own private property. So out Geoffrey went again, this time armed with a handful of cars, one for each of his playmates. But that "solution" didn't work either. In a short time, they were all broken again.

I remember having a very adult conversation with my three-year-old son about our dilemma. I asked him, "What's the most important thing for us living here in this community? Is it to get along and be friends with our neighbors or for you to protect your Matchbox cars?" He thought about it for a moment and then said with childlike wisdom, "Well, I like my Matchbox cars, but I also want to get along with my friends. I think people are more important than toys." That settled it, and the cars were never a problem again. Geoffrey learned an important lesson that day, and I came face-to-face with a deep underlying worldview theme that was firmly ensconced in my mind—namely, the importance of private property to Americans. The problem with personal possessions is that they can easily possess us, and we can become prisoners of our own making. Don't get me wrong. Private property is a good thing—as long as the owners are willing to share it with others in need.

We all have things we want to hang on to. Many American missionaries, when they go to other cultures, want to take as much stuff as they can pack

1. He told me this on October 28, 2022.

into their "missionary barrels" or crates. Sometimes it is kitchen appliances or household items that we think will make our life easier and our ministry more effective overseas. If we aren't careful, however, these items can become idols, and we can't imagine living without them.

I had to face this in my own life as we prepared to move to Papua New Guinea. In my study in the United States, I didn't have wallpaper. Instead, my books lined the walls, and I became prone to idolatry, "worshiping" my books. At the time, I had three thousand books and journals, and I "knew" I needed them all for my ministry. I could easily make fun of missionaries who needed to have a microwave oven, but give up my books? No way. My ministry depended on them, so I thought. I ended up leaving most of them behind for others to benefit from (but I still took several hundred books that I was sure I would need).

Frequently, missionaries tell me they are willing to give up a lot of their stuff, but is it right to ask their children to give up their favorite toys, books, games, and so on? The question to ask each member of the family is "Will your stuff increase or decrease your capacity to identify with the host community?" Incarnational identification is not just for Mom and Dad. It is a way of living that we enter into as a family. And when we do, it won't be long before we realize that what we have gained in fulfilling interpersonal relationships with people in our host society far outweighs any stuff we may have given up. The goal here is to keep our things from getting in the way of establishing deep personal relationships with others, and to let our things be used for this purpose, rather than trying to perpetuate our lifestyle in another culture.

Absolute Truth as Cultural Baggage

Our view of absolute truth can easily get in the way of understanding and relating to people who are culturally different from us. To many Americans, the word "compromise" is more of a negative than a positive attribute. To them it can denote weakness and not standing up for the truth. Moreover, if we baptize our personal perspective as "Christian," then we can easily justify our attitude and behavior toward those who are different or who hold a different perspective, and we can easily pass judgment without understanding the other person's perspective.

Anthropologists Conrad Arensberg and Arthur Niehoff, in their very helpful book *Introducing Social Change: A Manual for Americans Overseas* (1964),[2]

2. The initial publication in 1964 went through multiple printings, and then a second edition was published in 2017.

have an insightful chapter titled "American Cultural Values" that demonstrates some of the cultural baggage we Americans bring with us when we want to introduce social and cultural change into a society. The book is designed primarily for community development workers, but their insights are very useful for cross-cultural witnesses as agents of change. Although they don't use the term "cultural baggage," they write, "The most hazardous tendency in the way of thinking that Americans take with them into other cultural situations is that of making two-fold judgments based on principle. The structure of the Indo-European languages seems to foster this kind of categorization. [Therefore] two-fold judgments are the rule in American and Western life: moral-immoral, legal-illegal, right-wrong, success-failure, clean-dirty, modern-outmoded, civilized-primitive, developed-underdeveloped, practical-impractical, introvert-extrovert, secular-religious, Christian-pagan" (159–60).

This either/or thinking, on the basis of principle, seems to force Americans into positions of exclusiveness. If one position is accepted, then the other must be rejected.[3] This either/or mentality also causes us to polarize values. This is playing out in the United States in the political arena as I write this chapter. Arensberg and Niehoff help us understand why we carry this cultural baggage into different cultural contexts. "The average Western [person], including the American, conducts [their] personal life and [their] maintenance of law and order in the community on principles of right and wrong, rather than on sanctions of shame, dishonor, ridicule, or horror of impropriety. [They are] forced to categorize [their] conduct in universal, impersonal terms. The 'law is the law,' and 'right is right' regardless of other considerations" (1964, 161).

This tendency to think in either/or categories can cause Americans much frustration and mental anguish when we encounter people in other parts of the world who can hold two contradictory ideas in their heads, and they have no difficulty in doing so. For example, in Buddhism and Hinduism, you have many disparate, local folk beliefs that exist right alongside those derived from the main, formal theology. This is why we find it hard to find "pure" examples of Buddhism or Hinduism or Islam except in textbooks, since many people in these cultures practice a form of folk religion in addition to the formal religion.

Christianity is not immune to this phenomenon. For example, Father Jaime Bulatao points to the phenomenon called split-level Christianity in the Philippines, which is the coexistence within the same person of two or more thought-and-behavior systems that are inconsistent with each other (1966). Split-level Christianity means that Filipinos turn to Christianity for answers to their ques-

---

3. In his book *Digital, Diverse & Divided*, social scientist and cultural intelligence expert David Livermore gives us some very practical guidelines on how to encounter and engage a diverse world and break through the cultural barriers that divide us (Livermore 2022).

Figure 13.1
Split-Level Christianity

Spiritual Issues Like Ultimate Destiny

━ ━ ━ ━ ━ ━ ━ ━ ━ ━ ━ ━ ━

Mundane Issues Like Everyday Concerns

tions about issues like personal salvation and ultimate destiny. But the form of Christianity that was introduced doesn't seem to deal effectively with everyday problems, such as why our child got sick, why my wife had a miscarriage, and why the drought destroyed our garden. Bulatao observed that since Filipinos do not see that Christianity provides answers to the questions arising out of this everyday dimension of their world, they therefore turn to traditional answers and practices that seem to have worked in the past. This helps explain why during times of crisis Christians may therefore resort to magic and traditional practices. They do so not because they are bad Christians but because they have never found answers to their everyday problems in formal Christianity, at least in the way it is presented to them. Hence, they end up with a split-level form of Christianity. The split between spiritual and mundane issues is depicted in figure 13.1.

Before we point accusing fingers at our Filipino brothers and sisters and call them bad Christians, we need to examine whether we also have a form of split-level Christianity. Instead of magic and witchcraft, which we Americans scoff at, we use science and medicine to deal with our everyday concerns.

On a trip to Japan, I was taken to a Shinto shrine by a Baptist missionary, and I observed something fascinating. Out in front of the shrine was a place to write your concerns on small wooden plaques, and the Shinto priest would pray for them. The requests were written in both Japanese and English. I said to the missionary who was with me, "Why don't you make a list of these requests and then pray for these people, that God will bless them? Here are their obvious felt needs, and they are crying out for supernatural help in the best way they know how." I don't know if he took my suggestion seriously, but I hope he did. What better way to respond to the felt needs of these people who are hoping to do well on the national exam, the results of which will be life-changing for many of them.

As mentioned earlier, the word "compromise" more often than not tends to be viewed negatively by Americans because it can be construed as being wishy-washy, not standing up for your rights, and not having strong convictions. But to many in Asia, the idea of compromise is very positive indeed. That is what life is all about, compromising to obtain balance and harmony between people, between people and the natural world, and between humans and the supernatural world.

So, there is indeed Truth, and all truth is God's Truth, but we come to understand and articulate truth as it is understood and expressed through our language and culture. If we are not aware of this, then we may think we are communicating God's Truth, but in fact we are communicating our understanding of truth, which is not absolute but culturally defined and understood.

As noted earlier in this book (chap. 1, under the heading "The Structure of This Book"), sometimes our Christian faith is shaped and influenced by our cultural beliefs and values as much as it is by biblical values. For example, caste discrimination in India continues to be alive and well among Christians, despite the biblical teaching (Gal. 3:28) that in God's sight we are all equal and are all one in union with Christ. Another example is the "health and wealth gospel" that originated in America but has now spread around the world. That "gospel" taps into two dominant American values—individualism and prosperity—as a sign of God's blessing. The biblical value of suffering, implied in Jesus's injunction to "take up [your cross] and follow me" (Matt. 16:24 NIV) has gotten lost or suffocated by many American cultural values that encourage us to pursue wealth and fame.

CHAPTER SUMMARY

In this chapter, we argued that people in every culture carry cultural baggage with them when they enter another culture. I was not aware of my own cultural baggage of self-sufficiency when living in Rwanda in 1971 until I learned that the Africans had given me a nickname—Bwana Itsitungu, the man who can take care of himself. Cultural baggage can be carried by a person from northeast India serving as a cross-cultural witness in Kenya, a German missionary living in Papua New Guinea, a Han Chinese living among the Lisu in Yunnan Province, or an American missionary living in Indonesia. The appropriate beliefs, attitudes, and lifestyles that cross-cultural witnesses have in their home culture don't become cultural baggage until those witnesses enter a different culture. In fact, once we begin living in another culture, we begin to discover that we carry some unhelpful and even harmful cultural baggage. Therefore, becoming aware of the cultural baggage we carry is essential to effectively crossing cultures with the gospel.

I wrote this book for people serving in missions from all over the world, from everywhere to everywhere. Because Americans will presumably be reading this book, I offer additional resources that highlight American values and cultural patterns. These may also be helpful for many non-Western cross-cultural witnesses who have been unconsciously influenced by American values and beliefs, perhaps in their theological education and training or through American colleagues and churches with whom they have a relationship. Non-Americans may find them useful in understanding the context from which Americans come.

Althen, Gary. 2022. *American Ways: A Guide for Foreigners in America.* Boston: Intercultural Press.

Hiebert, Paul G. 1985. "Cultural Assumptions of Western Missionaries." In *Anthropological Insights for Missionaries*, 111–37. Grand Rapids: Baker.

Nussbaum, Stan. 2005. *American Cultural Baggage: How to Recognize and Deal with It.* Maryknoll, NY: Orbis Books.

Stewart, Edward C. 1972. *American Cultural Patterns: A Cross-Cultural Perspective.* Boston: Intercultural Press.

14

Strategies for Effectively Crossing Cultural Boundaries

If you want to go quickly, go alone. If you want to go far, go together.

Ghanaian proverb

After all of the learning you gained from the previous chapters, I want to leave you with the most important practical pieces of advice for crossing cultural boundaries. I have already mentioned lessons learned from my mistakes along the way. At the risk of repeating myself, I am providing the rest of the story in order to leave you with the most important pieces of wisdom that I have gained over my forty-five years in cross-cultural ministry. Let's begin with a story.

My wife and I had pulled together all our financial resources just to make it from Seattle to the Solomon Islands, where we would spend the next year doing fieldwork as we studied the social and cultural impact of the indigenous Anglican Melanesian Mission. The Anglican Church of Melanesia welcomed us, and Dudley Tuti, the bishop of Santa Isabel, had made arrangements for us to live in the village of Gnulahage on the island of Santa Isabel. In the capital city of Honiara, on the island of Guadalcanal, where ferocious fighting had occurred between Americans and Japanese in World War II, we purchased mosquito nets, a gas burner, and some foam rubber mattresses to set up in the house the villagers had constructed for us out of bamboo poles and sago palm leaves. We also picked up a kitten in Honiara because we had heard that the village was full of rats. The DDT that had been sprayed on the houses to kill mosquitoes in an effort to combat malaria had also killed off all the cats.

We made the twelve-hour boat ride from Guadalcanal to Santa Isabel, practicing what little of the Melanesian lingua franca we picked up from Peace Corps workers. We were totally reliant on the goodwill of the people because we couldn't speak their language, didn't understand their customs, and didn't know how to survive in this hot and humid tropical climate. The day we arrived in the village I was feeling insecure and anxious, wondering if I really knew how to do ethnographic research and discover the impact that Christianity had on the lives of these villagers. I remember being taken to the edge of the village and overlooking a valley where the local school was. As Laurie and I were standing there, feeling anxious and wondering how living here would unfold, suddenly out of the jungle came two large, brightly colored parrots, who flew straight toward us and then passed just above our heads and disappeared. I turned to Laurie and said, "We're going to be okay." I believed in that moment that God had sent those parrots as a sign to welcome us and assure us that even though we had very little knowledge of life there, we would eventually learn what we needed to know to survive and to tell the story of the impact of Anglican Christianity in the Solomon Islands.

Within weeks, we began to feel at home, to get out and about, and to learn more and more Cheke Holo, the local language. We felt adopted by the villagers, and the first baby girl born in Gnulahage after we arrived, they named Laurie, followed by the first baby boy, whom they named Darrell.

What had happened to make this transition so smooth and for us to feel at home so quickly? Without realizing it, we had bonded with the local people. The concept of bonding as a short-term strategy for relating to local people in a different culture had not even been birthed yet by Tom and Betty Brewster.

Writing this book has been a journey, and living it out around the world has been a lifetime adventure. As a cross-cultural witness trained in cultural anthropology and deeply influenced by the field of missiology, I have experienced much joy (and sometimes pain) in the journey as I've joined God's mission in the world. The concepts, ideas, biblical insights, and personal stories in this book have been shared with thousands of people around the world. I trust that your journey of reading and interacting with this book has been sobering and challenging but also encouraging and hopeful as you reflect on your own cross-cultural ministry.

When we face the realities of crossing so many different cultural boundaries, we can feel overwhelmed. Without the capacity for resilience[1] and a deeply

---

1. For research on resilience among cross-cultural witnesses, see Whiteman, Edwards, Savelle, and Whiteman 2020, 65–75; Whiteman and Whiteman 2022, 27–29; and K. Whiteman 2023a and 2023b.

rooted sense of being called by God, many people abandon their commitment to cross-cultural ministry and seek a different vocation. This final chapter is filled with encouraging information about two strategies that will enable us to *thrive*, not just survive, in cross-cultural ministry.[2] The first is a short-term strategy that begins as soon as we arrive in our host society. It is the process of bonding with the local people and their culture. The second strategy is long-term and can even take a lifetime. It is the process of becoming a bicultural person. Here is an example of a cross-cultural witness becoming thoroughly bicultural.

I once interviewed George Wilson, a Southern Baptist missionary in Hong Kong. He mentioned that he was going to give a speech in Cantonese the following week and had given his manuscript to his tutor to look over to make sure it was correct. I was shocked and said to him, "You still have a tutor after living twenty-five years in Hong Kong and mastering the language like no other missionary has done before?" He smiled. "Learning Cantonese and Chinese culture has been a lifetime endeavor, and I still have more things to learn." George Wilson had truly become a bicultural person. He also told me in that interview that humility was the most important characteristic for young missionaries coming from America to Hong Kong, because without it, they wouldn't become learners. Perhaps humility is one of the key components to becoming bicultural.

Bonding as a Way of Belonging

The late E. Thomas Brewster (Tom) and his wife, Elizabeth (Betty), have written on the concept of bonding in what I believe is one of the most significant missiological breakthroughs in terms of identification with our host society to appear in the last thirty to fifty years.[3] This concept of bonding has had a very positive impact on the missionary movement ever since the Brewsters identified it in 1982, but it has not always been clearly understood or correctly practiced. I have encountered many missionaries who think the idea of bonding with local people is simply impossible, and even if it were possible, they argue, it's not something a missionary should try to do. In my many years of training thousands of missionaries preparing to cross cultures with the gospel, I have found most of them eager to learn about the process of bonding but often fearful of doing it with a family. Some were frequently discouraged from attempting

2. See Carissa Alma's book ~~Surviving~~ Thriving in Cross-Cultural Ministry (2011) and her story of bonding with Indian people and becoming a bicultural person in India.

3. Their small booklet, Bonding and the Missionary Task: Establishing a Sense of Belonging (1982a), was reprinted as an abridged chapter titled "The Difference Bonding Makes" (2009).

to do it by missionaries who are already working in the area. Nevertheless, my wife and I can attest to the power of bonding in our own ministry. At times, we have bonded with local people, as we did in the Solomon Islands, and I'm sad to confess that other times we didn't. The difference in our ministry was a difference of day and night. When we bonded with local people, we were more fulfilled and effective. When we didn't bond, we weren't effective or fulfilled, and we felt disconnected and alienated from the culture and people.

In what follows, I'll begin by describing the process of bonding as the Brewsters developed it, and then I'll address some objections to and reservations about bonding that some people have raised.

The Process of Bonding

The concept of bonding as applied to the missionary task comes from what happens immediately after a baby is born. The baby is prepared psychologically and physiologically to bond with its parents. The Brewsters note, "The birth is essentially an entrance into a new culture with new sights, new sounds, new smells, new positions, new environment, and new ways of being held. Yet, at that particular time, he or she is equipped with an extraordinary ability to respond to these unusual circumstances and new stimuli" (2009, 465).

A generation or two ago, and in some places even today, many hospital births were not conducive to bonding for two reasons. First, the mother and baby were often groggy from the pain medicine given to the laboring mother. Second, after birth the baby was typically snatched away from its family and straightaway placed in the isolation of the nursery.

What happens when the normal bonding process does not occur? Rejection can result. In fact, studies show that child abuse is significantly greater for babies born prematurely and immediately whisked away to an incubator and given little if any opportunity for bonding with the parents.[4] The movement toward natural childbirth without drugs and with birthing rooms where the father is present for the birth have helped ameliorate these deficiencies in the bonding process.

Now, what does this have to do with missions? Fundamental to any effective cross-cultural ministry is the establishment of close personal relationships with people. Bonding helps facilitate these relationships from the beginning, when we come to live and work among a culturally distant people.

There are some important parallels between an infant's entrance into its new culture and an adult's entrance into a new, foreign culture. The psychic

---

4. The Brewsters draw on the research and work of Klaus and Kennell 1976, 2–10, for this discussion of the lack of bonding and the problem of child abuse. See also Bonding and Birth, n.d.

energy and spiritual readiness of a cross-cultural witness are frequently at an all-time high when they first enter a new culture. Like a newborn baby, they are ready to bond with someone. Will they bond with the host community? Or will they be whisked away by the other missionaries and deposited in the safety of a missionary compound, where they will bond with people who are like themselves? The Brewsters say that timing is critical (2009, 466). Cross-cultural witnesses will be in this state, ready to bond, for only a short time: "If a missionary is to establish a sense of belonging to the people among whom the missionary is called to serve, the way he or she spends the first few weeks can be of critical importance. It's not uncommon for a baby who is kept in the nursery to become bonded with hospital personnel instead of with his or her parents. New missionaries, as well, can fulfill their need for belonging by bonding with the expatriate community" (466).

The window of opportunity for maximum bonding for babies occurs in the first two or three hours. For missionaries, that same window of opportunity appears to be the first two or three weeks in their new country. What happens if the new missionary does not bond with the local people? Without bonding, they do not have a sense of feeling at home and of belonging within the new cultural context. They do not feel comfortable. They feel like outsiders looking in—because they are. Consequently, it is less likely they will pursue significant relationships in the community, and without these relationships, it is hard to imagine having a very effective ministry. Moreover, if bonding between the missionary and local people does not occur, rejection of the people, even abuse, can occur. The Brewsters say you must take the plunge immediately. "The individual who hopes to enter another culture in a gradual way faces greater obstacles and, in fact, may never enjoy the experience of belonging to the people. Better to plunge right in and experience life from the insiders' perspective" (2009, 466–67).

I remember teaching about the importance of timing and bonding with a large group of missionary candidates. I could see that one of the women was getting visibly shaken and worried by what she was hearing. She raised her hand and asked, "Can I just wait and do this bonding stuff after I get settled into my house, get the curtains hung, and get our routines established? Then we'll be more ready to spend time with the African people." I remember responding with something like, "If you wait until you are settled and your family life is organized, my fear is that it will be too late to really bond with the local people." Upon hearing those words, she broke down and cried and left the room in embarrassment. I felt so badly because I was trying to encourage her to develop a meaningful way of living cross-culturally, not to frighten or embarrass her. I decided to follow their progress, and unfortunately, it was as I had predicted. Within a couple years, they returned to the United States.

I recommend that arrangements be made ahead of time for you to be met at the airport by local people, not missionaries, and go and live immediately with a national host family. It is better if *no* other expatriate missionaries are around to help you through the first several days. It is important to rely on your host society right from the beginning. An ideal host family is one that understands why you are coming to their country and is supportive of your Christian commitments and ministry. It is also important that the host family understands their role in your bonding process. If English is your mother tongue and they speak English as a second language, then they should use it as little as possible with you, since right from the beginning it is important that you begin hearing the sounds of their language, not a different accent of your own language. This bonding experience will contribute significantly to your language learning, since we always learn language in a social context.[5]

What about missionary families that have children? Is it still possible to do this bonding experience? Yes, it is, but it may be more challenging, especially if you are living with a family in cramped quarters. Another concern is that a missionary family will put too much pressure on the limited resources of the host family. I suggest that you arrange for money to be given ahead of time to the host family so that they will have adequate resources to buy additional food and other necessary provisions.

How long should you stay with a host family? My rule of thumb is "the longer the better." Ideally, if a missionary family can stay three to four weeks, that will be a sufficient amount of time to begin to hear more of the language, to start to acclimate to new routines, to understand a small amount of the culture, and most importantly to begin to form what hopefully will become a lasting friendship with the host family.

Does it always go well? I have been recommending the bonding experience for missionaries for over thirty-five years, and in most every case it has been a good experience when they've actually done it. I am aware of only a few examples where it did not go well.

What happens if people don't bond at first? Can they attempt to bond later? The Brewsters ask, "Can a missionary who has lived overseas for a time without becoming a belonger and without learning the language very well change his/ her course?" (1982a, 14). The answer is yes, but it doesn't happen very often and will not be easy to do. Nevertheless, it is possible but takes intentionality. They recommend the following: "Acknowledge the potential and desirability of a belonging relationship with the local people; implement a decision to make

---

5. See Brewster and Brewster 1982b, as well as their very effective and practical guide for language learning titled *LAMP: Language Acquisition Made Practical* (1984).

such a commitment to the people; then, set a date and inform the missionary community, and any others who may be affected, of the scope and implications of the potential change in his/her relationships" (21).

Sadly, belated bonding doesn't happen very often. The Brewsters note:

> In the past decade our work has carried us to over seventy countries, giving us opportunity to observe missionary activity in many places. Only a small percent of these missionaries manifested the kinds of relationships with local people that would demonstrate that bonding had occurred. We would like to make it clear that *"bonding" and "identification" are not the same thing.* Maybe over 90% of all missionaries would say that they identify with the local people, but it is apparent that very few enjoy a sense of being at home with the people. It is not too difficult to tell the difference—*the bonded missionaries are typically the ones who feel that even their social needs are fulfilled in their relationships with local people.* (18–19)

Bonding has many advantages for helping people cross cultural boundaries with the gospel. As noted above, it facilitates language learning, but it is also a great aid in overcoming culture shock. More importantly, it reinforces the missionary's need to adopt the posture of a learner. This in turn fosters humility, which is an indispensable ingredient for successful cross-cultural ministry.

Opposition to Bonding

Not all mission people are enthusiastic about the idea of bonding, and some outright oppose it. Wherever I have encountered opposition to it, I frequently meet with excuses such as, "We couldn't find a host family to do it," "It was too much work," "It took too much time," and so on. When I have investigated the opposition more thoroughly, I have frequently discovered that the missionaries who oppose bonding are those who never bonded with local people. Hence, they feel threatened by those who do.

Flint Miller, in his doctoral research on Southern Baptist missionaries in East Asia, observed that oftentimes young missionary recruits were ready and willing to bond with local people and adopt an incarnational lifestyle, but they received pushback from other missionaries who had been there a while but had never bonded, and sometimes opposition came from mission administrators who were not supportive of such "radical identification" (1996). Miller notes some of the attitudes he documented: "Our missionaries travel half way around the world, learn the language, and work hard. . . . They are identifying! Can't we just be content to do business as usual? Aren't our present ministries working? Is it really necessary to further identify with the host people? If we try to more fully identify, would it make that much difference? Isn't further identification, especially with those more culturally distant (like the lower classes) just too much to ask of most Western missionaries?" (516–17).

Unfortunately, if we miss the opportunity to implement the short-term strategy of bonding with local people, it will make developing the long-term strategy of becoming a bicultural person even more difficult and challenging to accomplish.

Becoming Bicultural: A Long-Term Strategy for Relating to Others

Once a cross-cultural witness has bonded with local people, he or she has taken the first step on their way to becoming a bicultural (two-culture) person. Bicultural people have integrated more than one culture into their identity and therefore feel they belong and are at home in more than one culture. Most bicultural people are also bilingual, speaking fluently one or more languages.

However, becoming a bicultural person does not happen simply by living in another culture. We can live in another country for twenty-five years or more and simply repeat the first year twenty-five times. Sometimes immigrants in a country avoid becoming bicultural. They live in neighborhoods and interact with people from their home country and culture and avoid learning the local language and venturing out into what to them is an alien culture. Business expatriates frequently live in another society as foreigners, sometimes in gated communities in the "better parts" of the city, without ever becoming bicultural. Moreover, oftentimes they have no interest in doing so. Living in another country without becoming bicultural can easily occur with missionaries who serve in mission institutions such as Bible schools and seminaries, hospitals, and mission guesthouses. Mission personnel who fill roles of mission administration and technical support may also be less likely to become bicultural because they believe their "job" doesn't require it. However, for cross-cultural witnesses, this is not a viable option if they want to have an effective cross-cultural ministry.

When we become bicultural, we are able to detach ourselves in some measure from our home culture and translate cultural beliefs and practices from one culture to another. When this happens, we become "cultural brokers" or traders who move between cultures, bringing ideas and products from one culture to another. Don Larson notes that too often the roles missionaries have occupied may have given them power and position but have been perceived negatively by local people. So instead of the roles of teacher, seller, or accuser, he suggests that missionaries occupy roles that will be positively perceived and more readily received by local people. These are learner instead of teacher, trader instead of seller, and storyteller instead of accuser (Larson 1978).

As we discussed in chapter 11, Paul Hiebert notes that when we become bi-cultural people, we live with two worlds within us, and so we have to somehow reconcile those two worlds (1985, 105). He has observed four ways in which missionaries have attempted to do this.

The first "solution" is that we reject the local culture by not taking it seriously, branding it as primitive, seeing little redeeming value in the culture, and surrounding ourselves with people just like us. Hiebert says, "We can reconstruct our own culture within our homes and compounds, creating islands of security in an alien sea" (1985, 105).

In my research on cross-cultural adjustment of missionaries in Asia, I encountered a missionary who used this approach of rejection in dealing with Korean culture. She lived on a missionary compound and seldom left to venture into the Korean culture. Of course, she didn't do well in learning the language, understanding the culture, or developing close friendships with Koreans. Unfortunately, she had become a prisoner of her own making. In contrast, her husband did venture off the missionary compound and adapted well to the Korean culture and developed meaningful relationships with Koreans. This of course brought added stress to their marriage.

The second "solution" is the reverse of the first one. We try to turn our back on the culture in which we were raised and attempt to "go native." This doesn't and can't work simply because our parents weren't natives. We have developed deep within us a language, a culture, and a worldview, and we can't get rid of these things, even if we try. I have seldom seen cross-cultural witnesses who have tried to go native, but I do know of a few anthropologists who tried . . . and failed.

Australian missiological anthropologist Alan Tippett, in his classic book *Solomon Islands Christianity: A Study in Growth and Obstruction* (1967), compares the work of the Australian Methodist Mission with the work of the Anglican Melanesian Mission. He gives very high marks to the Anglicans for the way they related to the Solomon Islanders in more incarnational ways than the Methodists, who were ethnocentric and made little effort to connect the gospel to their culture. Charles Fox (whose story I told in chap. 11) is a wonderful example of a cross-cultural witness with the Anglican Melanesian Mission who was truly bicultural, and yet even after seventy years in the Solomon Islands, he never became a Solomon Islander but remained a New Zealander until his death at age ninety-nine.

I know of a cross-cultural witness who sat under my teaching and went with his family to central Asia to work among Muslims. He told me that he had come to the conclusion that in order to reach Muslims with the gospel, he would have to become a Muslim himself. As you can imagine, that strategy did not work in his attempt to identify with Muslims, nor did he receive his mission organization's blessing or endorsement. It wasn't long before he was back home.

Occasionally, I have seen Americans try to go native, and I have talked to local people about how they feel about these Americans. What I have discovered is that outsiders who try to become native are not respected and seldom appreciated. They are frequently pitied by local people because they appear not to know who they are and are confused about their own identity. So the first two "solutions," rejecting the local culture or attempting to reject our own culture and go native, turn out not to be appropriate solutions to the challenge of living in two worlds. They are especially inappropriate for cross-cultural witness.

A third "solution" to living in two worlds is compartmentalization (Hiebert 1985, 106–7). The catchphrase "When in Rome do as the Romans do" captures the essence of compartmentalization. But in the long term, this approach is not satisfactory or effective. Hiebert says, "The constant shift from one culture to the other can lead to confusion and insecurity and, in the extreme, to an identity crisis and cultural schizophrenia" (107).

The late Rick Love (1952–2019) talks about the challenges of serving in a post-9/11, globalized, pluralistic world in terms of our identity and the problem of compartmentalization. He notes, "This interconnectedness and globalization means that we are increasingly challenged to do three things simultaneously: present the gospel (in our primary setting, to the Muslim world), defend the gospel (to the secular world listening in), recruit for the gospel (within the church)" (2008, 32–33). In other words, we compartmentalize three different identities as we communicate with three different audiences, but these audiences are not isolated from each other. If we try to enter a country through a business platform or some other role that camouflages our true identity and mission, it often doesn't work. Moreover, we will be accused of duplicity, which dilutes or negates our message of Jesus as the way, the truth, and the life as we cross cultures with the gospel.

It's clear that compartmentalization as a "solution" to living in two worlds with multiple identities does not work, especially in the present age of globalization and the use of the internet that can reveal our identity to anyone who googles us. So, is there a better solution? Yes, and we turn to that next.

The fourth solution is indeed a real and lasting solution of how to live in two worlds as cross-cultural witnesses. That is the process of integration. Hiebert says, "In the long run and at the deepest levels, we need to work toward an integration between the two cultures within us. To do so we need a well-developed metacultural framework that enables us to accept what is true and good in all cultures and to critique what is false and evil in each of them" (1985, 107). And I would add, "including in our own." Rick Love states:

> A core identity speaks of "integrity" and "integration"—words that come from the same Latin root: to make whole. Integrity refers to consistency between inner

convictions and outward actions. We will be walking in integrity when we have "truth in the innermost being" (Ps. 61:6). Honesty, sincerity, lack of deceit, and guilelessness are other ways of describing it. We cannot continue to think of ourselves as missionaries in one context and aid workers, teachers, or businessmen in another. This reflects not only a split personality but a split spirituality—a false understanding that spiritual aspects of our life or our work are more important than the practical parts of life. (2008, 35)

Becoming a bicultural person is a long-term strategy because it takes time and deep involvement in the culture. I noted earlier how my wife and I bonded with the Solomon Islanders, but after living there initially for a year, we didn't become bicultural. That would have taken much more time and deeper involvement in the life of the people among whom we lived.

Limits to Becoming Bicultural

The question of how far we should go in identifying with a host culture frequently comes up in any discussion of adapting to other cultures.[6] Aren't there limits to how much we can adapt to cultures that are so different from our own? Are there some clearly defined boundaries beyond which we should not go lest we imperil our ministry and ourselves? These are important questions that are at the forefront of many cross-cultural witnesses' minds.

As I said in chapter 4, I suggest the following: we should go as far as we can in identifying with others without violating our conscience and while maintaining our sanity. However, sometimes our conscience needs to be educated and exposed to a wider understanding. T. Wayne Dye, in "Toward a Cross-Cultural Definition of Sin" (1976), and Robert J. Priest, in "Missionary Elenctics: Conscience and Culture" (1994), have given us very helpful guidelines to distinguish between how our conscience has been shaped by our culture in a specific time and place and universal principles of conscience that apply to all people in every culture. Priest argues that "missionaries need to understand the role that culture has played in the formation of their own conscience, and need help in distinguishing scruples grounded in transcendent biblical moral truth from scruples shaped at least in part, by conventional cultural meanings" (1994, 306).

What do we need to have in order to maintain our sanity? I remember a Bible translator in the Solomon Islands who was living in a very simple setting

---

6. After Harriet Hill's initial article (1990), McElhanon's (1991) response, and Hill's rejoinder (1993), Ken Baker (2002), J. Todd Billings (2012), and most recently Berdine van den Toren-Lekkerkerker and Benno van den Toren (2015) have contributed to the conversation, sometimes with fairly negative critiques.

on a rather isolated island. She claimed that if she needed X, Y, and Z in order to survive, then God would provide X, Y, and Z. One of the items on her list of things she needed for survival was her favorite shampoo. (I don't have a problem with missionaries who may feel they need a few things to help them with their transition to living in another culture and maintain their sanity. But I do have a problem with missionaries who need everything from A to Z and a few more things in order to survive.) She told me that the Lord had miraculously provided her with her favorite shampoo because, like the widow's jar of oil that never ran dry (1 Kings 17:8–16), her shampoo bottle never went empty.

Friendship as a Key to Becoming Bicultural

What can we do to become a bicultural person in another culture and enter deeply into meaningful relationships with others? In addition to feeling at home in our host society, learning the language and understanding the culture of the people, there are a number of techniques we can use in interacting with others. These include active listening, giving feedback, listening for feelings more than just hearing words, paying attention, and being 100 percent present and not distracted when engaged in conversations with others. These are all helpful things we can learn to do, but more important than learning specific techniques is a disposition to become a friend with a local person. What is your capacity for friendship? Those cross-cultural witnesses who have a large capacity for friendship are more likely to form cross-cultural friendships with local people and over time become bicultural in their host society. But can everyone do this? Aren't some people more gifted at forming friendships than others?

If we were to measure cross-cultural witnesses' ability to become bicultural people, we would probably discover something like a bell-shaped curve of distribution. At one end would be those who easily and readily adjust to the culture, form deep friendships and meaningful relationships, and effortlessly (it seems) are at home in their host culture and feel they belong. Charles Fox, whose story I told in chapter 11, is an example of this rare kind of person. In my travels, I have not encountered very many cross-cultural witnesses who fit this type. At the other end of the bell curve are those who never do become bicultural, do not develop friendships with local people, find it difficult to become incarnational, reject local food and entertainment, and remain outsiders. The Baptist missionary in Taiwan, who told me that the only Chinese food he liked was oranges, falls into this category. Unfortunately, I've met too many of this type. Those cross-cultural witnesses whose primary work is in institutions (schools, medical facilities, mission offices) and who seem to manage without learning the local language are less likely to adapt to the culture and become bicultural. But most of us cross-cultural witnesses find ourselves somewhere in the middle of these two ends of the bell curve. And so, we have to work at forming friendships. We have to be wholeheartedly convinced that God has called us to this work and ministry.

Thanks to the scholarship of mission historian Dana Robert, the importance of creating friendships in mission is gaining renewed attention. Robert notes, "Through deep relationships with other persons, the presence of God becomes concrete and tangible. At its best, friendship communicates the unshakable love of God through life's most challenging circumstances. The transitions of life and death, illness, social dislocation, and just the ordinary struggles of daily life can be transformed through the presence and prayers of friends. And if these friends are from another culture or ethnic group, the meaning of 'God with us' deepens" (2019, 56).

Robert's book is loaded with stories and examples of how friendship is such an important part of cross-cultural witnesses' successful journey into mission and becoming bicultural people. For example, Robert tells the story of Canadian Presbyterian missionary Caroline Macdonald, whose capacity for friendship led her to befriend Japanese prisoners and ultimately bring about prison reform. Robert quotes Macdonald's biographer, Margaret Prang (2002), to sum up the remarkable life of Caroline Macdonald: "While Macdonald's intelligence, education, and spirit of adventure all shaped her life, the definitive factor in her unusual career was her great capacity for friendship. This was rooted in her deep conviction that social and cultural differences were to be respected but were ultimately of little importance. For her the essential reality was that 'human nature is all one'" (Robert 2019, 63). Robert goes on to note that "Macdonald's capacity for friendship was expressed in her insistence that foreigners become fluent in Japanese and that they not criticize Japanese culture" (63).

Friendship with others can become a window into their culture. As we develop a relationship of mutuality that defies differences that might otherwise separate us, we come to know the deepest part of a person's culture, and we reveal our own cultural assumptions, including our prejudices and biases. Anthropologists refer to developing relationships with "key informants" in order to learn the language and culture. While these informants can be a good start, true friendship is not motivated by our need to find "key informants." Rather it comes from our commitment to the kingdom of God, principles of justice and equality, and our desire to know and to be known by others who are different from us.

Bible translator and missiologist Harriet Hill, in a provocative article titled "Lifting the Fog on Incarnational Ministry" (1993), recommends that cross-cultural witnesses develop incarnational empathy in relating to others. She notes, "How then do we develop incarnational empathy? One promising model of relationship to consider is friendship. In many ways, friendship is a role that honestly describes our relationships to the people. . . . Friendship allows for differences, but in an atmosphere of respect and acceptance, with a view to mutual enrichment. Friendship occurs in nearly all cultures and is sometimes more intimate than kin relations. It lends itself to ministry" (266).

Hill continues with seven characteristics of cross-cultural friendship:

1. *Cross-cultural friendship must be intentional.* In our home culture, we tend to gravitate toward people who are like us, so cross-cultural friendships require intentionality.

2. *Cross-cultural friendship requires proximity.* When we live near the people we serve, it is much easier to develop relationships with them than when we live at a distance and make periodic forays into their community.

3. *Cross-cultural friendship must appreciate differences and similarities.* Anthropology gives us tools and a perspective to discover differences, but we also must look for and celebrate our common humanness.

4. *Cross-cultural friendship will cross economic classes.* Crossing economic barriers is often a greater challenge than crossing cultural barriers, especially for cross-cultural witnesses from wealthy countries. Our economic status can create a certain lifestyle that divides us further from those we serve.

5. *Cross-cultural friendship also involves vulnerability.* Genuine friendships involve both persons sharing deeply and freely, willingness to expose needs and weakness, sharing joys and sorrows, and giving to and receiving from each other.

6. *Cross-cultural friendship must be selective.* Meaningful relationships in any culture are generally limited to a handful of people. Benjamin Franklin wrote that we should be civil to all, friendly with many, and intimate with a very few. We can't be best friends with every person in our host society, so we'll have to be selective and trust the Holy Spirit to guide us.

7. *Cross-cultural friendship must be flexible.* Missionaries will form friendships in different ways based on their personality, lifestyle, and role in the society. The goal is friendship. The way to achieve it varies from person to person and context to context. (1993, 266–68)

What is the goal and purpose of developing cross-cultural friendships, which can be very rich and meaningful? What is the purpose of bonding with the local people and over time becoming a bicultural person in our host society? In a classic article that is as relevant today as when it was first published in *Practical Anthropology* near the end of the colonial period of mission, William Reyburn writes, "The basis of missionary identification is not to make the native feel more at home around a foreigner nor to ease the materialistic conscience of the missionary, but to create a *communication* and a *communion* where together they seek out what Saint Paul in 2 Corinthians 10:5 calls the 'arguments and obstacles'—We pull down every proud obstacle that is raised against the knowledge of God; we take every thought captive and make it obey Christ" (1978, 760).

CHAPTER SUMMARY

Hopefully, this chapter has shown you the wisdom of the Ghanaian proverb "If you want to go quickly, go alone. If you want to go far, go together." We need cross-cultural relationships and friendships in order to become bicultural people, and we need to become bicultural with the people among whom we are living and serving if we are to experience the joy of effective and long-lasting cross-cultural ministry.

CONCLUSION TO PART 5

We have come to the end of this book, and hopefully you have gleaned some anthropological wisdom along the way. In this last part, "Growing into Effective Communicators," I have focused on the challenges and rewards in crossing cultures with the gospel. The good news is that it is indeed possible for cross-cultural witnesses to grow in their understanding and cultural competence when they live and minister in a culture that is different from their own. Unfortunately, today not many stay long enough to acquire a deep and thorough understanding of the culture, language, and worldview of the people among whom they are living and serving.

The dominant theme throughout this book is that in order to have an effective and long-lasting ministry we have to develop meaningful relationships with people, and this takes time and intentionality. We therefore have to discover the cultural differences that exist. In chapter 12 we introduced a number of practical skills and anthropological tools that enable us to discover cultural difference among the people with whom we live. These are skills that all cross-cultural witnesses can learn. I suggested that the anthropological research method of participant observation is ideally suited for cross-cultural witnesses to learn the language and culture of their host society. Cross-cultural witnesses should become good ethnographers in writing up what we are learning. This will enable us to learn how to ask good questions, make accurate observations, and interpret them correctly. When we practice being curious about the new culture we're in, we can discover cultural differences, but we'll need to suspend judgment and become aware of our bias and prejudice. Adopting a posture of cultural relativism will enable us to suspend judgment to understand why people do what they do in the context in which they live, instead of quickly passing judgment on them because their culture is different from our own.

In addition to discovering cultural differences in our host society, we also need to uncover our own cultural baggage. This was the topic of chapter 13, where we discussed uncovering our assumptions and worldview—things that often lead us to make premature judgments and false assumptions about others. In addition, our lifestyle can either thwart or facilitate our cross-cultural ministry, but too often we are unaware of this. Part of the cultural baggage we carry into cross-cultural settings, often without realizing it, is that sometimes our faith is shaped more by our cultural values and worldview than by biblical values.

Finally, in chapter 14 I suggested two strategies that all cross-cultural witnesses should adopt in order to develop deep and meaningful relationships with local people. The first is the concept of bonding, which is a short-term strategy that begins the moment we step off the plane and into the new culture. The second is becoming bicultural. Bicultural people have learned to live in two or more worlds that are integrated within their minds. They can move freely between worlds, with a sense of belonging and being at home in more than just one of them. This is an ideal posture for cross-cultural witnesses because it enables them to develop meaningful relationships with others and to effectively cross cultures with the gospel.

Conclusion

In my teaching and training seminars, I frequently tell the participants that what I'm going to read in the final minutes of our class is more important than anything else I have said or taught throughout the course. I note that we can be filled with a lot of anthropological wisdom, but if we miss the most important ingredient of cross-cultural ministry, then we've missed the very purpose of our calling. So, I will end this book in the same way I close many of my teaching and training experiences around the world. I invite you to reflect on the "Meditations of a Missionary."

Though I speak in the dialect of the people I serve and can preach with the eloquent power of a fiery evangelist; though I'm endowed with anthropological wisdom; though as a surgeon I can operate with skill; though as an agriculturalist I can raise high-grade river rice; though as a teacher I can deliver spell-binding lectures, but do not have love, my message is empty.

And though I have the talent of a diplomatic organizer and administrator in councils and meetings; though I have all the confidence that I need to raise large funds, but do not have love, I am good for nothing.

And though I share my possessions and give money to the poor, but do not help my brother and sister to become an interdependent follower of Christ, I achieve absolutely nothing.

Love, if it is genuine in the life and work of a missionary, is patient and constructive; it does not seek for position and prestige. Love is glad to see a competent national in charge, and envies not. Love seeks to train an indigenous leadership; it does not cherish inflated ideas of its own importance; it is never anxious to impress. Love tries to identify itself with local people and is never arrogant or ethnocentric.

Love that is genuine does not belittle. It does not compile statistics of another's mistakes. Love seeks to bear joy and sorrow, failure and success in helpful ways. Love is not easily provoked when there is a difference of opinion or when cultural differences arise, and when unknown rumors are spread, love does not contribute to the gossip but instead believes the very best.

Love that is genuine is a partnership. It is much better to fail with a national in charge than to succeed without him or her. Love is not touchy; it never hides hurt feelings or disappointments. Love never barricades understanding; it rejoices in sharing the truth.

Love keeps an open mind; it is willing to attempt new methods and ways of doing things. Love does not consider the past so precious that it limits new vision. Love gives courage to change old ways when necessary; it is flexible in adapting tried and trusted forms from the missionary's culture to fit the cultural context of the national's society. Unless we are prepared to adapt and change, we shall have defenders of an old system but no new voice; institutional caretakers but no truth seekers; we shall have plenty of preachers but no prophets. We shall keep the bush primly pruned by hired gardeners, using expensive equipment, but within the bush there will be no burning fire.

Love that trusts like little children never fails. Large institutions may cease, even heavily subsidized schools and colleges that impart knowledge may close. But if wisdom gained there fails to lead students to Christ the Savior, it would be better to entrust such education to the government; for our knowledge is always incomplete without him who is "the Way, the Truth, and the Life." Love that has no other desire but to trust never fails.

We are in a period of change and transition. The postcolonial and postmodern era are upon us. And tell me, where is the person who knows where we are going or what will happen in the globalized world of mission and evangelization? But now, here on earth, we can only vaguely comprehend.

When Christian missions were yet at the stage of childhood, the methods of proclaiming Christ's gospel were simple and sometimes naive. Authority was in the hands of a few. But now that missions have grown for over a century toward maturity, they must now put away childish dependence. There must be planted deep within the soil of every people group a new, vibrant, indigenous church of the Master; one that is not only self-supporting, self-governing, and self-propagating but also self-theologizing.

But, whatever happens, whatever direction the winds of change may take, there is this certainty: our Lord has not and will not leave himself without a witness in every culture, among every people group, and in every era. Through his creation and redemption, God is perfecting God's plan in and through history, though everything now looks confused, baffling, and sometimes hopeless.

Be sure of this: institutions will pass away, but labor wrought by hands which have shared with those in need and proclaimed the message of the saving love of Christ, who died and rose again and lives as Lord of life, will never, never, never pass away. In this life there are only three enduring qualities: Faith, Hope, and Love, these three. But the greatest of these is Love.[1]

---

1. This is a slight revision of an earlier version of "Meditations of a Missionary" that I wrote and sent to Paul Hiebert, which he used in *Anthropological Insights for Missionaries*, copyright 1985, pp. 297–98. Used by permission of Baker Academic, a division of Baker Publishing Group.

Bibliography

Achebe, Chinua. 1959. *Things Fall Apart*. Greenwich, CT: Fawcett Publications, Inc.

Adeney, Bernard T. 1995. *Strange Virtues: Ethics in a Multicultural World*. Downers Grove, IL: InterVarsity.

Adeney, Miriam. 2002. *Daughters of Islam: Building Bridges with Muslim Women*. Downers Grove, IL: InterVarsity.

———. 2009. *Kingdom without Borders: The Untold Story of Global Christianity*. Downers Grove, IL: InterVarsity.

———. 2015. "Why Cultures Matter." *International Journal of Frontier Missiology* 32 (2): 93–97.

Alma, Carissa. 2011. ~~Surviving~~ Thriving in Cross-Cultural Ministry. Lexington: Pavilion Books.

Althen, Gary. 2002. *American Ways: A Guide for Foreigners in America*. 2nd ed. Yarmouth, ME: Intercultural Press.

Anderson, Gerald H., ed. 1998. *Biographical Dictionary of Christian Missions*. New York: Macmillan Reference.

———. 2009. "Prevenient Grace in World Mission." In *World Mission in the Wesleyan Spirit*, edited by Darrell Whiteman and Gerald Anderson, 43–52. American Society of Missiology Series 44. Franklin, TN: Providence House.

Anderson, Linda E. 1994. "A New Look at an Old Construct: Cross-Cultural Adaptation." *International Journal of Intercultural Relations* 18 (3): 293–328.

Anderson, Tawa J., W. Michael Clark, and David K. Naugle. 2017. *An Introduction to Christian Worldview: Pursuing God's Perspective in a Pluralistic World*. Downers Grove, IL: IVP Academic.

Apfelthaler, Gerhard. 1999. *Interkulturelles Management: Die Bewältigung kultureller Differenzen in der internationalen Unternehmenstätigkeit*. Vienna: Manz Verlag Schulbuch.

Arbuckle, Gerald A. 1990. *Earthing the Gospel: An Inculturation Handbook for Pastoral Workers*. London: Geoffrey Chapman.

Arensberg, Conrad M., and Arthur H. Niehoff. 1964. *Introducing Social Change: A Manual for Americans Overseas*. Chicago: Aldine.

Azadipour, Shiva. 2019. "Personality Types and Intercultural Competence of Foreign Language Learners in Education Context." *Journal of Education and Health Promotion* 8 (236). https://www.ncbi.nlm.nih.gov/pmc/articles/PMC6904958/.

Backues, Lindy. 2017. "Humility: A Christian Impulse as Fruitful Motif for Anthropological Theory and Practice." In *On Knowing Humanity: Insights from Theology for Anthropology*, edited by Eloise Meneses and David Bronkema, 101–36. New York: Routledge.

Bailey, Kenneth E. 2005. *The Cross and the Prodigal: Luke 15 through the Eyes of Middle Eastern Peasants*. 2nd ed. Downers Grove, IL: InterVarsity.

———. 2008. *Jesus through Middle Eastern Eyes: Cultural Studies in the Gospels*. Downers Grove, IL: IVP Academic.

———. 2011. *Paul through Mediterranean Eyes: Cultural Studies in 1 Corinthians*. Downers Grove, IL: IVP Academic.

Baker, Ken. 2002. "The Incarnational Model: Perception or Deception?" *Evangelical Missions Quarterly* 38 (1): 16–24.

Barna, George, and Mark Hatch. 2001. *Boiling Point: How Coming Cultural Shifts Will Change Your Life*. Glendale, CA: Regal Books.

Barna Research Group. 2009. "Changes in Worldview among Christians over the Past 13 Years." March 9, 2009. https://www.barna.com/research/barna-survey-examines-changes-in- worldview-among-christians-over-the-past-13-years/.

Baxter, L. A. 2004. "Relationships as Dialogues." *Personal Relationships* 11 (1): 1–22.

Baxter, L. A., and B. M. Montgomery. 1996. *Relating: Dialogues and Dialects*. New York: Guilford.

Beech, Geoff. 2018. "Shame/Honor, Guilt/Innocence, Fear/Power in Relationship Contexts." *International Bulletin of Mission Research* 42 (4): 338–46.

Berger, Peter L., and Thomas Luckmann. 1966. *The Social Construction of Reality: A Treatise in the Sociology of Knowledge*. New York: Anchor Books.

Billings, J. Todd. 2004. "Incarnational Ministry and Christology: A Reappropriation of the Way of Lowliness." *Missiology* 32, no. 2: 187–201.

———. 2012. "The Problem with 'Incarnational Ministry.'" *Christianity Today*, July–August, 58–63. https://www.christianitytoday.com/ct/2012/july-august/the-problem-with-incarnational-ministry.html.

Black, J. Stewart, and Hal Gregersen. 1999. "The Right Way to Manage Expats." *Harvard Business Review*, March–April. https://hbr.org/1999/03/the-right-way-to-manage-expats.

Blue, Ron, with Michael Blue. 2016. *Master Your Money: A Step-by-Step Plan for Experiencing Financial Contentment*. Chicago: Moody.

Bonding and Birth. n.d. "About Marshall and Phyllis Klaus." Accessed March 2, 2023. https://www.bondingandbirth.org/marshall-and-phyllis-klaus.html.

Bradley, Keith. 1994. *Slavery and Society at Rome*. Cambridge: Cambridge University Press.

Brewster, E. Thomas, and Elizabeth S. Brewster. 1972. "Involvement as a Means of Second Culture Learning." *Practical Anthropology* 19 (1): 27–44.

Brewster, Elizabeth S., and E. Thomas Brewster. 1982a. *Bonding and the Missionary Task: Establishing a Sense of Belonging*. Pasadena, CA: Lingua House.

————. 1982b. *Language Learning Is Communication—Is Ministry*. Pasadena, CA: Lingua House.

————. 1984. *LAMP: Language Acquisition Made Practical; Field Methods for Language Learners*. Pasadena, CA: Lingua House.

————. 2009. "The Difference Bonding Makes." In *Perspectives on the World Christian Movement*, edited by Ralph D. Winter and Steven C. Hawthorne, 465–69. 4th ed. Pasadena, CA: William Carey Library.

Brightman, Robert. 1995. "Forget Culture: Replacement, Transcendence, Relexification." *Cultural Anthropology* 10 (4): 509–46.

Brislin, R. W., and H. VanBuren. 1974. "Can They Go Home Again?" *International Educational and Cultural Exchange* 9:19–24.

Brown, Robert McAfee. 1984. *Unexpected News: Reading the Bible with Third World Eyes*. Louisville: Westminster John Knox.

Bruner, Edward M. 1956. "Cultural Transmission and Cultural Change." *Southwestern Journal of Anthropology* 12, no. 2 (Summer): 191–99. Reprinted in *Readings in Anthropology*, edited by Jesse Jennings and Edward A. Hoebel, 338–42. New York: McGraw-Hill, 1966.

Bulatao, Jaime C. 1966. *Split-Level Christianity*. Manila: Ateneo de Manila University Press.

Burnett, David. 1992. *Clash of Worlds: A Christian's Handbook on Cultures, World Religions, and Evangelism*. Nashville: Oliver Nelson Books.

Carey, William. 1792. *An Enquiry into the Obligation of Christians to Use Means for the Conversion of the Heathens*. Reprinted in *Perspectives on the World Christian Movement*, edited by Ralph Winter and Steven Hawthorne, 312–18. 4th ed. Pasadena, CA: William Carey Library, 2009.

Carroll, John B. 1956. *Language, Thought and Reality: Selected Writings of Benjamin Lee Whorf*. Cambridge, MA: MIT Press.

Conklin, Harold. 1955. "Hanunóo Color Categories." *Southwestern Journal of Anthropology* 11 (4): 339–44.

Conn, Harvie M. 1984. *Eternal Word and Changing World: Theology, Anthropology, and Mission in Trialogue*. Phillipsburg, NJ: Presbyterian and Reformed.

Corbett, Steve, and Brian Fikkert. 2009. *When Helping Hurts: How to Alleviate Poverty without Hurting the Poor . . . and Yourself*. Chicago: Moody.

Costas, Orlando. 1982. "Contextualization and Incarnation: Communicating Christ amid the Oppressed." In *Christ Outside the Gate: Mission beyond Christendom*, 3–20. Maryknoll, NY: Orbis Books.

Cozens, Simon. 2018. "Shame Cultures, Fear Cultures, and Guilt Cultures: Reviewing the Evidence." *International Bulletin of Mission Research* 42 (4): 326–36.

Crown Financial Ministries. 2007. *Crown Biblical Financial Study*. Knoxville: Crown Financial Ministries.

Cupsa, Iona. 2018. "Culture Shock and Identity." *Transactional Analysis Journal* 48 (2): 181–91.

deNeui, Paul H., ed. 2017. *Restored to Freedom from Fear, Guilt, and Shame: Lessons from the Buddhist World*. Pasadena, CA: William Carey Library.

DeWalt, Kathleen M., and Billie R. DeWalt. 2011. *Participant Observation: A Guide for Fieldworkers*. 2nd ed. Walnut Creek, CA: AltaMira.

Donne, John. 2014. *Holy Sonnets with an introduction by John Daniel Thieme*. Newton, NJ: Vicarage Hill.

Donovan, Vincent. 1978. *Christianity Rediscovered*. Maryknoll, NY: Orbis Books.

Dye, T. Wayne. 1974. "Stress-Producing Factors in Cultural Adjustment," *Missiology* 2 (1): 61–77.

———. 1976. "Toward a Cross-Cultural Definition of Sin." *Missiology* 4 (1): 27–41.

Edgerton, Robert. 1992. *Sick Societies: Challenging the Myth of Primitive Harmony*. New York: Free Press.

Ekechi, F. K. 1971. "Colonialism and Christianity in West Africa: The Igbo Case, 1900–1915." *Journal of African History* 12 (1): 103–15.

Elmer, Duane. 2002. *Cross-Cultural Connections: Stepping Out and Fitting In around the World*. Downers Grove, IL: IVP Academic.

Elmer, Vickie. 2013. "More Than 40% of Managers That Are Sent Abroad Fail." *Quartz*, June 4. https://qz.com/90816/more-than-40-of-managers-that-are-sent-abroad-fail.

Emerson, Robert M., Rachel I. Fretz, and Linda L. Shaw. 2001. "Participant Observation and Fieldnotes." In *Handbook of Ethnography*, edited by Paul Atkinson, Amanda Coffey, Sara Delamont, John Lofland, and Lyn Lofland, 356–57. Thousand Oaks, CA: Sage.

———. 2011. *Writing Ethnographic Fieldnotes*. 2nd ed. Chicago: University of Chicago Press.

Feldman, Daniel C., and Holly B. Tompson. 1992. "Entry Shock, Culture Shock: Socializing the New Breed of Global Managers." *Human Resource Management* 31 (4): 345–62.

Fikkert, Brian, and Kelly M. Kapic. 2019. *Becoming Whole: Why the Opposite of Poverty Isn't the American Dream*. Chicago: Moody.

Fischer, Michael M. J. 2007. "Culture and Cultural Analysis as Experimental Systems." *Cultural Anthropology* 22 (1): 1–65.

Flanders, Christopher, and Werner Mischke, eds. 2020. *Honor, Shame, and the Gospel: Reframing Our Message and Ministry*. Littleton, CO: William Carey.

Fox, Charles E. 1910. *An Introduction to the Study of Oceanic Languages*. Norfolk Island: Melanesian Mission Press.

———. 1924. *Threshold of the Pacific: An Account of the Social Organization, Magic and Religion of the People of San Cristoval in the Solomon Islands*. London: Kegan Paul.

———. 1958. *Lord of the Southern Isles, Being the Story of the Anglican Mission in Melanesia 1849–1949*. London: A. R. Mowbray.

———. 1962. *Kakamora*. London: Hodder & Stoughton.

Fox, Richard G., and Barbara J. King, eds. 2020. *Anthropology beyond Culture*. New York: Routledge.

Frost, Michael. 2014. *Incarnate: The Body of Christ in an Age of Disengagement*. Downers Grove, IL: IVP Books.

Frost, Michael, and Alan Hirsch. 2003. *The Shaping of Things to Come: Innovation and Mission for the 21st-Century Church*. Peabody, MA: Hendrickson.

Frost, Michael, and Christina Rice. 2017. *To Alter Your World: Partnering with God to Rebirth Our Communities*. Downers Grove, IL: IVP Books.

Garrison, David. 2014. *A Wind in the House of Islam: How God Is Drawing Muslims around the World to Faith in Jesus Christ*. Monument, CO: WIGTake Resources.

Geertz, Clifford. 1973. *The Interpretation of Cultures*. New York: Basic Books.

Georges, Jayson. 2017. *The 3D Gospel: Ministry in Guilt, Shame, and Fear Culture*. Columbia, SC: Time Press.

———. 2019. *Ministering in Patronage Cultures: Biblical Models and Missional Implications*. Downers Grove, IL: IVP Academic.

Georges, Jayson, and Mark D. Baker. 2016. *Ministering in Honor-Shame Cultures*. Downers Grove, IL: IVP Academic.

Germann, W. 1869. *Genealogy of the South Indian Gods: A Manual of the Mythology and Religion of the People of Southern India. Including a Description of Popular Hinduism*. Madras: Higginbotham.

Goodenough, Ward. 1971. *Culture, Language, and Society*. An Addison-Wesley Module in Anthropology 7. Reading, MA: Addison-Wesley.

———. 1981. *Culture, Language, and Society*. 2nd ed. Menlo Park, CA: Benjamin/ Cummings.

Gordon, S. D. 1906. *Quiet Talks about Jesus*. New York: A. C. Armstrong.

Greenwood, Allan W. 1992. "Coping with Cross-Cultural Re-entry Stress." MA thesis, University of British Columbia.

Grunlan, Stephen A., and Marvin K. Mayers. 1979. 2nd ed., 1988. *Cultural Anthropology: A Christian Perspective*. Grand Rapids: Zondervan.

Guder, Darrell. 2004. *The Incarnation and the Church's Witness*. Eugene, OR: Wipf & Stock.

Guest, Kenneth J. 2018. *Essentials of Cultural Anthropology: A Toolkit for a Global Age.* 2nd ed. New York: Norton.

Guthrie, George. 1966. "Cultural Preparation for the Philippines." In *Cultural Frontiers of the Peace Corps,* ed. Robert B. Textor, 357–67. Cambridge, MA: MIT Press.

Haas, J. W. 2016. *Public Speaking in a Global Context.* 2nd ed. Plymouth, MI: Hayden-McNeil.

Hall, Edward T. 1959. *The Silent Language.* Greenwich, CT: Fawcett.

Haughey, John C. 1973. *The Conspiracy of God: The Holy Spirit in Us.* Garden City, NJ: Doubleday.

Hay, Rob, Valerie Lim, Detlef Blocher, Jaap Ketelaar, and Sarah Hay. 2007. *Worth Keeping: Global Perspectives on Best Practices in Missionary Retention.* World Evangelical Fellowship Missions Commission, Globalization of Mission Series. Pasadena, CA: William Carey Library.

Headlee, Celeste. 2015. "10 Ways to Have a Better Conversation." Filmed May 2015. TED video, 11:21. https://www.ted.com/talks/celeste_headlee_10_ways_to_have _a_better_conversation.

Herskovits, Melville. 1955. *Cultural Anthropology.* New York: Knopf.

Hiebert, Paul G. 1978. "Form and Meaning in Contextualization of the Gospel." In *The Word among Us: Contextualizing Theology for Mission Today,* edited by Dean Gilliland, 101–20. Dallas: Word.

———. 1983. *Cultural Anthropology.* 2nd ed. Grand Rapids: Baker Books.

———. 1985. *Anthropological Insights for Missionaries.* Grand Rapids: Baker Books.

———. 2008. *Transforming Worldviews: An Anthropological Understanding of How People Change.* Grand Rapids: Baker Academic.

Hill, Harriet. 1990. "Incarnational Ministry: A Critical Examination." *Evangelical Missions Quarterly* 26 (2): 196–201.

———. 1993. "Lifting the Fog on Incarnational Ministry." *Evangelical Missions Quarterly* 29 (3): 262–69.

Hirsch, Alan. 2006. *The Forgotten Ways: Reactivating the Missional Church.* Grand Rapids: Brazos.

History.com. 2022. "Rwandan Genocide." Originally posted October 14, 2009. Updated April 19, 2022. https://www.history.com/topics/africa/rwandan-genocide.

Holmes, Thomas H., and Minoru Masuda. 1974. "Life Change and Illness Susceptibility." In *Stressful Life Events: Their Nature and Effects,* edited by Barbara Dohrenwend and Bruce Dohrenwend, 45–72. New York: Wiley.

Horizon Unknown. 2019. "5 Stages of Culture Shock—How to Recognize, Overcome and Enjoy a Culture Shock." Posted February 16, 2019. https://horizonunknown .com/5-stages-culture-shock-how-to-overcome/.

Hovey, Kevin George. 2019. *Guiding Light: Contributions of Alan R. Tippett toward the Development and Dissemination of Twentieth-Century Missiology.* American Society of Missiology Monograph Series 38. Eugene, OR: Pickwick.

Howell, Brian M., and Jenell Williams Paris. 2019. *Introducing Cultural Anthropology: A Christian Perspective*. 2nd ed. Grand Rapids: Baker Academic.

Huffman, Douglas S., ed. 2011. *Christian Contours: How a Biblical Worldview Shapes the Mind and Heart*. Grand Rapids: Kregel.

Hull, Brian, and Patrick Mays. 2022. *Youth Ministry as Mission: A Conversation about Theology and Culture*. Grand Rapids: Kregel Academic.

Hunt, Peter. 2018. *Ancient Greek and Roman Slavery*. Chichester, UK: Wiley-Blackwell.

Hunter, George G. 2000. *The Celtic Way of Evangelism: How Christianity Can Reach the West . . . Again*. Nashville: Abingdon.

International Relations EDU. n.d. "The 7 Symptoms of Culture Shock—Identifying Them and Getting Ahead of the Problem." https://www.internationalrelationsedu .org/the-7-symptoms-of-culture-shock-indentifying-them-and-getting-ahead-of -the-problem/.

Jeyaraj, Daniel. 2005. *Genealogy of the South Indian Deities: An English Translation of Bartholomäus Ziegenbalg's Original German Manuscript with a Textual Analysis and Glossary*. New York: RoutledgeCurzon.

———. 2006. *Bartholomaus Ziegenbalg: The Father of the Modern Protestant Mission*. Delhi: Indian Society for Promoting Christian Knowledge.

Johnson, C. Neal. 2009. *Business as Mission: A Comprehensive Guide to Theory and Practice*. Downers Grove, IL: InterVarsity.

Johnson, Todd M., and Gina A. Zurlo, eds. 2020. *World Christian Encyclopedia*. 3rd ed. Edinburgh: Edinburgh University Press.

Just, Arthur A., Jr. 2003. *Luke: Ancient Christian Commentary on Scripture*. Downers Grove, IL: InterVarsity.

Kairos Central America: A Challenge to the Churches of the World. (1988). 3rd ed. New York: Circus.

Kearney, Michael. 1984. *World View*. Novato, CA: Chandler and Sharp.

Keener, Craig. 2011. *Miracles: The Credibility of the New Testament Accounts*. Grand Rapids: Baker Academic.

Kim, Young Yun. 2001. *Becoming Intercultural: An Integrative Theory of Communication and Cross-Cultural Adaptation*. Thousand Oaks, CA: Sage.

Kirby, Jon P. 1995. "Language and Culture Learning IS Conversion . . . IS Ministry." *Missiology* 23 (2): 131–43.

Kirner, Kimberly, and Jan Mills. 2020. *Doing Ethnographic Research: Activities and Exercises*. Thousand Oaks, CA: Sage.

Klaus, John H., and Marshall H. Kennell. 1976. *Maternal Infant Bonding*. St. Louis: Mosby.

Kluckhohn, Clyde. 1949. *Mirror for Man: The Relation of Anthropology to Modern Life*. New York: McGraw-Hill.

Kluckhohn, Clyde, and W. H. Kelly. 1945. "The Concept of Culture." In *The Science of Man in the World Crisis*, edited by Ralph Linton, 78–105. New York: Columbia University Press.

Koyama, Kosuke. 1990. "The Role of Translation in Developing Indigenous Theologies—an Asian View." In *Bible Translation and the Spread of the Church: The Last 200 Years*, edited by Philip C. Stine, 95–107. New York: Brill.

Kraft, Charles H. 1979. *Christianity in Culture*. Maryknoll, NY: Orbis Books.

———. 1991. *Communication Theory for Christian Witness*. Rev. ed. Maryknoll, NY: Orbis Books.

———. 1996. *Anthropology for Christian Witness*. Maryknoll, NY: Orbis Books.

———. 2005. *Christianity in Culture*. Rev. 25th anniv. ed. Maryknoll, NY: Orbis Books.

———. 2008. *Worldview for Christian Witness*. Pasadena, CA: William Carey Library.

Kraft, Marguerite. 1978. *Worldview and the Communication of the Gospel*. Pasadena, CA: William Carey Library.

Kroeber, A. L. 1917. "The Superorganic." *American Anthropologist* 19 (2): 163–213.

Kroeber, A. L., and Clyde Kluckhohn. 1952. *Culture: A Critical Review of Concepts and Definitions*. New York: Vintage Books.

Lai, Patrick. 2015. *Business for Transformation: Getting Started*. Pasadena, CA: William Carey Library.

Lane, Harlan. 1979. *The Wild Boy of Aveyron*. Cambridge, MA: Harvard University Press.

Langmead, Ross. 2004. *The Word Made Flesh: Towards an Incarnational Missiology*. Lanham, MD: University Press of America.

Larson, Donald N. 1978. "The Viable Missionary: Learner, Trader, Storyteller." *Missiology* 4 (2): 155–63.

Lévy-Bruhl, Lucien. 1910. *How Natives Think*. Reprinted 1985. Princeton: Princeton University Press.

———. 1923. *Primitive Mentality*. Reprinted 1978. New York: AMS.

Lewis, Julian. 2023. "Spiritual Depression: Signs, Causes, Coping, and Treatment." *ZellaLife* (blog), January 26, 2023. https://www.zellalife.com/blog/spiritual-depression-signs-causes-coping-and-treatment/.

Lingenfelter, Sherwood, and Julie Green. 2022. *Teamwork Cross-Culturally: Christ-Centered Solutions for Leading Multinational Teams*. Grand Rapids: Baker Academic.

Lingenfelter, Sherwood, and Marvin K. Mayers. 2016. *Ministering Cross-Culturally: A Model for Effective Personal Relationships*. 3rd ed. Grand Rapids: Baker Academic.

Linton, Ralph. 1936. *The Study of Man*. New York: Appleton Century Crofts.

Livermore, David. 2006. *Serving with Eyes Wide Open: Doing Short-Term Missions with Cultural Intelligence*. Grand Rapids: Baker Books.

———. 2009. *Cultural Intelligence: Improving Your CQ to Engage Our Multicultural World*. Grand Rapids: Baker Academic.

———. 2015. *Leading with Cultural Intelligence: The Real Secret to Success*. 2nd ed. New York: American Management Association.

———. 2022. *Digital, Diverse & Divided: How to Talk to Racists, Compete with Robots, and Overcome Polarization*. Oakland, CA: Berrett-Koehler.

Loss, Myron. 1983. *Culture Shock: Dealing with Stress in Cross-Cultural Living*. Winona Lake, IN: Light & Life.

Love, Rick. 2008. "Blessing the Nations in the 21st Century: A 3D Approach to Apostolic Ministry." *International Journal of Frontier Missiology* 25 (1): 31–37.

Lupton, Robert D. 2012. *Toxic Charity: How Churches and Charities Hurt Those They Help, and How to Reverse It*. New York: HarperCollins.

Luzbetak, Louis. 1970. *The Church and Cultures: An Applied Anthropology for the Religious Worker*. Techny, IL: Divine Word Publications. Originally published 1963.

———. 1988. *The Church and Cultures: New Perspectives in Missiological Anthropology*. Maryknoll, NY: Orbis Books.

Maclachlan, Matthew. 2017. "7 Tips to Take the Shock Out of Culture Shock." Learnlight. Accessed September 5, 2022. https://www.communicaid.com/cross-cultural-training/blog/top-tips-overcoming-culture-shock/.

Malinowski, Bronislaw. 1922. *Argonauts of the Western Pacific: An Account of Native Enterprise and Adventure in the Archipelagoes of Melanesian New Guinea*. London: Routledge & Sons.

———. 1944. *A Scientific Theory of Culture and Other Essays*. Chapel Hill: University of North Carolina Press.

Manning, Jimmie. 2014. "A Constitutive Approach to Interpersonal Communication Studies." *Communication Studies* 65:432–40.

Manz, Sonja. 2003. "Culture Shock—Causes, Consequences and Solutions: The International Experience." https://www.grin.com/document/108360.

Maranz, David E. 2015. *African Friends and Money Matters*. 2nd ed. Dallas: SIL International.

Marx, Elisabeth. 2001. *Breaking through Culture Shock: What You Need to Succeed in International Business*. London: Nicholas Brealey.

Mayers, Marvin K. 1974. *Christianity Confronts Culture: A Strategy for Cross-Cultural Evangelism*. Grand Rapids: Zondervan. Revised edition published 1987.

Mbiti, John. 1979. "The Gospel in the African Context." In *Toward Theology in an Australian Context*, edited by Victor C. Hayes, 18–26. Bedford Park: Australian Association for the Study of Religion.

McElhanon, Kenneth. 1991. "Don't Give Up on the Incarnational Model." *Evangelical Missions Quarterly* 27 (4): 390–93.

Mead, Margaret. 1928. *Coming of Age in Samoa*. New York: William Morrow.

Mehrabian, Albert. 1971. "Nonverbal Communication." *Nebraska Symposium on Motivation* 19:107–61.

———. 1981. *Silent Messages: Implicit Communication of Emotions and Attitudes*. Belmont, CA: Wadsworth.

———. 2008. *Communication without Words*. 2nd ed. New York: Routledge.

Mejudhon, Ubolwan. 1994. "The Way of Meekness: Being Thai and Christian in the Thai Way." DMiss diss., Asbury Theological Seminary.

Miller, Flint. 1996. "Mixed Messages: A Study of Southern Baptist Missionaries in East Asia and Their Attempt to Interpret and Apply the Concept of Ministering Incarnationally." DMiss diss., Asbury Theological Seminary.

Mischke, Werner. 2015. *The Global Gospel: Achieving Missional Impact in Our Multicultural World*. Scottsdale, AZ: Mission ONE.

Moon, W. Jay. 2017. *Intercultural Discipleship: Learning from Global Approaches to Spiritual Formation*. Grand Rapids: Baker Academic.

Moon W. Jay, and W. Bud Simon. 2021. *Effective Intercultural Evangelism: Good News in a Diverse World*. Downers Grove, IL: InterVarsity.

Moreau, Scott, Evvy Hay Campbell, and Susan Greener. 2014. *Effective Intercultural Communication: A Christian Perspective*. Grand Rapids: Baker Academic.

Muller, Roland. 2000. *Honor and Shame: Unlocking the Door*. Self-published, Xlibris Corporation.

Myers, Bryant. 2017. *Engaging Globalization: The Poor, Christian Mission, and Our Hyperconnected World*. Grand Rapids: Baker Academic.

Naugle, David. 2002. *Worldview: The History of a Concept*. Grand Rapids: Eerdmans.

Nehrbass, Kenneth. 2016. *God's Image and Global Cultures: Integrating Faith and Culture in the Twenty-First Century*. Eugene, OR: Cascade Books.

Newbigin, Lesslie. 1986. *Foolishness to the Greeks: The Gospel and Western Culture*. Grand Rapids: Eerdmans.

New Hebrides Mission. 1875. *Twelfth Annual Report of the New Hebrides Vessel* Day Spring: *1875*. Sydney: S. T. Leigh. https://catalogue.nla.gov.au/Record/8542109.

Nicotera, Anne Maydan. 2009. "Constitutive View of Communication." In *Encyclopedia of Communication Theory*, edited by Stephen W. Littlejohn and Karen A. Foss, 175–78. London: Sage.

Nida, Eugene. 1954. *Customs and Cultures: Anthropology for Christian Mission*. New York: Harper & Brothers.

Nussbaum, Stan. 2005. *American Cultural Baggage: How to Recognize and Deal with It*. Maryknoll, NY: Orbis Books.

———. 2007. *Breakthrough! Steps to Research and Resolve the Mysteries in Your Ministry*. Colorado Springs: GMI Research Services.

Oates, Lynette. 1992. *Hidden People: How a Remote New Guinea Culture Was Brought Back from the Brink of Extinction*. Sutherland, NSW: Albatross Books.

Oberg, Kalervo. 1960. "Culture Shock." *Practical Anthropology* 7 (4): 177–82.

Okesson, Gregg. 2020. *A Public Missiology: How Local Churches Witness to a Complex World*. Grand Rapids: Baker Academic.

Opler, Morris. 1945. "Themes as Dynamic Forces in Culture." *American Journal of Sociology* 51:198–206.

Osmer, Richard. 2021. *The Invitation: A Theology of Evangelism*. Grand Rapids: Eerdmans.

Ott, Craig. 2022. "Talking about Cultural Differences in an Age of Globalization and Hybridization: Between Obelix and Stephen Colbert." *Missiology* 50:63–77.

Pachuau, Lalsangkima. 2018. *World Christianity: A Historical and Theological Introduction*. Nashville: Abingdon.

Paracletos. 2015. "The Sad Facts about Missionary Attrition." Posted March 25, 2015. https://paracletos.org/the-sad-facts-about-missionary-attrition/.

Pearce, W. B., and W. E. Cronen. 1980. *Communication, Action, and Meaning: The Creation of Social Realities*. New York: Praeger.

Pike, Eunice, and Florence Cowan. 1959. "Mushroom Ritual versus Christianity." *Practical Anthropology* 6 (4): 145–50.

Prang, Margaret. 2002. *A Heart at Leisure from Itself: Caroline Macdonald of Japan*. Vancouver: University of British Columbia Press.

Priest, Robert J. 1994. "Missionary Elenctics: Conscience and Culture." *Missiology* 22 (3): 291–315.

———. 2008. *Effective Engagement in Short-term Missions: Doing It Right*. Pasadena, CA: William Carey Library.

Pullinger, Jackie. 2007. *Chasing the Dragon: One Woman's Struggle against the Darkness of Hong Kong's Drug Dens*. Grand Rapids: Chosen.

Reyburn, William D. 1978. "Identification in the Missionary Task." In *Readings in Missionary Anthropology II*, edited by William A. Smalley, 746–60. Pasadena, CA: William Carey Library. Originally published in *Practical Anthropology* 7, no. 1 (1960).

Richards, E. Randolph, and Richard James. 2020. *Misreading Scripture with Individualist Eyes: Patronage, Honor, and Shame in the Biblical World*. Downers Grove, IL: IVP Academic.

Richards, E. Randolph, and Brandon J. O'Brien. 2012. *Misreading Scripture with Western Eyes: Removing Cultural Blinders to Better Understand the Bible*. Downers Grove, IL: InterVarsity.

Robert, Dana. 2019. *Faithful Friendships: Embracing Diversity in Christian Community*. Grand Rapids: Eerdmans.

Rosenthal, Paul. 2009. "The Concept of the Paramessage in Persuasive Communication." *Quarterly Journal of Speech* 58, no. 1: 15–30.

Russell, Mark L. 2010. *The Missional Entrepreneur: Principles and Practices for Business as Mission*. Birmingham, AL: New Hope.

Rynkiewich, Michael. 2011. *Soul, Self, and Society: A Postmodern Anthropology for Mission in a Postcolonial World*. Eugene, OR: Cascade Books.

———. 2020. "The Challenge of Teaching Mission in an Increasingly Mobile and Complex World." *International Bulletin of Mission Research* 44 (4): 335–48.

Sanneh, Lamin. 2009. *Translating the Message: The Missionary Impact on Culture*. Revised and expanded edition. Maryknoll, NY: Orbis Books.

Sapir, Edward. 1921. *Language: An Introduction to the Study of Speech*. New York: Harcourt, Brace.

———. 1929. "The Status of Linguistics as a Science." *Language* 5 (4): 207–14. http://www.jstor.org/stable/409588.

Satter, Ralph. 1991. "Discovering the Gift of God: The Impact of American Worldview on Salvation by Grace." DMiss diss., Asbury Theological Seminary.

Sears, Andrea. 2020. "New Data Confirms That Team Conflict Is One of the Primary Factors in Missionary Attrition." *A Life Overseas* (blog). Posted February 18. https://www.alifeoverseas.com/new-data-confirms-that-team-conflict-is-one-of-the-primary-factors-in-missionary-attrition/.

Sigman, S. J. 1992. "Do Social Approaches to Interpersonal Communication Constitute a Contribution to Communication Theory?" *Communication Theory* 2:347–56.

Silverman, Sydel. 2020. Foreword to *Anthropology beyond Culture*, edited by Richard G. Fox and Barbara J. King, 1–4. New York: Routledge.

Simons, Gary. 2023. *Ethnologue: Languages of the World*. 26th ed. https://www.ethnologue.com.

Sire, James W. 2015. *Naming the Elephant: Worldview as a Concept*. 2nd ed. Downers Grove, IL: IVP Academic.

———. 2020. *The Universe Next Door: A Basic Worldview Catalog*. 6th ed. Downers Grove, IL: IVP Academic.

Slocum, Marianna. 1988. *The Good Seed*. Orange, CA: Promise.

Smalley, William A. 1963. "Culture Shock, Language Shock, and the Shock of Self-Discovery." *Practical Anthropology* 10 (2): 49–56. Reprinted in 1978 in *Readings in Missionary Anthropology II*, edited by William Smalley, 693–700. Pasadena, CA: William Carey Library.

———, ed. 1967. *Readings in Missionary Anthropology*. Tarrytown, NY: Practical Anthropology.

———, ed. 1978. *Readings in Missionary Anthropology II*. Pasadena, CA: William Carey Library.

Spradley, James P. 2016a. *The Ethnographic Interview*. Long Grove, IL: Waveland.

———. 2016b. *Participant Observation*. Long Grove, IL: Waveland.

Spradley, James P., and David McCurdy. 1975. *Anthropology: The Cultural Perspective*. Long Grove, IL: Waveland.

Spradley, James P., and Mark Phillips. 1972. "Culture and Stress: A Quantitative Analysis." *American Anthropologist* 74 (3): 518–29.

Starke, John. 2011. "The Incarnation Is about a Person, Not a Mission." The Gospel Coalition. May 16. https://www.thegospelcoalition.org/article/the-incarnation-is -about-a-person-not-a-mission/.

Steffen, Tom, and Mike Barnett, eds. 2006. *Business as Mission: From Impoverished to Empowered*. Pasadena, CA: William Carey Library.

Stewart, Edward. 1972. *American Cultural Patterns: A Cross-Cultural Perspective*. Chicago: Intercultural Press.

Stewart, Louise, and Peter A. Leggat. 1998. "Culture Shock and Travelers." *Journal of Travel Medicine* 5:84–88.

Stine, Philip C. 2004. *Let the Words Be Written: The Lasting Influence of Eugene A. Nida*. Atlanta: Society of Biblical Literature.

Strelan, John G. 1977. *Search for Salvation: Studies in the History and Theology of Cargo Cults*. Adelaide, Australia: Lutheran Publishing House.

Taber, Charles R. 1971. "The Missionary Ghetto." *Practical Anthropology* 18 (5): 193–96.

———. 1990. "Review of *The Church and Cultures: New Perspectives in Missiological Anthropology*, by Louis J. Luzbetak, SVD." *Missiology* 18:103–4.

Talman, Harley, and John Travis, eds. 2015. *Understanding Insider Movements: Disciples of Jesus within Diverse Religious Communities*. Pasadena, CA: William Carey Library.

Taylor, John V. 1963. *The Primal Vision*. Philadelphia: Fortress.

Taylor, William D. 1997. *Too Valuable to Lose: Exploring the Causes and Cures of Missionary Attrition*. World Evangelical Fellowship Missions Commission, Globalization of Mission Series. Pasadena, CA: William Carey Library.

Thomas, William I., and Dorothy S. Thomas. 1928. *The Child in America: Behavior Problems and Programs*. New York: Knopf.

Tiénou, Tite. 1991. "The Invention of the 'Primitive' and Stereotypes in Mission." *Missiology* 19 (3): 295–303.

———. 2016. "Reflections on Michael A. Rynkiewich's 'Do Not Remember the Former Things.'" *International Bulletin of Mission Research* 40 (4): 318–24.

Tippett, Alan R. 1967. *Solomon Islands Christianity: A Study in Growth and Obstruction*. New York: Friendship Press.

———. 1971. *People Movements in Southern Polynesia*. Chicago: Moody.

———. 1980. *The Transmission of Information and Social Values in Early Christian Fiji, 1836–1905*. Canberra, Australia: St. Mark's Library.

———. 2013. *The Ways of the People: A Reader in Missionary Anthropology*. Pasadena, CA: William Carey Library.

Towler, Sonya. 2020. "How Much of Communication Is Really Nonverbal?" Premier Global Services, Inc. March 30. https://www.pgi.com/blog/2020/03/how-much -of-communication-is-really-nonverbal/.

Tylor, Edward Burnett. 1871. *The Origins of Culture*. Vol. 1 of *Primitive Culture*. New York: Harper & Row. Reprinted 1958.

USDA. 2022. "Rural Classifications." USDA Economic Research Service. Last up-
    dated November 29, 2022. https://www.ers.usda.gov/topics/rural-economy
    -population/rural-classifications/.

van den Toren-Lekkerkerker, Berdine, and Benno van den Toren. 2015. "From Mis-
    sionary Incarnate to Incarnational Guest: A Critical Reflection on Incarnation as a
    Model for Missionary Presence." *Transformation: An International Journal of Holis-
    tic Mission Studies* 32 (2): 81–96.

van der Zee, Karen, and Jan Pieter van Oudenhoven. 2013. "Culture Shock or Chal-
    lenge? The Role of Personality as a Determinant of Intercultural Competence."
    Journal of Cross-Cultural Psychology 44 (6): 928–40.

Walls, Andrew F. 1996. "The Gospel as Prisoner and Liberator of Culture." In *The
    Missionary Movement in Christian History: Studies in the Transmission of Faith*,
    3–15. Maryknoll, NY: Orbis Books.

Walton, John H., and Craig S. Keener, eds. 2016. *NIV Cultural Backgrounds Study
    Bible*. Grand Rapids: Zondervan.

Ward, Colleen, Stephen Bochner, and Adrian Furnham. 2001. *The Psychology of Cul-
    ture Shock*. 2nd ed. New York: Routledge.

Watt, Agnus. 1896. *Twenty-Five Years' Mission Life on Tanna, New Hebrides*. Edin-
    burgh: John Menzies.

Weiss, Gerald. 1973. "A Scientific Concept of Culture." *American Anthropologist* 75
    (5): 1376–1413.

Wells, Samuel. 2018. *Incarnational Mission: Being with the World*. Grand Rapids:
    Eerdmans.

Whelchel, Michael. 1996. "The Relationship of Psychological Type to the Missionary
    Calling and Cross-Cultural Adjustment of Southern Baptist Missionaries." DMiss
    diss., Asbury Theological Seminary.

Whiteman, Darrell L. 1983. *Melanesians and Missionaries: An Ethnohistorical Study of
    Social and Religious Change in the Southwest Pacific*. Pasadena, CA: William Carey
    Library.

———. 1985. *Missionaries, Anthropologists, and Cultural Change*. Studies in Third
    World Societies 25. Williamsburg, VA: Department of Anthropology, William and
    Mary College.

———. 1990. "Bible Translation and Social and Cultural Development." In *Bible
    Translation and the Growth of the Church: The Last 200 Years*, edited by Philip C.
    Stine, 120–41. Leiden: Brill, 1990.

———. 1992. "The Legacy of Alan R. Tippett." *International Bulletin of Missionary
    Research* 16:163–66.

———. 1993. "Presenting the Lamb of God in a Country with No Sheep." *Mission
    Advocate: A Publication of the Mission Society for United Methodists* (Summer): 2–3.

———. 1994. "Alan R. Tippett 1911–1988: Anthropology in the Service of Mis-
    sion." In *Mission Legacies: Biographical Studies of Leaders of the Modern Missionary*

Movement, edited by Gerald H. Anderson, Robert T. Coote, Norman A. Horner, and James M. Phillips, 532–38. Maryknoll, NY: Orbis Books.

———. 1997. "Contextualization: The Theory, the Gap, the Challenge." *International Bulletin of Missionary Research* 21 (1): 2–7.

———. 2003. "Anthropology and Mission: The Incarnational Connection." Third Annual Louis J. Luzbetak Lectures on Mission and Culture, Catholic Theological Union. Reprinted in *Mission and Culture: The Louis J. Luzbetak Lectures*, edited by Stephen B. Bevans, 59–98. Maryknoll, NY: Orbis Books, 2012.

———. 2005. "'Incarnational Identification': Reflections on Philippians 2:5–8." *Faith in Action Study Bible: Living God's Word in a Changing World*. Grand Rapids: Zondervan.

———. 2006. "The Role of Ethnicity and Culture in Shaping Western Mission Agency Identity." *Missiology* 34 (1): 59–70.

———. 2010. "Response to Paul G. Hiebert: The Gospel in Human Context: Changing Perceptions of Contextualization." In *MissionShift: Global Mission Issues in the Third Millennium*, edited by David J. Hesselgrave and Ed Stetzer, 114–28. Nashville: B&H Academic.

———. 2018. "Shame/Honor, Guilt/Innocence, Fear/Power: A Missiological Response to Simon Cozens and Geoff Beech." *International Bulletin of Mission Research* 42 (4): 348–56.

———. 2019. Review of *Incarnational Mission: Being with the World*, by Samuel Wells. *Missiology* 47 (1): 85.

———. 2021. "Contextualization: A Passing Fad, a Syncretistic Danger, or a Biblical Model?" *Doon Theological Journal* 18 (2): 21–39.

———. 2023a. "Why Is Christianity Perceived as a Foreign Religion?" In *Leave the Farm and Follow Me: Festschrift in Honour of Rev. Dr. Graham Whitfield Houghton: Essays on Theology and Mission*, edited by Richard Howell, 385–406. Farrukh Nagar, India: Caleb Institute.

———. 2023b. "The Conversion of a Missionary: A Missiological Study of Acts 10." *Missiology* 51 (1): 19–30.

———. 2023c. "My Pilgrimage in Mission." *International Bulletin of Mission Research* 47 (4): 536–47.

Whiteman, G., E. Edwards, A. Savelle, and K. Whiteman. 2020. "How Do Missionaries Become Resilient?" In *Relentless Love: Living Out Integral Mission to Combat Poverty, Injustice, and Conflict*, edited by Graham Joseph Hill, 65–75. Carlisle, UK: Langham Global Library.

Whiteman, Geoff, and Heather Pubols, eds. 2023. *Essentials for People Care and Development*. Wheaton, IL: Missio Nexus.

Whiteman, Geoff, and Kriss Whiteman. 2022. *Supporting Today's Global Workers Toward Missional Resilience*. EMQ 58 (2): 27–29.

Whiteman, Kristina. 2023a. "A Treasured History: Listening to and Learning from Global Workers' Stories of Resilience." PhD diss., Asbury Theological Seminary.

———. 2023b. "A Treasured History: Stories of Resilience." In G. Whiteman and Pubols, *Essentials for People Care*, 17–31. Wheaton, IL: Missio Nexus.

Wikipedia. S.v. "Participant Observation." Last modified January 2, 2023, 19:29. https://en.wikipedia.org/wiki/Participant_observation.

William, J. D. n.d. *Bartholomeus Ziegenbalg: First Protestant Missionary to India*. Nasik, India: Genesis Books.

Winkelman, Michael. 1994. "Culture Shock and Adaptation." *Journal of Counseling & Development* 73:121–26.

Winter, Ralph D., and Steven C. Hawthorne, eds. 2009. *Perspectives on the World Christian Movement*. 4th ed. Pasadena, CA: William Carey Library.

Wolcott, Harry. 2005. *The Art of Fieldwork*. 2nd ed. Walnut Creek, CA: AltaMira.

———. 2008. *Ethnography: A Way of Seeing*. 2nd ed. Lanham, MD: AltaMira.

World Evangelicals. 2003. "US Report of Findings on Missionary Retention." December. http://www.worldevangelicals.org/resources/rfiles/res3_95_link _1292358708.pdf.

Wright, N. T. 1992. *The New Testament and the People of God*. Minneapolis: Fortress.

Wu, Jackson. 2019. *Reading Romans with Eastern Eyes: Honor and Shame in Paul's Message and Mission*. Downers Grove, IL: IVP Academic.

Yale, Brandie. 2017. "Understanding Culture Shock in International Students." *Academic Advising Today* 40 (4). https://nacada.ksu.edu/Resources/Academic -Advising-Today/View-Articles/Understanding-Culture-Shock-in-International -Students.aspx.

Yamamori, Tetsunao, and Kenneth Eldred, eds. 2003. *On Kingdom Business: Transforming Missions through Entrepreneurial Strategies*. Carol Stream, IL: Crossway Books.

Yavetz, Zvi. 1988. *Slaves and Slavery in Ancient Rome*. New Brunswick, NJ: Transaction.

Zahniser, A. H. Mathias. 1997. *Symbol and Ceremony: Making Disciples across Cultures*. Monrovia, CA: MARC.

Ziegenbalg, Bartholomäus. 1984. *Genealogy of the South-Indian Gods: A Manual of the Mythology and Religion of the People of Southern India. Including a Description of Popular Hinduism*. New Delhi: Unity Book Service.

Zurlo, Gina A., Todd M. Johnson, and Peter F. Crossing. 2020. "World Christianity and Mission 2020: Ongoing Shift to the Global South." *International Bulletin of Mission Research* 44 (1): 8–19.

Index